First World War

and Army of Occupation

War Diary

France, Belgium and Germany

40 DIVISION
119 Infantry Brigade
Welsh Regiment
17th Battalion
10 December 1915 - 2 November 1917

WO95/2607/1

The Naval & Military Press Ltd
www.nmarchive.com
Published in association with The National Archives

Published by

The Naval & Military Press Ltd

Unit 10 Ridgewood Industrial Park,

Uckfield, East Sussex,

TN22 5QE England

Tel: +44 (0) 1825 749494

www.naval-military-press.com

www.nmarchive.com

This diary has been reprinted in facsimile from the original. Any imperfections are inevitably reproduced and the quality may fall short of modern type and cartographic standards.

Contents

Document type	Place/Title	Date From	Date To
Heading	WO95/2607/1		
Heading	40th Division 119th Infy Bde 17th Bn Welsh Regt Jun 1916-Feb 1918		
Heading	17th Bn. The Welsh Rgt. War Diary June 1916		
War Diary	Blackdown	02/06/1916	02/06/1916
War Diary	Havre	03/06/1916	04/06/1916
War Diary	Lillers	05/06/1916	05/06/1916
War Diary	St Hilaire	06/06/1916	09/06/1916
War Diary	Houchin	10/06/1916	10/06/1916
War Diary	Maroc	11/06/1916	14/06/1916
War Diary	Houchin	15/06/1916	18/06/1916
War Diary	Maroc	19/06/1916	21/06/1916
War Diary	Houchin	22/06/1916	22/06/1916
War Diary	Divion	23/06/1916	30/06/1916
Miscellaneous	D.A.G. 3rd Echelon.	09/07/1916	09/07/1916
Miscellaneous	17th Service Battalion. The Welsh Regiment. Appendix 1		
Miscellaneous	To Headquarters, 17th Welsh Regt. Appendix 2	07/06/1916	07/06/1916
Miscellaneous	Attachment Of 17th And 18th Welsh (119th Brigade). Appendix 3	09/06/1916	09/06/1916
Operation(al) Order(s)	1st Infantry Brigade. Relief Order No. 74 Appendix 4	13/06/1916	13/06/1916
Miscellaneous	O.C. 17th Welch. Appendix 5	20/06/1916	20/06/1916
Miscellaneous	O.C. 17th Welsh Appendix 5	20/06/1916	20/06/1916
Miscellaneous	O.C. 18th Welch. Appendix 6	21/06/1916	21/06/1916
Heading	17th Bn The Welsh Regt. War Diary July 1916.		
War Diary	Divion	01/07/1916	02/07/1916
War Diary	Barlin	03/07/1916	03/07/1916
War Diary	Bully Grenay	04/07/1916	07/07/1916
War Diary	Calonne	08/07/1916	19/07/1916
War Diary	Bully Grenay	20/07/1916	30/07/1916
War Diary	Calonne	31/07/1916	31/07/1916
Miscellaneous	17 Battalion, The Welsh Regiment. Appendix 6	17/07/1916	17/07/1916
Operation(al) Order(s)	Extract From Routine Orders No 52. By Major General H.G. Ruggles Brise. G.B. M.V.O. Commanding 40th Division Appendix 7	27/07/1916	27/07/1916
Heading	War Diary 17th Bn. (S) Welsh Regt. August 1916		
War Diary	Calonne	07/08/1916	10/08/1916
War Diary	Bully Grenay	14/08/1916	16/08/1916
War Diary	Les Brebis	17/08/1916	23/08/1916
War Diary	Loos	24/08/1916	31/08/1916
War Diary	Calonne	01/09/1916	13/09/1916
War Diary	Loos	01/09/1916	06/09/1916
War Diary	N. Maroc	07/09/1916	10/09/1916
War Diary	Les Brebis	11/09/1916	19/09/1916
War Diary	Maroc	20/09/1916	30/09/1916
Miscellaneous	Headquarters, 119th Infantry Brigade.	26/09/1916	26/09/1916
Heading	17th The Welsh Regiment		
Operation(al) Order(s)	Operation Order No. 16. By Lieut Col G.Y. Wilkie Commanding 17th Service Battalion The Welsh Regiment.	23/09/1916	23/09/1916

Miscellaneous	Headquarters, 119th Infantry Brigade.	26/09/1916	26/09/1916
War Diary	N E Maroc	01/10/1916	04/10/1916
War Diary	Maroc	05/10/1916	09/10/1916
War Diary	Les Brebis	10/10/1916	12/10/1916
War Diary	N Maroc	13/10/1916	16/10/1916
War Diary	N.E. Maroc	16/10/1916	19/10/1916
War Diary	N.E. Maroc Right Loos	20/10/1916	20/10/1916
War Diary	Right Loos	21/10/1916	28/10/1916
War Diary	Right Loos Les Brebis	29/10/1916	29/10/1916
War Diary	Les Brebis	30/10/1916	30/10/1916
War Diary	Les Brebis Bruay	31/10/1916	31/10/1916
Heading	War Diary Of 17th (S) Bn SW Of Welsh Regiment From Nov 1st. 1916 To Nov 30th 1916.Volume 6		
War Diary	Bruay La Thieuloye	01/11/1916	01/11/1916
War Diary	La Thieuloye Ternas	02/11/1916	02/11/1916
War Diary	Ternas	03/11/1916	03/11/1916
War Diary	Ternas Bonnieres	04/11/1916	04/11/1916
War Diary	Bonnieres	05/11/1916	05/11/1916
War Diary	Bois Bergues	06/11/1916	14/11/1916
War Diary	Noeux	15/11/1916	16/11/1916
War Diary	Barly	17/11/1916	17/11/1916
War Diary	Brevillers	18/11/1916	21/11/1916
War Diary	Gezaincourt	22/11/1916	22/11/1916
War Diary	Franqueville	23/11/1916	23/11/1916
War Diary	Vauchelles Les Quesnoy	24/11/1916	30/11/1916
Heading	War Diary Of The 17th (S) Bn The Welsh Regt For Period Dec 1st To Dec 31st. 1916		
Miscellaneous	HQ. 110, Inf Bde.	31/12/1916	31/12/1916
War Diary	Vauchelles-Les-Quesnoy	01/12/1916	09/12/1916
War Diary	Camp 12 (Bois Celestins)	10/12/1915	25/12/1915
War Diary	Camp 21	26/12/1916	26/12/1916
War Diary	Trenches S. Of Rancourt	27/12/1916	27/12/1916
War Diary	Trenches	28/12/1916	31/12/1916
Heading	War Diary Of 17th (S) Bn The Welsh Regt From January 1st 1917 To January 31st 1917 Volme		
War Diary	Rancourt Sector	01/01/1917	04/01/1917
War Diary	Camp 21	05/01/1917	08/01/1917
War Diary	Right Front Bouchavesnes N. Sector.	08/01/1917	12/01/1917
War Diary	Reserve Line Asquith Flats	13/01/1917	13/01/1917
War Diary	Reserve Asquith Flats	15/01/1917	15/01/1917
War Diary	Right Front Sub. Sector Bouchavesnes	16/01/1917	17/01/1917
War Diary	Camp 21.	18/01/1917	22/01/1917
War Diary	Maurepas Ravine	22/01/1917	22/01/1917
War Diary	Maurepas Ravine	23/01/1917	25/01/1917
War Diary	Right Sub Sector Rancourt Sector	25/01/1917	27/01/1917
War Diary	Camp 124 (West)	28/01/1917	31/01/1917
Heading	War Diary Of 17th (Service) Battalion The Welsh Regiment. From 1-2-1917. To 28-2-1917.		
War Diary	Camp 24 West.	01/02/1917	09/02/1917
War Diary	Camp 21	10/02/1917	10/02/1917
War Diary	Rancourt Sector	11/02/1917	15/02/1917
War Diary	Right Sub Sector	15/02/1917	15/02/1917
War Diary	Rancourt Sector	16/02/1917	19/02/1917
War Diary	Maurepas Ravine	20/02/1917	21/02/1917
War Diary	Camp III	22/02/1917	28/02/1917
Miscellaneous	H.Q. 119th Infantry Brigade.	31/03/1917	31/03/1917

War Diary	Camp III Belair	01/03/1917	06/03/1917
War Diary	From Camp. 19. Suzanne Into Support Clery Sector	07/03/1917	07/03/1917
War Diary	From Support 18th Rifle Sub. Sector Of Clery Sector.	08/03/1917	08/03/1917
War Diary	Right Sub Sector Clery Sector	09/03/1917	12/03/1917
War Diary	Support Clery Sector	13/03/1917	15/03/1917
War Diary	Camp. 17	16/03/1917	16/03/1917
War Diary	Linger	17/03/1917	17/03/1917
War Diary	Camp. 164.	18/03/1917	20/03/1917
War Diary	Haut-Allaines	21/03/1917	25/03/1917
War Diary	Bouchavesnes	26/03/1917	31/03/1917
Heading	War Diary Of The 17th (S) Bn The Welsh Regiment From April 1st 1917 To April 30th 1917. Volume II		
War Diary	Bouchavesnes	01/04/1917	07/04/1917
War Diary	Etricourt	08/04/1917	17/04/1917
War Diary	Fins	18/04/1917	24/04/1917
War Diary	R 14 C. 8.0 Is R. 14 B. R.8 (Ref. Map T.S. 52 1/20,000)	25/04/1917	29/04/1917
War Diary	Gouzeaucourt	30/04/1917	30/04/1917
War Diary		24/04/1917	24/04/1917
Heading	War Diary Of 17th (S) Bn The Welsh Regiment. From 1.5.17 To 31.5.17.		
War Diary	Equancourt	01/05/1917	04/05/1917
War Diary	Fins	05/05/1917	05/05/1917
War Diary	Right Of La Vacquerie	05/05/1917	06/05/1917
War Diary	Gouzeaucourt	06/05/1917	14/05/1917
War Diary	Gouzeaucourt Front Line	14/05/1917	22/05/1917
War Diary	Gouzeaucourt	22/05/1917	22/05/1917
War Diary	Fins	23/05/1917	23/05/1917
War Diary	Equancourt	24/05/1917	29/05/1917
War Diary	Sorel-Le-Grand	30/05/1917	31/05/1917
Heading	17th (S) Bn The Welsh. Regt. War Diary From 1st June 1917 To 30th June 1917.		
War Diary	Sorel-Le-Grand	01/06/1917	02/06/1917
War Diary	Gouzeaucourt	03/06/1917	11/06/1917
War Diary	Left. Sub Sector Villers Plouich	12/06/1917	20/06/1917
War Diary	Dessart Wood Near Fins	21/06/1917	27/06/1917
War Diary	Gonnelieu Sector	28/06/1917	30/06/1917
War Diary	La Vacquerie	05/05/1917	18/05/1917
Miscellaneous	17th Bn The Welsh Regt List Of Honours And Awards M.C.O's And Men		
War Diary	Gonnelieu Sector	01/07/1917	04/07/1917
War Diary	Gonnelieu Right Sub-Sector	05/07/1917	13/07/1917
War Diary	Sergeant Thomas Thomas L/Cope Arthur John Davies Private Walter Furlong		
War Diary	Gonnelieu Right Sub-Sector	14/07/1917	31/07/1917
Miscellaneous	17th Bn. The Welsh Regt.-List Of Honours And Awards.		
Heading	War Diary 17th (S) Bn The Welsh Regt. August 1917.		
War Diary	Gonnelieu Right Sub Sector	01/08/1917	02/08/1917
War Diary	Left Sub Sector Villers Plouich	03/08/1917	14/08/1917
War Diary	Gouzeaucourt	15/08/1917	23/08/1917
War Diary	Left Subsector Villers Plouich	24/08/1917	31/08/1917
Miscellaneous	Lift Of Honours And Awards.		
Heading	War Diary 17th. (S) Bn. The Welsh Regiment. September 1917.		
War Diary	Villers-Plouich Left Subsector	01/09/1917	30/09/1917

Heading	War Diary 17th. (S) Bn. The Welsh Regt. October 1917.		
War Diary	Villers Plouich Left Subsector	01/10/1917	06/10/1917
War Diary	Sorrel-Le-Grand	07/10/1917	07/10/1917
War Diary	Doingt	08/10/1917	10/10/1917
War Diary	Simencourt	11/10/1917	28/10/1917
War Diary	Coullemount	29/10/1917	31/10/1917
Miscellaneous	17th. (Service) Battalion The Welsh Regt. Training Programme For Wednesday October 31st. 1917.	31/10/1917	31/10/1917
Miscellaneous	17th. (Services) Battalion The Welsh Regiment. Training Programme For Week Ending 27th October 1917.	27/10/1917	27/10/1917
Miscellaneous	17th. (Service) Battalion. The Welsh Regiment Training Programme For Week Ending 27th October 1917.	24/10/1917	24/10/1917
Operation(al) Order(s)	17th Bn. The Welsh Regiment Order No. 50		
Miscellaneous	O.C. 17th Welsh.	05/10/1917	05/10/1917
Miscellaneous	O.C.	05/10/1917	05/10/1917
War Diary	Q.C.	05/10/1917	05/10/1917
Miscellaneous	First Omnibus Train. (1 Coach, 30 Covered Wagons, 17 Flats)		
Miscellaneous	First Coaching Train Appendix 'B'		
Operation(al) Order(s)	119th Infantry Brigade Order No. 120	07/10/1917	07/10/1917
Miscellaneous	Time Tables To Accompany 119th Infantry Brigade Order No. 120		
Operation(al) Order(s)	17th (Service) Battalion The Welsh Regiment. Order No. 52.	07/10/1917	07/10/1917
Miscellaneous	Time Table To Accompany. Order No. 52 Movement Of The 119th Infantry Brigade Group By Boust Decanalle On 8th Oct. 1917.	08/10/1917	08/10/1917
Operation(al) Order(s)	17th (Ser.) Battalion The Welsh Regiment. Order No. 51.		
Map			
Operation(al) Order(s)	17 Welsh Regt. Order No.		
Operation(al) Order(s)	119th Infantry Brigade Order No. 121	28/10/1916	28/10/1916
Miscellaneous	March Table "B" To Accompany 119th Infantry Brigade Order No. 121		
Miscellaneous	With Reference To 17th. Welsh Order No. 52 Dated October 22nd. 1917	22/10/1917	22/10/1917
Operation(al) Order(s)	17th. Welsh Regiment Order No. 52	22/10/1917	22/10/1917
Heading	War Diary 17th (S) Bn. The Welsh Regiment November 1917		
War Diary	Coullemont	01/11/1917	15/11/1917
War Diary	Simencourt	16/11/1917	16/11/1917
War Diary	Sommicourt	17/11/1917	18/11/1917
War Diary	Barastre	19/11/1917	21/11/1917
War Diary	Sraincourt	22/11/1917	23/11/1917
War Diary	Bourlon Wood	24/11/1917	26/11/1917
War Diary	Pommier	27/11/1917	30/11/1917
Miscellaneous	17th (Service) Battalion The Welsh Regt. Training Programme For Friday November 2nd. 1917		
Miscellaneous	To All Concerned. Reference the attached. Brigade Scheme.	11/11/1917	11/11/1917
Operation(al) Order(s)	17th. Bn. The Welsh Regt Order No 54.	14/11/1917	14/11/1917
Miscellaneous	O.C. Companies. Transport Officer. Quartermaster. Signalling Officer.	08/11/1917	08/11/1917
Miscellaneous		11/11/1917	11/11/1917

Heading	War Diary 17th. (S.) Bn. The Welsh Regiment. Dec 1917		
War Diary	Pommier	01/12/1917	02/12/1917
War Diary	Croisilles	03/12/1917	20/12/1917
War Diary	Ervillers	21/12/1917	21/12/1917
War Diary	Iniskilling Camp	22/12/1917	26/12/1917
War Diary	Croisillers	27/12/1917	31/12/1917
Heading	War Diary 17th. Bn Welsh Regt January 1918		
War Diary	Croisilles (Sector)	01/01/1918	09/01/1918
War Diary	Mory	10/01/1918	13/01/1918
War Diary	Croisilles	14/01/1918	25/01/1918
War Diary	Mory	26/11/1917	27/11/1917
War Diary	Croisilles	31/01/1918	31/01/1918
War Diary	Mory	28/01/1918	29/01/1918
War Diary	Croiselles	30/01/1918	31/01/1918
Heading	War Diary February 1918. 17th Welsh Regt.		
Miscellaneous	List Of O.R. Presented With Military Medal. For Gallantry In Bourlon Wood November 23rd 24th 25th 1917		
War Diary	Croisilles	01/02/1918	05/02/1918
War Diary	Mory	06/02/1918	08/02/1918
War Diary	Mory And Bailleulmont (9 Miles S.W. Of Arras.)	09/02/1918	09/02/1918
War Diary	Bailleulmont	10/02/1918	16/02/1918
Miscellaneous	The Attack On Bourlon Wood		
Miscellaneous	O.C. 13th. G.W.O. 17th Welsh.	10/11/1917	10/11/1917
Miscellaneous	Special Order Of The Day. By Brigadier-General F.P. Crozier., D.S.O. Commanding 119th Infantry Brigade.	27/11/1917	27/11/1917
Miscellaneous	17th (S). Battalion The Welsh Regiment Officers Casualties		
Miscellaneous	Special Divisional Order	28/11/1917	28/11/1917
Miscellaneous	17th. (Service) Battalion The Welsh Regiment. Training Programme For Thursday November 1st. 1917.	01/11/1917	01/11/1917
War Diary	17th. (Service) Battalion The Welsh Regt. Training Programme For Friday November 2nd. 1917.	02/11/1917	02/11/1917
Miscellaneous	17th (Service) Battalion The Welsh Regt. Training Programme For Saturday. November 3rd. 1917.	03/11/1917	03/11/1917
Miscellaneous	17th (S). Bn. The Welsh Regt. Training Programme For Monday Nov 5th 1917.	05/11/1917	05/11/1917
Miscellaneous	17th. (S) Battalion The Welsh Regiment Training Programme For Tuesday November 6th 1917.	06/11/1917	06/11/1917
Operation(al) Order(s)	17th. Welsh Order No. 8.	06/11/1917	06/11/1917
Miscellaneous	17th. (Service) Battalion The Welsh Regiment. Training Programme For Wednesday 7/11/17.	07/11/1917	07/11/1917
Miscellaneous	17th. (S) Battalion The Welsh Regiment Training Programme For Thursday November 8th 1917	08/11/1917	08/11/1917
Miscellaneous	17th (Service) Bn The Welsh Regt. Training Programming For Friday Nov 9th 1917	09/11/1917	09/11/1917
Operation(al) Order(s)	17th Welsh Order No. X2	12/11/1917	12/11/1917
Miscellaneous	17th (Service) Battn The Welsh Regt Training Programme For Week Ending 17th November 1917	17/11/1917	17/11/1917
Operation(al) Order(s)	17th Welsh Order No X. 2.	12/11/1917	12/11/1917

40TH DIVISION
119TH INFY BDE

17TH BN WELSH REGT

JUN 1916-FEB 1918

DISBANDED

17th Bn The Welsh Regt

War Diary

June 1916

Army Form C. 2118

WAR DIARY
or
~~INTELLIGENCE SUMMARY~~
(Erase heading not required.)

Instructions regarding War Diaries and Intelligence Summaries are contained in F. S. Regs., Part II. and the Staff Manual respectively. Title Pages will be prepared in manuscript.

Place	Date	Hour	Summary of Events and Information	Remarks and references to Appendices
Blackdown	2/6/16	5.30	Right half Battalion marched out of AISNE BARRACKS, BLACKDOWN for entraining at FRIMLEY.	For list of Officers embarking and left behind see Appendix 1
		7.10	Train departed.	
		7.30	Left half Battalion marched out	
		9.10	Train departed.	
			The Battalion detrained at SOUTHAMPTON DOCKS. Strength 35 Officers, including Chaplain, and other ranks 995 including 4 A.S.C. Drivers attached.	
			The Commanding Officer, Adjutant, eight other Officers and 135 Other ranks embarked on S.S. CITY of BENARES. The second in command and remainder of the Battalion embarked on S.S. CONNAUGHT.	
			Both ships left SOUTHAMPTON WATER during night 2/3 June 1916. H.M.B.	
HAVRE.	3/6/16		The Battalion disembarked during the morning of 3/6/16, marched to No 5 REST CAMP, HAVRE and there spent the night.	
			Capt. C. T. YOUNG and Sec. Lt. G. R. JACKMAN attached to H.Q. 119th Inf. Bde. H.M.B.	
HAVRE	4/6/16		The Battalion, less 'A' Coy and M-Gun Section No 1, entrained at HAVRE, Point 3, leaving at 8.5 en route for LILLERS.	
			'A' Coy and No 1 M-G. Section entrained at HAVRE, Point 1, leaving at 10.5 also en route to LILLERS. H.M.B.	
LILLERS	5/6/16		Battalion, less 'A' Coy. and M-G. Section No 1, arrived LILLERS at 1.30 and proceeded by march route to take up billets at St HILAIRE.	
			'A' Coy. and M-G. Section No 1 arrived LILLERS at 3.10 and also proceeded to billets in St HILAIRE. Billets were occupied by 6.30 H.M.B.	

1375 Wt. W593/826 1,000,000 4/15 J.B.C. & A. A.D.S.S./Forms/C. 2118.

Instructions regarding War Diaries and Intelligence Summaries are contained in F. S. Regs., Part II. and the Staff Manual respectively. Title Pages will be prepared in manuscript.

WAR DIARY
or
~~INTELLIGENCE SUMMARY~~
(Erase heading not required.)

Army Form C. 2118

Place	Date	Hour	Summary of Events and Information	Remarks and references to Appendices
St HILAIRE	6/6/16		Nothing to record.	
St HILAIRE	7/6/16		Received orders from H.Q. 119th Inf. Bde. to proceed, on 9/6/16, to 1st Div. area for attachment and instruction.	appendix 2 ~~appendix~~
St HILAIRE	8/6/16		Preparations for move on 9/6/16.	
St HILAIRE	9/6/16		March from St HILAIRE to HOUCHIN, via LILLERS, ALLOUAGNE and cross roads N.E of HAILLICOURT, arriving at HOUCHIN at 2.30 p.m. The march was completed between breakfast and dinner.	
HOUCHIN	10/6/16		Battalion attached to 1st Brigade for instruction in trenches in MAROC sector. A + B Coys attached to 2nd Bn. Black Watch. C + D to 8th Royal Berks. Attachment throughout on man to man principle. No casualties, quiet night, rain.	appendix 3
MAROC.	11/6/16		Attachment as on 10/6/16. Quiet. Much rain. Casualties – 1 O.R. Wounded	

1875 Wt. W593/826 1,000,000 4/15 J.B.C. & A. A.D.S.S./Forms/C. 2118.

Instructions regarding War Diaries and Intelligence Summaries are contained in F. S. Regs., Part II. and the Staff Manual respectively. Title Pages will be prepared in manuscript.

WAR DIARY
or
INTELLIGENCE SUMMARY
(Erase heading not required.)

Army Form C. 2118

Place	Date	Hour	Summary of Events and Information	Remarks and references to Appendices
MAROC	12/6/16		Attachment on Platoon principle. Slight hostile shelling. Rain. Casualties 2 O.R. wounded.	H.M.S.
MAROC.	13/6/16		Attachment as on 12/6/16. Rain. Casualties 4 O.R. wounded	H.M.S.
MAROC.	14/6/16		Battalion left the trenches and assembled at LES BREBIS by 16.30 o'clock. Tea was provided for the men by the Black Watch and Royal Berks. After tea men marched back to HOUCHIN. Men tired and feet sore after four days almost continuous in the trenches. No stragglers but two men dropped at Field Ambulance in NOEUX LES MINES.	Appendix 4 H.M.S.
HOUCHIN	15/6/16		Day spent in cleaning up after tour of duty in trenches.	H.M.S.
"	16/6/16		Company work. Physical Drill, musketry etc.	H.M.S.
"	17/6/16		As for 16/6/16.	H.M.S.

Instructions regarding War Diaries and Intelligence Summaries are contained in F. S. Regs., Part II. and the Staff Manual respectively. Title Pages will be prepared in manuscript.

WAR DIARY
or
INTELLIGENCE SUMMARY
(Erase heading not required.)

Army Form C. 2118

Place	Date	Hour	Summary of Events and Information	Remarks and references to Appendices
HOUCHIN	18/6/16		Battalion attached to 2nd Brigade for instruction in MAROC trenches. A+B Coys to 2nd R Sussex	Appendix 5
			'A' Coy took over the front line from CRASSIER Sap to Allie's Lane.	
			'B' Coy in reserve line, SOUTH STREET.	
			2nd Bde bombers held double crassier on right of 'A' Coy & 'B' Coy 2nd Royal Sussex continued line on their left.	
			C+D Coys. were attached to 2nd K.R.R.C in South MAROC.	
			Quiet day. Casualties – nil	H.P.B.S.
MAROC.	19/6/16		Attachment as for 18/6/16	
			Some hostile shelling. Casualties 2 O.R. killed, 1 O.R. wounded	H.P.B.S.
MAROC.	20/6/16.		Attachment as for 18/6/16	
			Some hostile shelling. Casualties. 4 O.R. wounded.	H.P.B.S.
MAROC.	21/6/16		Bn. left trenches on relief by 18th Welsh and marched back to Houchin.	H.P.B.S. Appendix 6.

1875 Wt. W593/826 1,000,000 4/15 J.B.C. & A. A.D.S.S./Forms/C. 2118.

Army Form C. 2118

Instructions regarding War Diaries and Intelligence Summaries are contained in F. S. Regs., Part II. and the Staff Manual respectively. Title Pages will be prepared in manuscript.

WAR DIARY
or
INTELLIGENCE SUMMARY
(Erase heading not required.)

Place	Date	Hour	Summary of Events and Information	Remarks and references to Appendices
HOUCHIN	22/6/16		Proceeded by march Route to take up billets at DIVION. No stragglers and Battalion well closed up on arrival.	H.M.S.
DIVION.	23/6/16		Battalion proceeded by companies to Baths at AUCHEL after being inspected by medical officer. Numerous cases of itch, in early stage of development reported. Itch probably due to dirty billets in St HILAIRE and men having had no bath since leaving England.	H.M.S.
DIVION	24/6/16 to 27/6/16		Route marches and company training.	H.M.S.
"	28/6/16		Bn inspected by G.O.C. 119th Inf. Bde.	H.M.S.
"	29/6/16 & 30/6/16		Route marches and company training.	H.M.S.

1875 Wt. W593/826 1,000,000 4/15 J.B.C. & A. A.D.S.S./Forms/C. 2118.

To D.A.G. 3rd Echelon.

I.D.
15 sheets

Herewith War Diary for June for the Battalion under my command.

9/7/16

Lt. COLONEL.

Appendix 1.

17th Service Battalion. The Welsh Regiment.

Lieut Colonel.
Wilkie, C.J.

Majors.
Gilbert, E.H.St.G.
Appleby, D.

Captains.
Sheppard, H.N.
Lyne, C.V.
Stratton, W.P.
Jeffreys, E.W.
Young, C.T. Attached 119 Bde.
Grant, A.E.
Evans, I.A.E.
Williams, E.

Lieutenants.
Dunn, C.M.
Wallace, T.
Jones, A.T.
Ettley, P.K.
Evans, C.R.
Rees, A.J.L.
Enser, J.C.
Higson, F.S.
Evans, G.J.

2nd Lieutenants.
Lloyd, A.P.
Walters, D.K.
Williams M.M.
Lewis, D.T.
Jackman, G.R. Attached 119 Brigade.
Walton, L.A.
Farmer, P.J.
Hammond, E.W.
Hughes, J.L.
O'Donnell, H.N.
Thomas, H.H.M.
Waring, C.

Adjutant:- Captain Gough, H.P.B.
Quartermaster:- Hon.Lieut. Walters A.
Medical Officer:- Lieut Proctor R.

appendix 2

119th INFANTRY
11 (G.L)
17 JUN. 1916
BDE.

17th (GLAM.) Bn.
JUN 1916
No. 17/W/17.
THE WELSH REGT.

S E C R E T.

To Headquarters,

17th Welsh Regt.

The unit under your command will march to Divisional Area as under for attachment and instruction. Detailed orders will follow.

To 1st Divisional Area.

JUNE 9th.

17th Welsh Regt.

[signature]

Captain,

Brigade Major,

7-6-16. 119th Infantry Brigade.

Appendix 3

1st Brigade No. 2600.

ATTACHMENT of 17th and 18th WELCH (119th BRIGADE).

(a) June 10th - Two Companies 17th Welch report to 8th Berks at PETIT SAINS.
Two Companies 17th Welch report to The Black Watch at LES BREBIS.

(b) June 14th - Four Companies 17th Welch march back to Billets at HOUCHIN.
Two Companies 18th Welch report to Cameron Head Quarters N. MAROC.
Two Companies 18th Welch report to 10th Gloster Head Quarters N. MAROC.

(c) June 18th - Four Companies 18th Welch march back to Billets at HOUCHIN.
Two Companies 17th Welch report to 8th Berks Head Quarters N. MAROC.
Two Companies 17th Welch report to The Black Watch Head Quarters N. MAROC.

(d) June 21st - Two Companies 18th Welch relieve two Companies 17th Welch with 8th Berks.
Two Companies 18th Welch relieve two Companies 17th Welch with The Black Watch.
Four Companies 17th Welch, on relief, march to Billets in HOUCHIN.

(e) June 22nd - 8th Berks, on relief, hand over two Companies 18th Welch to 10th Glosters.
The Black Watch, on relief, hand over two Companies 18th Welch to Camerons.
17th Welch march from HOUCHIN to 40th Divisional Area.

(f) June 24th - Four Companies 18th Welch march back to Billets at HOUCHIN.

(g) June 25th - 18th Welch march from HOUCHIN to 40th Divisional Area.

N.B. - Reference (a) and (b) for the first 48 hours Companies of 17th and 18th Welch will be attached on the man to man basis i.e. Company Commander to Company Commander, Platoon Commander to Platoon Commander and one man of the Welch to one man of the 1st Brigade etc.
For the second 48 hours they will be attached as Platoons.

Reference (c) and (d) the 17th and 18th Welch during this attachment will retain their Company formation.

The Head Quarters, Signallers, Lewis Gunners, Stretcher Bearers etc of the 17th and 18th Welch during the first four days of their attachments will be distributed amongst the Battalions of the 1st Brigade.

V.M. Fortune, Major,
Brigade Major 1st Infantry Brigade.

9th June 1916.

Issued to :- 4 Battalions
1st Divn. (G)
1st Divn. (Q)
Staff Captain
17th Welch
18th Welch
119th Infty. Brigade.

Appendix 3 (Cont.)

1st Brigade No. 2600/1.

ATTACHMENT of 17th and 18th WELCH (119th Brigade).

Reference 1st Brigade No. 2600 dated 9th June 1916.

1. 'A' and 'B' Companies 17th Welch will march from HOUCHIN tomorrow June 10th, with Cookers, so as to arrive at FOSSE 2 L.34.a.9.5. at 12 Noon.
 A Guide from the 1st Brigade will meet them there and will direct them to the spot where they will have dinners. After dinners Black Watch guides will meet them and lead them to Black Watch Head Quarters where they will be split up amongst Black Watch Companies.

2. 'C' and 'D' Companies 17th Welch will march from HOUCHIN tomorrow June 10th to PETIT SAINS when they will report to 8th Berks Head Quarters at 3 p.m. with Cookers.
 After tea they will be split up amongst 8th Berks Companies.

3. Head Quarters 17th Welch will be attached as follows :-

2nd in Command	-	The Black Watch.
Lewis Gun Officer	-	The Black Watch.
Grenade Officer	-	The Black Watch.
Adjutant	-	8th Berks.

Medical Officer and 8 Stretcher Bearers - 8th Berks.
N.C.O. and 7 Stretcher Bearers - The Black Watch.
Signal Officer and 8 Signallers - 8th Berks.
Signalling Sergeant and 7 Signallers - The Black Watch.
7 Lewis Gunners-to each Battalion.
 With the exception of the Lewis Gunners and the Lewis Gun Officer(who will report at the Mine Build--ings LES BREBIS at 11 a.m. tomorrow where the 1st Brigade Lewis Gun Officer will meet them), all Officers, N.C.O's and Men attached to The Black Watch should accompany 'A' and 'B' Companies (para 1), those attached to the 8th Berks with 'C' and 'D' Companies (para 2).

4. The 17th Welch will wire as soon as possible to 1st Brigade Head Quarters giving strength of Officers and Other Ranks by Companies.

V.M. Fortune, Major,
Brigade Major 1st Infantry Brigade.

9th June 1916.

Issued to :-

4 Battalions
119th Infty. Brigade
17th Welch
Staff Captain.

Appendix Ep.

1st INFANTRY BRIGADE.

- RELIEF ORDER No. 74 -

Copy No.

Reference :-

Trench Map 1/10,000.

13th June 1916.

1. The following Internal Reliefs will take place tomorrow June 14th in the MAROC SECTION.

The Reliefs will be carried out under arrangements to be made between Commanding Officers concerned and will be completed by 7 p.m. :-

(a) 10th Glosters will relieve 8th Berks in the Left Subsection.
(b) 8th Berks will move into Brigade Reserve in NORTH MAROC.
(c) Camerons will relieve The Black Watch in Right Subsection.
(d) The Black Watch (less one Company) will move into Support with - One Company in SOUTH STREET.
One Company in O.G.1.
One Company in Billets in N.MAROC.

2. The Black Watch will detail one Company to proceed to I Corps Head Quarters as Corps Troops.

They will move out of the Line tomorrow under orders already received.

3. The 17th Welch will move out of the Line by Platoons and will be guided, by the Battalions they are attached to, to their Quarter Master's Store in LES BREBIS.

4. The 18th Welch will join 10th Glosters and Camerons (2 Companies each) tomorrow, for attachment vide 1st Bde. No.2600 dated 9th instant.

The 10th Glosters will detail 8 Platoon Guides to report at their Battalion Quarter Master's Store in LES BREBIS at 1-30 p.m.

The Camerons will detail 8 Platoon Guides to report at their Battalion Quarter Master's Store in LES BREBIS at 2 p.m.

5. All Bombing Posts will be relieved by 12 Noon.

6. Completion of Relief to be reported to 1st Brigade Head Quarters.

V.M. Fortune, Major,
Brigade Major 1st Infantry Bde.

Issued to :-

10th Gloster Regt	1.	No. 2 Coy. Train	18.
1st The Black Watch	2.	Bde Supply Officer	19.
8th Royal Berks	3.	Left Group	20.
1st Cameron Highlanders	4.	Captain Sparrow	21.
4 Quarter Masters	5 - 8.	1/1 T.M. Battery	22.
No. 1 Coy.M. Gun Corps	9.	Y/1 -do-	23.
Bde Scout Officer	10.	X/1 -do-	24.
1st Div. (G)	11.	Staff Captain	25.
1st Div. (Q)	12.	Signals	26.
2nd Brigade	13.	War Diary	27 - 28.
3rd Brigade	14.	Office	29.
48th Brigade	15.		
C.R.E.	16.		

SECRET

Appendix 5

2nd INFANTRY BRIGADE. No. 91331 Date 20.6.16

O.C.
17th Welch.

2nd Brigade No. G. 1319 is hereby cancelled. The following will now be the system of reliefs :-

Date.	Right Front.	Left Front.	Support.	Reserve.
June 18/19.	K.R.R.C.	R. Sussex.	L.N.Lancs.	Northants.
June 25/26.	Northants.	L.N.Lancs.	R. Sussex.	K.R.R.C.

Details of reliefs for further dates will be issued later.

The following will be the attachments of Units 40th Division.-

June 18th.

To Royal Sussex. Headquarters and A and B Companies 17th Welch.

To K. R. R. C. Second in Command and C and D Companies 17th Welch.

June ~~22nd~~ *21st*. (Early morning). 17th Welch relieved by 18th Welch and march to 40th Division area. Route :- NOEUX-LES-MINES, South of HOUCHIN, BRUAY thence either MARLES LES MINES or DIVION.

To Royal Sussex. Headquarters and A and B Companies 18th Welch.

To K. R. R. C. Second in Command and C and D Companies 18th Welch.

18th Welch relieved ~~xxx~~ by 20th Middlesex Regiment on June 24th and march to 40th Division area. Route :- As for 17th Welch.

NOTE :- Both 17th and 18th Welch are to go in as Companies in front and support, having completed their man to man and platoon to platoon attachments.

20th Middlesex Regiment due to arrive on June 24th are a new Battalion and will do man to man attachment for the first 48 hours and platoon to platoon attachment for second 48 hours.

Details of attachments of 20th Middlesex Regiment will be notified later.

[signature]

Major, A/Brigade Major,
2nd Infantry Brigade.

20th June, 1916.

Appendix 5

2nd INFANTRY BRIGADE.
No. A49/1/2.
Date 20/6/16.

O.C. 17th Welch

Reference my 1331 (G) of todays date.

The attachments of Units of 40th Division should be amended to read as follows :-

June 21st. 17th Welch relieved by 18th Welch and proceed to HOUCHIN, rejoining 40th Division on 22nd instant via BRUAY to DIVION or MARLES LES MINES.

To Royal Sussex. Headquarters and A and B Companies 18th Welch.

To K.R.R.C. Second in Command and C and D Companies 18th Welch.

18th Welch relieved by 20th Middlesex Regiment on June 24th and march to HOUCHIN, rejoining 40th Division on 25th instant via BRUAY to DIVION or MARLES LES MINES.

20th June, 1916.

Major, A/Brigade Major,
2nd Infantry Brigade.

~~O.C.~~

For your information.

119th Brigade Headquarters close at BULLY at 8 a.m. and re-opens at MARLES LES MINES at noon, 23rd instant.

Probable hour of your arrival in 40th Division area on 22nd to be reported to them.

[signature]

20th June, 1916.

Major, A/Brigade Major,
2nd Infantry Brigade.

SECRET appendix 6.

2nd INFANTRY BRIGADE.
No. ...
Date 21.6.16

O.C. 18th Welch.
O.C. 17th Welch.

Reference relief of 17th Welch by 18th Welch to-night :-

1. Headquarters and A and B Companies 17th Welch attached to Royal Sussex will be relieved by Headquarters and A and B Companies 18th Welch.

2. Second in Command and C and D Companies 17th Welch attached to K.R.R.C. will be relieved by Second in Command and C and D Companies 18th Welch.

3. All details to be arranged between Commanding Officers concerned.

4. Four Guides per Company 17th Welch will be at IRON GATES, MAROC at 10 p.m.

5. Completion of relief to be reported to 2nd Brigade Headquarters at LES BREBIS.

[signature]

Major, A/Brigade Major,
2nd Infantry Brigade.

21st June, 1916.

Copies to.

Royal Sussex.)
Loyal N. Lancs.)
Northamptons.) for information.
K.R.R.C.)
119th Brigade.)

40 July

17. Welsh Reg

Vol 2

17th Bn The WELSH Regt

WAR DIARY

JULY 1916.

2. D.
10 sheets

Instructions regarding War Diaries and Intelligence Summaries are contained in F. S. Regs., Part II. and the Staff Manual respectively. Title Pages will be prepared in manuscript.

WAR DIARY
or
~~INTELLIGENCE SUMMARY~~
(Erase heading not required.)

Army Form C. 2118

Place	Date	Hour	Summary of Events and Information	Remarks and references to Appendices
DIVION.	1/7/16	–	In Billets at DIVION. Nothing to report.	
DIVION.	2/7/16	3.35pm	Telegram received from 119th Inf Bde as follows – 'Take your Bn as early as possible to BARLIN, occupying billets vacated by 1 Bn. 121st Bde. You will move up to trenches tomorrow. Send officer at once to report to 121st Bde H.Q. at BARLIN to obtain billets. ---- Nothing will be left at DIVION by you ----.'	
	"	7.15pm	The battalion marched via HOUDAIN – MAISNIL LES RUITZ – CITÉ LIAUTEY, to take over billets in CITÉ No 9 and CITÉ JEANNE D'ARC. Found these billets occupied by 20th Middlesex. Eventually got into billets at CITÉ D'ARRAOUAC.	
BARLIN.	3/7/16		Instructions received to proceed to BULLY GRENAY, leading platoon to reach the GRAND PLACE at 4 p.m., to take over billets occupied by Black Watch.	
	"	10.30am	The battalion proceeded to BULLY GRENAY via HERSIN – PETIT SAINS – road junction at L.35.a.8.0, arriving at GRANDE PLACE at 2.55 p.m. Billets taken over and Battalion placed under orders of G.O.C. 1st Inf Bde until the relief of ~~that~~ Brigade by ~~the~~ 119th Bde was completed on 5/7/16.	
BULLY GRENAY.	4/7/16 – 5/7/16		Work done on CHAPTEL ALLEY and ALGIERS TRENCH with a view to deepening to 7', setting trench boards in order, revetting where necessary, and digging sump pits.	

Instructions regarding War Diaries and Intelligence Summaries are contained in F. S. Regs., Part II. and the Staff Manual respectively. Title Pages will be prepared in manuscript.

WAR DIARY
or
~~INTELLIGENCE~~ SUMMARY
(Erase heading not required.)

Army Form C. 2118

Place	Date	Hour	Summary of Events and Information	Remarks and references to Appendices
BULLY GRENAY	6/7/16		Work on CHAPTEL ALLEY and ALGIERS TRENCH continued.	
		10 p.m.	Village line occupied between R.12.c.6.2 to R.8.a.2½.½. for purpose of familiarising Officers and O.R. with stations and routes to same by night.	
BULLY GRENAY	7/7/16	12.30a.m	Shell burst in billet of 'C' Coy. 6 men wounded.	
			Battalion relieved ~~the~~ 9th Bn. R.W.F. in right subsection CALONNE. 'D' Coy in front line from Boyau 200 to Pickaxe corner, 'A' Coy from Pickaxe corner to HAUNTED HOUSE, 'B' Coy thence to PITTROP CORNER. 'C' Coy. in support. Completed 6.45 p.m. Naval Division on our right and 18th Bn Welsh Rgt on our left.	
CALONNE	8/7/16.		Front line about HAUNTED HOUSE corner from Boyau 212 to Boyau 210 is very badly battered and in most places untenable. This part ~~of the~~ line is guarded at night by bombing posts on 'A' Coys left - 'B' Coys right respectively. Until this line is reestablished a back line is to be established and firebays made along the trench running from WALL St through DOWTY'S POST to BIRDCAGE walk. The 12th S.W.B., with R.E. assistance have been detailed to carry this out during the night of July 8/9, 1916, the 17th Welsh providing covering parties and patrols between DOWTY'S post and HAUNTED HOUSE.	
			While this work was in progress heavy enemy trench mortar fire commenced with the result that 2 of the 17th Welsh, 3 of the S.W.B and 1 R.E. were killed and several others wounded. On this occasion 37852 L-Cpl. E.J.B. Stiff, 17th Welsh Rgt. behaved with great gallantry.	see 27/7/16.
			During the night A + D Coys lines were also bombarded by trench mortars and several casualties occurred. Enemy trench mortar appeared to fire from M.6.7.4. Artillery retaliation	

Instructions regarding War Diaries and Intelligence Summaries are contained in F. S. Regs., Part II. and the Staff Manual respectively. Title Pages will be prepared in manuscript.

WAR DIARY
or
INTELLIGENCE SUMMARY
(Erase heading not required.)

Army Form C. 2118

Place	Date	Hour	Summary of Events and Information	Remarks and references to Appendices
			was called for and hostile trench mortars silenced in early hours of 9/7/16.	
			Casualties to 12 noon 8/7/16 — 1 O.R. killed and 6 O.R. wounded.	
CALONNE	9/7/16		Damaged caused by previous nights bombardment repaired and work on new trench continued.	
			Casualties from noon 8/7/16 to noon 9/7/16 — 4 O.R. killed, Capt Sheppard and 9 O.R. wounded.	
"	10/7/16		Quiet day.	
			Casualties from noon 9/7/16 to noon 10/7/16 — 5 O.R wounded.	
"	11/7/16		Battalion relieved by 19th Bn R.W.F. and went into billets in CALONNE vacated by ~~the~~ latter.	
			No casualties.	
			'No mans' land from Boyau 200 to Pit Prop corner patrolled nightly. No enemy patrols seen and no mining parties found at work during period 7/7/16 to 11/7/16.	
"	12/7/16		Work done remaking Boyaux 237, 235 and 234, deepening HOXTON Road between Boyaux 230 and 237. Working party putting firebays along BIRDCAGE WALK from Boyau 210 ~~to the~~ trench leading to DOWTY'S Post and cleaning Boyau 210.	

1375 Wt. W593/826 1,000,000 4/15 J.B.C. & A. A.D.S.S./Forms/C. 2118.

Army Form C. 2118

Instructions regarding War Diaries and Intelligence Summaries are contained in F. S. Regs., Part II. and the Staff Manual respectively. Title Pages will be prepared in manuscript.

WAR DIARY
or
INTELLIGENCE SUMMARY
(Erase heading not required.)

Place	Date	Hour	Summary of Events and Information	Remarks and references to Appendices
CALONNE	13/7/16		Work continued as on 12/7/16. Casualties – wounded, 3 O.R.	
"	14/7/16		Work continued as on 12/7/16 and 13/7/16.	
"	15/7/16		The battalion relieved the 19th Bn. R.W.F. in the right subsection CALONNE. Relief completed 6.30 p.m. Naval Division on our right & 18th Bn Welsh Regt on left. 'C' Coy hold line from Boyau 200 to junction of M.20.2 and M.20.3., 'A' Coy thence to junction of M.20.3 and M.20.4., 'B' Coy thence to Pitprop Corner. 'D' Coy. in support in CALONNE.	
	16/7/16		Considerable enemy artillery and trench mortar fire on B Coy's front and support line during early hours of morning.	
		3.15 a.m.	Our artillery retaliated and did considerable damage to enemy front line in CITE DES CORNAILLES, with the result that enemy trench mortars ceased firing about 3.40 a.m. A and C companies report quiet night July 15/16	
		6.30 pm.	Camouflet blown about M.20.b.3½.4½ – no crater formed. Considerable Trench Mortar, rifle grenade and M-Gun activity on our side with view to preventing rescue work by enemy. Orders received from 119th Inf. Bde to make careful reconnaissance of enemy wire opposite our front with a view to organising a raid. Patrol reports attached Casualties – 3 O.R. wounded.	appendix 6

Instructions regarding War Diaries and Intelligence Summaries are contained in F. S. Regs., Part II. and the Staff Manual respectively. Title Pages will be prepared in manuscript.

WAR DIARY
or
INTELLIGENCE SUMMARY
(Erase heading not required.)

Army Form C. 2118

Place	Date	Hour	Summary of Events and Information	Remarks and references to Appendices
CALONNE	17/7/16		Considerable amount of work done on Boyaux 207 and 208, the Morgan Trench and on Boyaux 214 and 215.	
			Patrols report enemy front line in CITÉ DES CORNAILLES to be unoccupied at night, very lights fired from enemy support line. No enemy patrols or working parties met.	
			2/Lt L.C. Walters wounded.	
	18/7/16		4 enemy loophole plates between M.20.b.5.4 and M.20.b.8.6 fired on by our four snipers with an elephant gun. All four plates penetrated.	
			Orders received to send out patrols during the night with a view to intercepting enemy attempts to repair his wire in front of the N.W. corner of the CITE DES CORNAILLES and procuring a prisoner.	
			Three parties were sent out under 2/Lt H.M. Thomas, 2/Lt C. Waring and Sgt J. Rees. All three patrols reported no trace of enemy patrol or working party. Patrol on left reports enemy line in CITÉ DES CORNAILLES unoccupied, patrols on centre and right report lines strongly held.	
	19/7/16	4 a.m.	Camouflet blown at 4 a.m at M.20.b.5.5. Our snipers had been warned and claim 3 hits in enemy trenches at this hour. No crater was found but considerable amount of smoke & flame observed.	
			The Battalion was relieved by the 19th Bn R.W.F. and took up billets in BULLY GRENAY vacated by "the 12" S.W.B.	

1373 Wt. W593/826 1,000,000 4/15 J.B.C. & A. A.D.S.S./Forms/C. 2118.

Instructions regarding War Diaries and Intelligence Summaries are contained in F. S. Regs., Part II. and the Staff Manual respectively. Title Pages will be prepared in manuscript.

WAR DIARY
or
~~INTELLIGENCE~~ SUMMARY
(Erase heading not required.)

Army Form C. 2118

Place	Date	Hour	Summary of Events and Information	Remarks and references to Appendices
BULLY GRENAY	20/7/16		Rest and cleaning up in billets	
			Orders received ~~that~~ 119th Brigade will be relieved by 120th Brigade in CALONNE on 21st and 22nd July. 17th Welsh to take over billets occupied by 14th Bn A & S Highrs in LES BREBIS. (119th Brigade Order No 10 of 20/7/16).	
			Extracts from amendments to 119th Bde. Order No 10 of 20/7/16 —	
			Owing to readjustments of 1st Corps front whereby 40th Division takes over additionally the LOOS Section from ~~the~~ 16th Division, the CALONNE section is extended to M. 4. c. 5. 6.	
			17th Bn Welsh Regt. will remain in present billets in BULLY.	
			On completion of the relief ~~the~~ 17th Bn Welsh Regt. will form the Brigade Reserve, at call, for tactical purposes, of G.O.C. 121st Brigade.	
" "	21/7/16		Work done on BAJOLLE LINES between CHAPTEL ALLEY and CALONNE SOUTH, repairing fire bays, renewing sump holes and duck boards.	HPSS
" "	22/7/16			
" "	23/7/16		Also on CHAPTEL ALLEY from RUE BERTHELOT to TAMWORTH; cleaning, deepening and repairing Trench boards.	HPSS
" "	24/7/16		2Lt L.G. Walton, wounded on 17/7/16, returned to duty.	
			Lieut. A. HUMPHREYS, Late 12th Welsh, reported for duty & is posted to 'D' Coy.	
			Work as on 21/7/16.	HPSS

1875 Wt. W593/826 1,000,000 4/15 J.B.C. & A. A.D.S.S./Forms/C. 2118.

Army Form C. 2118

Instructions regarding War Diaries and Intelligence Summaries are contained in F. S. Regs., Part II. and the Staff Manual respectively. Title Pages will be prepared in manuscript.

WAR DIARY
or
~~INTELLIGENCE SUMMARY~~
(Erase heading not required.)

Place	Date	Hour	Summary of Events and Information	Remarks and references to Appendices
BULLY GRENAY	25/7/16		Work as on 21/7/16. Casualties – 2 men wounded by shrapnel outside billet.	
" "	26/7/16		Work as on 21/7/16. 2nd Lt E. Hammond, late 22nd Welsh, reported for duty & was posted to 'B' Coy.	
" "	27/7/16		Military medal awarded to 37852 L.Cpl. E. J. B. Stiff for gallantry on night of July 8/9. Work as on 21/7/16	See Appendix
" "	28/7/16		2Lt P. K. Lloyd-Williams (late 12th Welsh) reported for duty and was posted to 'C' Coy. 3 O.R. wounded, one at BULLY GRENAY and 2 at LES BREBIS. [illegible] attached to 119th Inf. Bde. Work as on 21/7/16.	
" "	29/7/16		Instructions received that 119th Brigade relieve 120th Bde in CALONNE sector on 29th and 30th insts. Bn Signallers and Lewis Gunners relieved 14th H.L.I.	
" "	30/7/16		Bn relieved the 14th H.L.I. in right centre CALONNE. 'D' Coy held front line from Boyau 211 exclusive to PITPROP CORNER (M.14 C.20.07) inclusive. A B & C Coys (less 2 platoons of C) in CALONNE, 2 platoons of 'C' Coy in BAJOLLE LINE between CALONNE NORD and Railway in M.8.d. Shortly after the relief had taken place heavy artillery and trench mortar fire	

1875 Wt. W593/826 1,000,000 4/15 J.B.C. & A. A.D.S.S./Forms/C. 2118.

Instructions regarding War Diaries and Intelligence Summaries are contained in F. S. Regs., Part II. and the Staff Manual respectively. Title Pages will be prepared in manuscript.

WAR DIARY
or
~~INTELLIGENCE~~ SUMMARY
(Erase heading not required.)

Army Form C. 2118

Place	Date	Hour	Summary of Events and Information	Remarks and references to Appendices
			was directed on our front line and on MORGAN trench. Boyau 214 and MORGAN trench were badly damaged.	
			Casualties Lt. T. Wallace and 11 O.R. wounded.	
			19th Bn. R.W.F. hold line on our right and 12th Bn S.W.B on our left. O.C 17th Bn Welsh Regt. in charge of CALONNE Defences.	
CALONNE	31/7/16		A large number of winged grenades fell in our lines round about Boyau 214. All these bear July date. Our Snipers claim 3 hits about M.20.b.8.7 and M.20.b.9.5½.	
			Capt. Sheppard, wounded 9/7/16, rejoined ~~the~~ Battalion.	

1875 Wt. W593/826 1,000,000 4/15 J.B.C. & A. A.D.S.S./Forms/C. 2118.

Appendix 6

[illegible] — The [illegible]

Report [illegible]

1. Section from [illegible] to M.20.c.[illegible]

Wire Entanglement [illegible] Gap at M.20.c.[illegible] about [illegible] [illegible] from M.20.c.[illegible] to M.20.c.[illegible] [illegible] M.20.c.[illegible] to M.20.c.[illegible]

[illegible] 2 gaps [illegible]

Route [illegible] bearing 150° (Magnetic). [illegible] the gap [illegible] from the German trench.

2. Section from M.20.c.[illegible] to M.20.b.[illegible]

[illegible] Gap at M.20.b.[illegible] about [illegible] yds. [illegible]

[illegible] 2 gaps [illegible]

Route [illegible]

3. Section M.20.b.[illegible] to M.21.a.[illegible]

[illegible] From M.20.b.[illegible] to M.20.b.[illegible] the German wire is [illegible] [illegible] M.20.b.[illegible] to M.21.a.[illegible] the wire is [illegible] but not high.

[illegible] Gap near [illegible]

Route [illegible] from the German [illegible] from HAUNTED HOUSE

4. General

A Patrol from left Coy reached the German wire at about M.20.b.[illegible] [illegible]

(Signed) [illegible] Lt Col.

[illegible] Comdg [illegible] Welsh Regiment

Appendix 7.

Extract from Routine Orders No 52.

by

Major General H. G. Ruggles Brise. C.B. M.V.O.

Commanding 40th Division

Headquarters, 40th Division

27th July 1916

342. Military Medal.

The Corps Commander has awarded the Military Medal to:-

No 37852. Lance Corporal Ernest John Burman Stiff.
17th Battalion, The Welsh Regiment.

for the following act of gallantry:-

A working party was buried during a hostile bombardment. Lance Corporal Stiff sent a messenger for assistance and at once single handed, under heavy fire, set to work to dig out the buried men. On arrival of Officer and a relief party, Lance Corporal Stiff stood on the parapet amidst severe bombardment from Trench Mortars and indicated by whistle the direction of approaching shells throughout the time taken to dig out the buried men, thereby saving many lives.

Subsequently, during a second bombardment on the same night, Lance Corporal Stiff in charge of a post found himself, owing to casualties, without a man available for look out. Cut off by destruction of the communication, he himself acted as sentry until relieved on cessation of the bombardment.

Vol 3

WAR DIARY

17th Bn. (S) WELSH REGT.

AUGUST 1916.

Instructions regarding War Diaries and Intelligence Summaries are contained in F. S. Regs., Part II. and the Staff Manual respectively. Title Pages will be prepared in manuscript.

WAR DIARY
or
~~INTELLIGENCE SUMMARY~~
(Erase heading not required.)

Army Form C. 2118

Place	Date	Hour	Summary of Events and Information	Remarks and references to Appendices
CALONNE	7/8/16.		'B' Coy relieved 'A' Coy in front line, the latter coy. taking up billets vacated by ~~the~~ former in CALONNE Much work done in improving the sanitary condition of CALONNE area. Deep trenches have been dug to take empty tins and refuse matter, far too much of which was scattered broadcast round about the billets. Casualties – 1. O.R. wounded	H.W.S.
"	8/8/16		Deep drainage pit – about 25 ft deep & 8 ft diameter – completed near water supply tanks. This pit should have great effect in draining ground here which is at present in a very unsanitary condition.	H.W.S.
"	9/8/16		Enemy rifle grenades directed on our trenches on the BURNING BING rather troublesome until we retaliated heavily on their front and support lines in CITE CORNAILLES. Prompt & heavy retaliation seems to be very effective in inducing ~~the~~ Boche to cease troubling us with grenades. A similar policy would doubtless prove effective with regard to his T. M's but unfortunately our T. M's do not seem to be able to do this. Casualties – 7. O. R. wounded.	H.W.S.
"	10/8/16		The 40th Div. front is being readjusted to its original line consisting of CALONNE and MAROC sections. In consequence of this ~~the~~ Battalion (A & D Coys) took over the front occupied by 2 coys 19th R.W.F in CALONNE right subsection. Disposition on relief as follows – D Coy from Boyau 200 inclusive to Boyau 206 inclusive, 'A' Coy thence to Boyau 211 exclusive, B Coy. from 211 inclusive to MERSEY TUNNEL exclusive. 'C' Coy. in support in BERTHELOT ST. Casualties – 3. O. R. wounded.	H.W.S.

1375 Wt. W593/826 1,000,000 4/15 J.B.C. & A. A.D.S.S./Forms/C. 2118.

Instructions regarding War Diaries and Intelligence Summaries are contained in F. S. Regs., Part II. and the Staff Manual respectively. Title Pages will be prepared in manuscript.

WAR DIARY
or
INTELLIGENCE SUMMARY
(Erase heading not required.)

Army Form C. 2118

Place	Date	Hour	Summary of Events and Information	Remarks and references to Appendices
BULLY GRENAY	14/8/16 15/8/16		} Nothing to report except — Casualties — 1.O.R. wounded on 14/8/16	[illegible]
" "	16/8/16.		The 120th Inf. Bde relieved the 119th Bde in the CALONNE section. The battalion was relieved by, and took over billets vacated by 14th A & S. Highrs in LES BREBIS.	H.W.R.
LES BREBIS	17/8/16 to 23/8/16.		Nothing to report except — Casualties — 1.O.R. wounded, 19/8/16. — 2/Lt. P.J. Farmer & 1.O.R., attached to 119th Bde. Bombing School, accidentally wounded. 20/8/16. — 1.O.R. wounded 21/8/16. — 1.O.R. killed 22/8/16.	H.W.R.
LOOS	24/8/16.		The 119th Bde relieved the 47th Bde in LOOS section. The battalion relieved the 6th Connaught Rangers in the right subsection LOOS from HAYMARKET inclusive to Piccadilly inclusive. Dispositions on relief as follows — 'B' Coy. from HAYMARKET inclusive to Boyau 33 inclusive, 'C' Coy, thence to Boyau 38 exclusive, 'D' Coy from Boyau 38 inclusive to PICCADILLY inclusive. 'A' Coy in support in the ENCLOSURE. HARRISON'S Crater and MANNING'S mound held by 'C' Coy, HART'S crater held by 'D' Coy. The whole system of trenches is in very bad order, very little shelter for men in the front line, in places none at all, and dugouts in support line quite insufficient. Boyaux connecting front & support line badly battered, firebays & traverses falling to pieces, firesteps in many places non existent.	

1375 Wt. W593/826 1,000,000 4/15 J.B.C. & A. A.D.S.S./Forms/C. 2118.

Instructions regarding War Diaries and Intelligence Summaries are contained in F. S. Regs., Part II. and the Staff Manual respectively. Title Pages will be prepared in manuscript.

WAR DIARY
or
~~INTELLIGENCE SUMMARY~~
(Erase heading not required.)

Army Form C. 2118

Place	Date	Hour	Summary of Events and Information	Remarks and references to Appendices
			There is practically no wire on our front but the enemy wire is thick & in very good order with no obvious gaps in it.	H.P.S.S.
LOOS.	25/8/16		Wiring commenced on all three company fronts and on sides of craters. Attempts made to improve trenches last night almost nullified by enemy T.M. bombardment today. The work of putting in order the front & support lines is likely to be slow and tedious.	
			Our patrols confirm the reports as to the bad state of our wire and the excellent state of the enemy's wire. Patrols also report that the enemy are working hard in their saps.	
			An Officers patrol consisting of 2Lt. H.M. Thomas, 1 N.C.O + 6 men left our trenches at M.6.d. 8.7½ at 10.50 p.m. with the intention of trying to get a prisoner from a working party which could be plainly heard opposite our right Coy. front. The patrol found it impossible to get through the enemy's wire. They encountered first, a trip wire, then a wide low belt of barbed wire, and beyond that a belt of thick high wire.	H.P.S.S.
			Casualties – 2. O.R. killed & 2. O.R. wounded.	
"	26/8/16		Work on trenches and wire continued but trenches battered in almost as quickly as they are put in order.	
			Casualties – 1 O.R. wounded	H.P.S.S.
"	27/8/16		Trenches, ~~both~~ both front & support lines of left and centre Coys heavily bombarded by T.M's. The trenches were knocked in in about 12 places. These trenches were cleared during the night & sides revetted as far as possible. The constant hammering of our support line is probably due to the fact ~~that~~ 2 of our Stokes guns fire from emplacements therein. It appears that if the support line is to be	

Instructions regarding War Diaries and Intelligence Summaries are contained in F. S. Regs., Part II. and the Staff Manual respectively. Title Pages will be prepared in manuscript.

WAR DIARY
or
~~INTELLIGENCE SUMMARY~~
(Erase heading not required.)

Army Form C. 2118

Place	Date	Hour	Summary of Events and Information	Remarks and references to Appendices
			occupied by the infantry emplacements for the stokes guns should be built at the ends of short saps leading out of the communication trenches.	H.H.B.S.
			Casualties – 3 O.R. wounded.	
LOOS.	28/8/16		The battalion was relieved by the 19th R.W.F. and took over billets vacated by the 18th Bn Welsh Regt as support battalion in LOOS right subsection.	
			Disposition as follows – A + B Coys. in Enclosure and DUKE'S ALLEY.	
			'C' Coy. less 1 platoon in DUKE STREET, one platoon of C. Coy. in 'Keep' (G.27.d). 'D' Coy + Headquarters in VILLAGE LINE from TRIVETE passage inclusive to LENS REDOUBT inclusive.	
			Condition of DUKE STREET bad, accommodation at Headquarters insufficient.	
			Lt. F. Badham, late of 21st Bn Welsh Regt, reported for duty and is posted to 'D' Coy.	
			Casualties – 1.O.R. wounded.	H.H.B.S.
"	29/8/16		Very heavy rainstorm. DUKE STREET flooded and many falls both in this trench and in the VILLAGE LINE.	
			2/Lt. H.C. Williams, late of 21st Bn Welsh Regt, reported for duty + is posted to 'D' Coy.	
			Casualties – 1. O R. killed.	H.H.B.S.
"	30/8/16		Heavy rain at intervals throughout day. Condition of trenches worse than ever. Men kept hard at work draining and rebuilding sides of trenches. Many new trench boards laid in bad places.	
"	31/8/16		Repair and drainage of DUKE STREET and VILLAGE LINE continued, much good work done.	H.H.B.S.

1875 Wt. W593/826 1,000,000 4/15 J.B.C. & A. A.D.S.S./Forms/C. 2118.

Instructions regarding War Diaries and Intelligence Summaries are contained in F. S. Regs., Part II. and the Staff Manual respectively. Title Pages will be prepared in manuscript.

WAR DIARY
or
~~INTELLIGENCE SUMMARY~~
(Erase heading not required.)

Army Form C. 2118

Place	Date	Hour	Summary of Events and Information	Remarks and references to Appendices
CALONNE	1/9/16.	28	WALL Street + MORGAN trench were frequently and heavily bombarded with aerial darts. The effect of these is very local and damage to trenches small so that light head cover, preferably in rear of traverses would probably provide efficient protection against these missiles. Our patrols report that the enemy has considerably strengthened his wire in front of the CITÉ CORNAILLES since our last occupation of these trenches. It has been decided to make a parapet on the CALONNE side of MORGAN trench. This parapet will be quite invisible to the enemy and will save many casualties due to blowback from darts and bombs falling in the open space between MORGAN trench and the NEW SUPPORT line. Casualties – 2. O. R. wounded.	HPBS.
"	2/9/16.		Good work done improving our wire at PITTROT corner and filling up gaps between existing knife rests in this vicinity. Deepening of MORGAN trench and building up of parapet commenced. The trench up the side of the BURNING BING needs deepening – this work has been taken in hand and about 6 yards of the worst portion has been dealt with and now affords complete protection against enemy snipers. Patrols have been sent out constantly during the last four nights but have not met any hostile patrols, nor have enemy working parties been seen in NO MAN'S LAND. These patrols on two occasions reported enemy at work in his saps in front of CITÉ CORNAILLES. Bombardment of these saps caused abrupt cessation of work. Casualties – 1. O. R. killed, 3. O. R. wounded.	HPBS.

1875 Wt. W593/826 1,000,000 4/15 J.B.C. & A. A.D.S.S./Forms/C. 2118.

Instructions regarding War Diaries and Intelligence Summaries are contained in F. S. Regs., Part II. and the Staff Manual respectively. Title Pages will be prepared in manuscript.

WAR DIARY
or
~~INTELLIGENCE SUMMARY~~
(Erase heading not required.)

Army Form C. 2118

Place	Date	Hour	Summary of Events and Information	Remarks and references to Appendices
CALONNE	3/9/16.		'A' Coy. relieved 'D' Coy. in front line, 'D' Coy. taking up billets vacated by 'A' Coy. in CALONNE. Instructions received from 119th Bde. to push on with work in Boyaux 210 + 211, to make a new T head on the site of an old trench leading out of STAFFORD trench and to put out wire for the protection of the mine head in Boyau 211. Wire was put out round the bombing post at the end of STAFFORD trench. This post is now fairly secure and is of great value for the protection it affords to the minehead in Boyau 211.	H.P.B.S.
"	4/9/16		Improvement of trenches continued with satisfactory results. Several portions of the front line were deepened and new wire put out. Usual collection of debris from Morgan trench disposed of. Casualties — 1 O.R. killed, 2 O.R. wounded.	H.P.B.S.
"	5/9/16		The bombers holding the end of STAFFORD trench were formerly much exposed to shrapnel and grenade fire. Cover has now been made by constructing a small 'bay' for each sentry. Our wiring parties were interfered with by M-Gun fire, but in spite of this a good deal of wire was put out in front of STAFFORD trench and the BURNING BING. Casualties — 3. O.R. wounded.	H.P.B.S.
"	6/9/16		Enemy bombardments with Minnies during the last few days have been heavy and frequent, but our sentries are now so well trained to use their whistles to such good advantage that losses among our men have been reduced to a minimum. Aerial darts and rifle grenades are now the greatest source of danger but provision of head cover should result in minimising this danger. Casualties 1 O.R. wounded.	H.P.B.S.

Instructions regarding War Diaries and Intelligence Summaries are contained in F. S. Regs., Part II. and the Staff Manual respectively. Title Pages will be prepared in manuscript.

WAR DIARY
or
~~INTELLIGENCE SUMMARY~~
(Erase heading not required.)

Army Form C. 2118

Place	Date	Hour	Summary of Events and Information	Remarks and references to Appendices
CALONNE	11/9/16		'C' Coy. relieved 'B' Coy. in front line, the latter taking up billets vacated by 'C' Coy in BERTHELOT Street. Other Coy. unchanged. 'No Man's' Land has been ~~constantly~~ patrolled by our men but no enemy patrols have been seen. On one occasion a small reconnoitring patrol of 1 N.C.O + 2 men did come across a large Bosh covering party but as our own men were busily engaged in wiring just opposite no hostile action was taken. The enemy has lately shown some disposition to work on his own wire, but as he never starts work until after our men are out there has not been much opportunity of doing him harm. It was decided to try the effect of expanded metal sheets with a layer of sandbags on top as head cover against aerial darts and rifle grenades. Casualties – 2. O. R. wounded.	H.P.B.S.
"	12/9/16.	–	The Dugouts in our left Coy. front are quite insufficient and unsuitable to house the company holding it. Representations have been made with a view to shoring up and rendering bomb proof the cellars off MORGAN trench. These cellars together with those in the NEW SUPPORT line, especially if both groups were connected by a tunnel, would provide good and reasonably safe cover in the event of a heavy bombardment. Casualties – 2. O. R wounded.	H.P.B.S.
"	13/9/16.		The battalion was relieved by the 19th R.W.F. and proceeded to take up billets vacated by the 18th ?Welsh Rgt. in BULLY GRENAY. Much has been done to improve the trenches in CALONNE right subsection during this tour of duty. Trenches have been deepened, new work continued & completed, firebays rebuilt & revetted, new wire put out & bombing posts made much more secure. Casualties – 3. O. R. wounded.	H.P.B.S.

1875 Wt. W593/826 1,000,000 4/15 J.B.C. & A. A.D.S.S./Forms/C. 2118.

Instructions regarding War Diaries and Intelligence Summaries are contained in F. S. Regs., Part II. and the Staff Manual respectively. Title Pages will be prepared in manuscript.

WAR DIARY or INTELLIGENCE SUMMARY

(Erase heading not required.)

Army Form C. 2118

17 Welsh Regt

Vol 4

Place	Date	Hour	Summary of Events and Information	Remarks and references to Appendices
LOOS	1/9/16.		Battalion relieved 19th Bn R.W.F. in right subsection LOOS. Disposition. 'A' Coy. from HAYMARKET inclusive to Boyau 33 inclusive, 'C' Coy. thence to Boyau 38 exclusive, 'D' Coy from Boyau 38 inclusive to PICCADILLY inclusive. 'B' Coy in support in the ENCLOSURE. One of the 3 dugouts in support line of centre Coy. completely blown in recently, being the Platoon in support having insufficient accomodation. Arrangements were made to send 1 Platoon down to the ENCLOSURE for rest during the day.	
"	2/9/16		Very heavy bombardment of our front and support lines by enemy Artillery and Heavy T.M. Portions of Support line beaten flat and communication trenches between Support and Front Line badly damaged. Casualties 1 O.R. killed and 1 O.R. wounded.	
"	3/9/16.		Enemy artillery and Heavy T.M's active. Enemy working parties very busy in their front line trenches and behind their wire. These parties were dispersed by L. Guns and Rifle Grenades. Losses inflicted unknown but all work stopped. Casualties – 1 O.R. wounded.	
"	4/9/16		Enemy Artillery and T.M. activity confined to our Front and Support lines between HARTS and HARRISONS craters. Boyaux connecting Front & Support lines almost	A. D. 12 sheets

1875 Wt. W593/826 1,000,000 4/15 J.B.C. & A. A.D.S.S./Forms/C. 2118.

Instructions regarding War Diaries and Intelligence Summaries are contained in F. S. Regs., Part II. and the Staff Manual respectively. Title Pages will be prepared in manuscript.

WAR DIARY
or
~~INTELLIGENCE~~ SUMMARY
(Erase heading not required.)

Army Form C. 2118

Place	Date	Hour	Summary of Events and Information	Remarks and references to Appendices
			obliterated. Our artillery retaliated and eventually succeeded in silencing enemy T.M's.	
			A patrol under 2Lt L.A. Walton left our trenches on the left of HARTS CRATER with the object of examining MODEL MOUND. 2Lt Walton reported that enemy were not holding MODEL MOUND but that they were hard at work on their front line trenches opposite. On his return a few well directed rifle grenades put an end to this activity.	
			A small patrol of 2 men left our trenches between HARTS and HARRISONS craters and soon met an enemy patrol of about 14 men. Our patrol got back unobserved and L-Gunners opened fire on the enemy with, it is believed, good results.	
			Casualties:— Killed O.R. 1 Wounded O.R. 9 (5 shell shock)	H.P.B.S.
LOOS	5/9/16		A patrol under 2Lt L.A. Walton went out at midnight to the right of HARTS CRATER for the purpose of reconnoitring GREEN MOUND and a small mound to the right of the same. 2Lt Walton reported both mounds unoccupied and no enemy saps leading to them. The patrol then worked up to the enemy wire, found it very strong and no gaps. Front line appeared to be very lightly held.	
			Casualties:— Wounded O.R. 5.	H.P.B.S.
LOOS.	6/9/16		The Battalion was relieved by the 19th Bn R.W.F. and took up billets vacated by 18th Welsh in Brigade Reserve in N. MAROC.	
			Casualties:— Killed O.R. 2 Wounded O.R. 2	H.P.B.S.

1875 Wt. W593/826 1,000,000 4/15 J.B.C. & A. A.D.S.S./Forms/C. 2118.

Instructions regarding War Diaries and Intelligence Summaries are contained in F. S. Regs., Part II. and the Staff Manual respectively. Title Pages will be prepared in manuscript.

WAR DIARY
or
~~INTELLIGENCE SUMMARY~~
(Erase heading not required.)

Army Form C. 2118

Place	Date	Hour	Summary of Events and Information	Remarks and references to Appendices
N. MAROC	7/9/16. 8/9/16. 9/9/16. 10/9/16.		In Brigade Reserve in N MAROC. Billets were good and much was done to improving them by [illegible] cellars and constructing beds for the men.	
			On 9/9/16 'A' Coy. proceeded to CLARQUES to dig trenches for the First Army T.M. School. Lt Col Wilkins proceeded to England on leave on 8/9/16 and Major [illegible] (12th S.W.B.) assumed the command. Casualties — Nil.	[illegible]
LES BREBIS	11/9/16		The 119th Bde was relieved by the 121st Bde in the LOOS Sector on 10th/11th inst. The 17th Bn Welsh was relieved by the 20th Middlesex in N MAROC and proceeded to LES BREBIS taking over billets vacated by the 13th Bn Yorks (Ann B).	
			The Corps Commander (1st Corps) has awarded the Military Medal to 26138 Cpl. Levi Davies, 17th Bn Welsh Regt for the following act of gallantry —	
			"On the night 3/4 September during a heavy bombardment the [illegible] 17th Welsh Regt was completely buried, Corporal Davies rushed to their assistance and despite the fact that he was three times blown off his feet – on one occasion being blown into a mine shaft – he carried on, and, although in a dazed condition assisted stretcher bearers 5 times, the time working under heavy fire, to extricate the [illegible]. Unfortunately the [illegible] subsequently died from his injuries."	
			The undermentioned Officers reported for duty and were posted as shown. 2Lt. H. B. Davies — 'D' Coy. 2Lt W. J. Griffiths — 'C' " 2Lt W. J. Mould — 'A' " 2Lt J. P. M. [illegible] — 'B' "	[illegible]

1875 Wt. W593/826 1,000,000 4/15 J.B.C. & A. A.D.S.S./Forms/C. 2118.

Instructions regarding War Diaries and Intelligence Summaries are contained in F. S. Regs., Part II. and the Staff Manual respectively. Title Pages will be prepared in manuscript.

WAR DIARY
or
~~INTELLIGENCE SUMMARY~~
(Erase heading not required.)

Army Form C. 2118

Place	Date	Hour	Summary of Events and Information	Remarks and references to Appendices
LES BREBIS	12/9/16 to 16/9/16		In billets in Les Brebis. Company training carried on daily. On 16/9/16 the undermentioned officers reported for duty and were posted as shown 2Lt A. J. Elmitt to 'C' Coy 2Lt S. T. Hennell to 'D' "	HPBS.
"	17/9/16		Billets in Les Brebis. Much has been done to improve these billets and to improve the Horse Shelters in PETIT SAINS. The health of the men suffered in Les Brebis through lying on stone floors. Work on beds has been continuous and arrangements made to carry on with this work while the Battalion is in the line. It is hoped that by the time the Battalion returns to Les Brebis all rooms with stone floors will be provided with beds.	HPBS.
"	18/9/16		The 119th Inf Bde. relieves the 120th Inf. Bde in the MAROC Sector on 18th & 19th inst. L. Guns of the 17th Welsh relieved the L. Guns of the 13th E. Surreys in the Right Subsection. Disposition — 6 guns in firing line, 2 in support.	HPBS.
"	19/9/16		The 17th Welsh relieved the 13th Bn. E. Surrey Rgt. in the MAROC Right Subsection. Disposition — 'B' Coy. from EDGWARE RD. inclusive to Boyau inclusive, 'C' Coy. thence to Boyau 18 inclusive. 'D' Coy. in NEUF and EDGWARE Keeps with remainder of men in billets. Details of 'A' Coy. in billets. 111th Bde. (37th Div.) on our right: 12th Bn S. W. B. on our left	

1875 Wt. W593/826 1,000,000 4/15 J.B.C. & A. A.D.S.S./Forms/C. 2118.

Instructions regarding War Diaries and Intelligence Summaries are contained in F. S. Regs., Part II. and the Staff Manual respectively. Title Pages will be prepared in manuscript.

WAR DIARY
or
INTELLIGENCE SUMMARY
(Erase heading not required.)

Army Form C. 2118

Place	Date	Hour	Summary of Events and Information	Remarks and references to Appendices
			Major E. H. St G. Gilbert proceeded to take up duty as Commandant of the Rest Camp [illegible].	
			~~Casualties~~ Lt. Col. C. J. Wilkie returned from leave and resumed command of the Battalion.	
			Casualties :- Nil	[illegible]
MAROC.	20/9/16		Patrols sent out to examine wire ~~[illegible]~~ report enemy's wire to be good with the exception that a number of gaps had been cut in it by our Artillery and Trench Mortars. Our wire is reported to be fair. It needs thickening and some repairing.	
			Trench is fairly good order except in [illegible] left near the [illegible] [illegible].	
			Casualties :- Nil	[illegible]
"	21/9/16		Two strong fighting patrols under 2/Lt. L. A. Walton and Sgt. [illegible] of 'B' Coy went out at about 8.40 p.m. with the intention of forcing a fight on any enemy patrol encountered. The patrols remained out about 3½ hours but they came in having seen no sign of the enemy either in front of or behind his wire.	
			Our T.M's (medium) and Stokes Guns heavily bombarded enemy front line [illegible] [illegible] with apparently very good results.	
			'A' Coy. returned from 1st Army T. M. School.	
			Casualties – ~~[illegible]~~ OR Wounded O.R. 2	[illegible]
"	22/9/16		Two fighting patrols, under Capt. Jeffreys and Lt. A. J. Rees, from left Coy. patrolled from 9.15 p.m. to 12.45 a.m. with the hope of meeting the enemy. An endeavour was made to entice enemy out by sending a small party of 3 to work along the enemy wire [illegible] [illegible]	

1375 Wt. W593/826 1,000,000 4/15 J.B.C. & A. A.D.S.S./Forms/C. 2118.

Instructions regarding War Diaries and Intelligence Summaries are contained in F. S. Regs., Part II. and the Staff Manual respectively. Title Pages will be prepared in manuscript.

WAR DIARY
or
~~INTELLIGENCE SUMMARY~~
(Erase heading not required.)

Army Form C. 2118

Place	Date	Hour	Summary of Events and Information	Remarks and references to Appendices
			Enemy Heavy T. M's very active doing much damage to our trenches. Casualties :- Nil	A.P.W.S
MAROC	23-9-16		Internal relief. 'B' Coy. relieved by 'A' Coy, 'C' Coy relieved by 'D' Coy. Casualties :- Wounded O.R. 1.	H.P.W.S
MAROC	24-9-16		Medium T.M. knocked the Tower of Puits 16 down. This tower is in the enemy's lines and overlooked the whole of this sector. Officers patrol out from left Coy at 9.30 pm reconnoitring enemy's wire. Returned at 11.15 pm without having seen or heard any hostile patrols or working parties. Casualties :- Nil	A.P.L.
MAROC	25-9-16	9.15 pm.	On the night of the 25/26 a raid was carried out by 2 Officers and 40 O.R. See Apendix I for Operation Order and Appendix II for the Commanding Officers Report together with comments of the Brigadier General commanding the 119th Inf Brigade. Casualties:- Nil	For operation order see appendix I For report see appendix II A.P.L.
MAROC	26-9-16		Artillery active on Hostile trenches from 3 pm to 3.30 pm. Enemy's artillery quiet but he retaliated with heavy aerial torpedoes. 2/Lt Dunn patrolled no man's land and after some considerable searching recovered the German equipment which had been dropped by one of the raiding party of last night who went to assist a wounded comrade. Six or seven Corps Signallers put out a cable across No Man's land and covering parties for the cable layers were found by the right & left Companies. No enemy patrols seen or heard. Casualties :- Missing O.R. 1. Wounded O.R. 5.	
MAROC	27-9-16		The Battalion was relieved in the Right Subsection MAROC by the 19th Bn. Royal Welsh Fusiliers. Relief complete at 3.55 pm. Battalion then moved into	A.P.L.

1875 Wt. W593/826 1,000,000 4/15 J.B.C. & A. A.D.S.S./Forms/C. 2118.

Instructions regarding War Diaries and Intelligence Summaries are contained in F. S. Regs., Part II. and the Staff Manual respectively. Title Pages will be prepared in manuscript.

WAR DIARY
or
INTELLIGENCE SUMMARY
(Erase heading not required.)

Army Form C. 2118

Place	Date	Hour	Summary of Events and Information	Remarks and references to Appendices
			Brigade Reserve occupying Billets vacated by the 15th (S) Bn The Welsh Regt The Corps Commander has awarded the Military Medal to 25633 Private Frederick Green 17th (S) Bn Welsh Regiment attd. 119th Trench Mortar Battery. for the following act of gallantry:— During the afternoon of the 21st September Private Green while serving his mortar during an organised bombardment of the enemy line noticed that the shell which he was about to place in his gun had started to fuse apparently due to a faulty pistol head. He immediately endeavoured to throw the shell out of the gun pit on to the parados, but the shell fell back into the pit. Pte Green without hesitation again picked up the shell and was this time successful in throwing it clear when it immediately exploded. The fuse was timed for 9 or 10 seconds only and as there were two other men in the emplacement besides over 100 detonated shells Pte Green's action doubtless saved his comrades from death or injury, and his mortar & emplacement from serious damage. After the incident Pte Green continued to serve his gun, firing some 50 more shells very rapidly, thus setting an excellent example to the other men at the gun. Casualties Wounded or. 1	
MAROC	28-9-16		In Brigade Reserve in S. MAROC	ARL
	29-9-16		Battalion busily engaged in supplying the various fatigues and carrying parties called for.	
	30-9-16		On 21/9/16 the following officer reported for duty & was posted to 'A' Coy 2/Lieut E. EVANS.	ARL

1875 Wt. W593/826 1,000,000 4/15 J.B.C. & A. A.D.S.S./Forms/C. 2118.

Headquarters,

119th Infantry Brigade.

- - - - - - - - - - - - - -

Reference to Raid on hostile trenches between M.10.c.09.48 and M.10.c.22.76 on night 25/26 Sept, by 17th (S) Bn The Welsh Rgt. I have to report as under :-

1. Infantry Advance. At 8-45 the Right party, 2 Sgts and 15 O.R. under Lt. A.J.L. Rees, emerged from Sap B; the Left party, 2 Sgts 21 O.R. under 2nd Lt. L.A. Walton from RUSSIAN SAP and crawled to gaps in hostile wire at M.10.c.13.58 (Right) and M.10.c.18.65 (Left). The advance was made in perfect order under cover of own Lewis Guns and parties were aligned at 9-11 p.m. close up against gaps without a single hostile shot.

2. Artillery and M.G. preparation. At 9-13 p.m. (-2) intense bombardment commenced with H.E. as arranged by O.C. Right Group and M.G. opened on flanks. The gunnery was of the best and close under the hostile wire as the raiders were none received the slightest injury from own gun fire. This must inspire the greatest confidence in future operations.

3. Infantry Attack. 5 seconds before ZERO (9-15 p.m) the order for assualt was given and both parties rushed the gaps and ran to appointed posts in and over the trenches which were found very much blown in. 3. O.R. were wounded by rifle bullets fired from Support or Communication trenches whilst they were on the hostile parados. Under cover of the flanking parties, who found no enemy, the driving parties under Lt Rees and 2nd Lt Walton proceeded along the front line trench.

APPENDIX III

Lt Rees (Right) with his driving party entered trench at a fire bay on the step of which was a rifle and skeleton set of equipment. They soon came upon entrance to a dug-out which was lighted. A bomb was thrown but before it exploded Sgt Abbott was wounded by rifle shot from dug-out. Nine bombs were thrown in and light extinguished. Party proceed round Bay and found another entrance which also showed light - nine bombs were thrown - Lt Rees then assisted Sgt Abbott over parapet and sent him back as he was unfit for further action. Lt Rees proceeded some 30 - 40 yards along trench but finding no Boches nor means of indentification returnedto dug-outs where there was no sign of life. The dug-outs were very deep and full of bomb gas. Reaching point of entry he threw the rifle and equipment, which had remained in the original positions, over the parapet to two men, names unknown as all faces were blackened, and told them to take the rifle and equipment back to own lines. Lt Rees then gave the signal to retire and collected his party.

2Lt Walton (Left) entered the trench with his driving party as arranged but found no Boches or means of identification. He found a lighted dug-out into which bombs were thrown. 2Lt Walton who is slightly deaf did not hear the signal to retire and was consequently the last to leave the hostile trench. On finding himself alone he got on to the parapet and saw both parties on their way back to own lines but three men had wandered to hostile Right flank, two together and one behind. Getting up to the one (Pte Lennon) he found him dazed so took him to Sap head and then returned to find the other two, who he knew from Pte Lennon to be L/C. Morgan and Pte A.Sheppard. He failed to find them so after long search he returned to his lines. Captains Lyne and Jeffries who know the ground well then went out with party but found the Boches lining their wire between wire and parapet so had to return.

~~In meantime~~

In meantime L/C Morgan had walked into left of a flank covering party under Lt Badham at about M.10.a.50.90. He reported that he and Pte A.Sheppard had lost their way and had mistaken hostile trench in M.10.a. as their own. Pte Sheppard got through wire in front of L/C. Morgan who warned him that he thought they were wrong. Pte Sheppard however saying "It all right our lads are here" jumped into the trench and was most likely killed at once, as three Boches fired at L/C.Morgan, who was in the wire and who fired back. Wounded in the arm he dropped his rifle and one Boche jumped out to capture him. L/C Morgan tore himself free of the wire and ran away.

Lt Badham and Lt Walton subsequently went out again with a party and thoroughly searched the whole ground in M.10.a. but found no trace of Pte Sheppard, but they saw a rifle in the wire.

General. The trenches in section raided are reported as wide and deep but much battered.

The raid itself was carried out according to programme without a hitch. The wounds are all by rifle bullets and are slight except in the case of Sgt Abbott who is wounded both in lower ~~in~~ part of lung and in arm. Total wounded 5.

Captain Lyne trained the Raiding Parties most successfully. Lt Rees and 2nd Lt Walton exhibited great coolness and handled their parties well. The ranks and file performed their tasks like clockwork. Being so close to the intense bombardment was a trying ordeal for young troops. 2nd Lt Walton showed great pluck and enterprise in twice conducting long searches for Pte Sheppard.

(sgd) C.J.WILKIE. Lt Col.
26-9-1916 Commanding 17th (S) Bn. The Welsh Regt.

- - - - - - - - - - - -

-2-

Headquarters (G)

40th Division.

- - - - - - - - - -

Forwarded.

I consider the raid was well carried out according to rehearsed programme, and that Capt Rees and Lt Walton led their parties well. The artillery intense bombardment was most accurate. It was unfortunate that no prisoners were taken, owing to front trench being unoccupied. Every endeavour was made by additional search parties to find Pte Sheppard the ~~missing~~ missing man, but no doubt he missed his way and was probably killed. For a first raid, I think it was well carried out.

(signed) C Cunliffe Owen
Brigadier General.

26-9-1916. Commanding 119th Infantry Brigade.

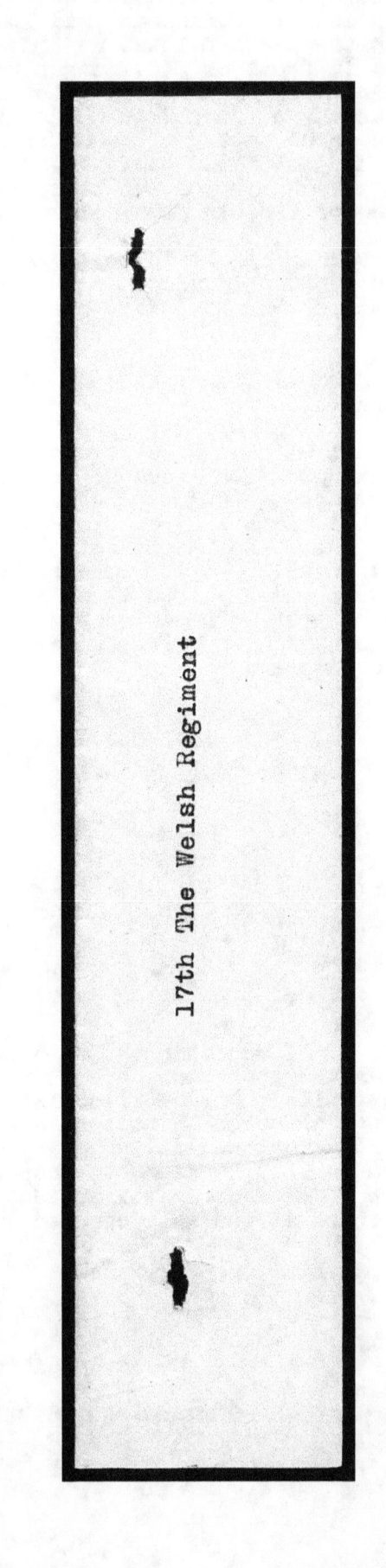

17th The Welsh Regiment

SECRET

Operation Orders [illegible] by [illegible] [illegible]
Commanding 19th Welsh [illegible] [illegible] [illegible]

[illegible]
[illegible] 1/10,000

Copy No. 18
[illegible]

[illegible] will be [illegible] on night [illegible] [illegible]
[illegible]

Object [illegible] [illegible] [illegible]
[illegible] [illegible] [illegible]
[illegible]

R. Party	Lieut. A.J.L. KEEN
	2 Sergeants
	[illegible]
L. Party	2/Lieut. LAWRENCE
	2 Sergeants
	2 O.R.

Programme. [illegible] ZERO [illegible] [illegible] [illegible] [illegible] [illegible] [illegible] [illegible] [illegible] 2 minutes [illegible] ZERO [illegible] bombardment [illegible] [illegible] ZERO [illegible] [illegible] [illegible] [illegible] [illegible] [illegible] Left party through [illegible] [illegible] [illegible] [illegible] 15 minutes [illegible] [illegible] [illegible] [illegible] [illegible] [illegible] [illegible] immediately [illegible] [illegible] [illegible] [illegible]

Arms. Bombers. [illegible] & [illegible]
Riflemen. Rifle & Bayonet (fixed.)

Code.
Cardiff — Raid coming off.
Newport — Raid NOT coming off.
[illegible] — Artillery barrage can slacken
Dish — [illegible] [illegible]
Cup — Resume normal conditions
Spoon — ZERO.

APPENDIX I

Medical. The M.O. will arrange for [illegible] [illegible] [illegible] [illegible] [illegible]

Prisoners. [illegible] [illegible] [illegible] [illegible]

General. [illegible]
[illegible] [illegible] [illegible] [illegible] [illegible]
[illegible]
All [illegible] [illegible] [illegible] [illegible] [illegible]
All [illegible] [illegible] [illegible] [illegible]
All [illegible] [illegible]
All [illegible] [illegible]

[illegible] 2/Lt & Adjt.
19th Ser. Bn. The Welsh Regiment

Copy No. 1	File	Copy No. 10	O.C. 119 M.G. Coy.
2	H.Q. 119th Bde.	11	O.C. [illegible] Artillery
3	2nd in Command	12	O.C. 12th S.W.B.
4	O.C. [illegible] Coy	13	O.C. 13th R. [illegible]
5	O.C. [illegible]	14	[illegible] Officer T.M.B.
6	O.C. [illegible]	15	[illegible]
7	O.C. [illegible]	16	[illegible]
8	[illegible]	17	[illegible]
9	M.O.	18	War Diary

Headquarters,

119th Infantry Brigade.

- - - - - - - - - - - - - -

Reference to Raid on hostile trenches between M.10.c.09.48 and M.10.c.22.76 on night 25/26 Sept, by 17th (S) Bn The Welsh Rgt. I have to report as under :-

1. Infantry Advance. At 8-45 the Right party, 2 Sgts and 15 O.R. under Lt. A.J.L. Rees, emerged from Sap B; the Left party, 2 Sgts 21 O.R. under 2nd Lt. L.A. Walton from RUSSIAN SAP and crawled to gaps in hostile wire at M.10.c.13.58 (Right) and M.10.c.18.65 (Left). The advance was made in perfect order under cover of own Lewis Guns and parties were aligned at 9-11 p.m. close up against gaps without a single hostile shot.

2. Artillery and M.G. preparation. At 9-13 p.m. (-2) intense bombardment commenced with H.E. as arranged by O.C. Right Group and M.G. opened on flanks. The gunnery was of the best and close under the hostile wire as the raiders were none received the slightest injury from own gun fire. This must inspire the greatest confidence in future operations.

3. Infantry Attack. 5 seconds before ZERO (9-15 p.m) the order for assualt was given and both parties rushed the gaps and ran to appointed posts in and over the trenches which were found very much blown in. 3. O.R. were wounded by rifle bullets fired from Support or Communication trenches whilst they were on the hostile parados. Under cover of the flanking parties, who found no enemy, the driving parties under Lt Rees and 2nd Lt Walton proceeded along the front line trench.

APENDIX II

Lt Rees (Right) with his driving party entered trench at a fire bay on the step of which was a rifle and skeleton set of equipment. They soon came upon entrance to a dug-out which was lighted. A bomb was thrown but before it exploded Sgt Abbott was wounded by rifle shot from dug-out. Nine bombs were thrown in and light extinguished. Party proceed round Bay and found another entrance which also showed light - nine bombs were thrown - Lt Rees then assisted Sgt Abbott over parapet and sent him back as he was unfit for further action. Lt Rees proceeded some 30 - 40 yards along trench but finding no Boches nor means of indentification returnedto dug-outs where there was no sign of life. The dug-outs were very deep and full of bomb gas. Reaching point of entry he threw the rifle and equipment, which had remained in the original positions, over the parapet to two men, names unknown as all faces were blackened, and told them to take the rifle and equipment back to own lines. Lt Rees then gave the signal to retire and collected his party.

2Lt Walton (Left) entered the trench with his driving party as arranged but found no Boches or means of identification. He found a lighted dug-out into which bombs were thrown. 2Lt Walton who is slightly deaf did not hear the signal to retire and was consequently the last to leave the hostile trench. On finding himself alone he got on to the parapet and saw both parties on their way back to own lines but three men had wandered to hostile Right flank, two together and one behind. Getting up to the one (Pte Lennon) he found him dazed so took him to Sap head and then returned to find the other two, who he knew from Pte Lennon to be L/C. Morgan and Pte A.Sheppard. He failed to find them so after long search he returned to his lines. Captains Lyne and Jeffries who know the ground well then went out with party but found the Boches lining their wire between wire and parapet so had to return.

In meantime

In meantime L/C Morgan had walked into left of a flank covering party under Lt Badham at about M.10.a.50.90. He reported that he and Pte A.Sheppard had lost their way and had mistaken hostile trench in M.10.a. as their own. Pte Sheppard got through wire in front of L/C. Morgan who warned him that he thought they were wrong. Pte Sheppard however saying "It all right our lads are here" jumped into the trench and was most likely killed at once, as three Boches fired at L/C.Morgan,who was in the wire and who fired back. Wounded in the arm he dropped his rifle and one Boche jumped out to capture him. L/C Morgan tore himself free of the wire and ran away.

Lt Badham and Lt Walton subsequently went out again with a party and thoroughly searched the whole ground in M.10.a. but found no trace of Pte Sheppard, but they saw a rifle in the wire.

General. The trenches in section raided are reported as wide and deep but much battered.

The raid itself was carried out according to programme without a hitch. The wounds are all by rifle bullets and are slight except in the case of Sgt Abbott who is wounded both in lower ~~ix~~ part of lung and in arm. Total wounded 5.

Captain Lyne trained the Raiding Parties most successfully. Lt Rees and 2nd Lt Walton exhibited great coolness and handled their parties well. The ranks and file performed their tasks like clockwork. Being so close to the intense bombardment was a trying ordeal for young troops. 2nd Lt Walton showed great pluck and enterprise in twice conducting long searches for Pte Sheppard.

(sgd) C.J.WILKIE. Lt Col.
26-9-1916 Commanding 17th (S) Bn. The Welsh Regt.

- - - - - - - - - - - -

-2-

Headquarters (G)

40th Division.

- - - - - - - - - -

Forwarded.

I consider the raid was well carried out according to rehearsed programme, and that Capt Rees and Lt Walton led their parties well. The artillery intense bombardment was most accurate. It was unfortunate that no prisoners were taken, owing to front trench being unoccupied. Every endeavour was made by additional search parties to find Pte Sheppard the ~~maissing~~ missing man, but no doubt he missed his way and was probably killed. For a first raid, I think it was well carried out.

(Signed) C Cunliffe Owen

Brigadier General.

26-9-1916. Commanding 119th Infantry Brigade.

Instructions regarding War Diaries and Intelligence Summaries are contained in F. S. Regs., Part II. and the Staff Manual respectively. Title Pages will be prepared in manuscript.

WAR DIARY
or
~~INTELLIGENCE SUMMARY~~
(Erase heading not required.)

Army Form C. 2118

VOES

Place	Date	Hour	Summary of Events and Information	Remarks and references to Appendices
N.E. MAROC	1-10-16		Relieved the 12th Bn SWB in Brigade Support in N.E. Maroc vacating Reserve Billets in S. Maroc into which the S.W.B. moved. Casualties :- nil.	APL
N.E. MAROC	2-10-16 3-10-16 4-10-16		In Brigade Support in N.E. Maroc with B and C Coys finding garrisons of TRAVERS and ST JAMES KEEPS respectively. Remainder of Battalion engaged in furnishing rations and many fatigues. Casualties :- nil.	APL
MAROC	5-10-16		Relieved the 19th RWF in Right Subsection MAROC. 'A' & 'D' Coys in front line with 'B' & 'C' Coys in Support. Casualties :- Nil.	APL
MAROC	6-10-16		At about 12.30 pm our own Heavy Trench Mortar fired some 8 shells after the front line had been cleared completely from EDGEWARE ROAD to BOYAU 10 B. 2 shells fell in No Mans Land, 2 in Bosche wire, 3 in Bosche trenches and 1 in our own front line destroying two bays & traverses of the right coy's (A) front. A large crater was formed. The uncertainty of the fire of these shells due to faulty charges and until others are obtained the front line will always have to be cleared of all personnel when the H.T.M. fires. 2/Lt WARING & 2/Lt MOULD of 'A' Coy and 4 O.R. patrolled between 2 am & 4 am at about M. 10 a 50 40. An officers patrol left D Coy and searched ground between BANK SAP & M 4 C 35.25. No hostile patrols or working parties seen. Lt BADHAM and 10 OR left D Coy at 10 pm from H Sap. Object being to discover any enemy saps or works between M 4 C 00.50 & M. 4 C 40.50. and to engage any enemy patrols which might be about. No patrol seen or heard but a trench reported at M 4 C 00.50 running towards CRASSIER. This trench was empty & had but little wire in front. A few Rum Jars fell around BANK SAP and LIVERPOOL ST. between 5 & 6 pm. Casualties :- Nil	APL 7 sheets

1875 Wt. W593/826 1,000,000 4/15 J.B.C. & A. A.D.S.S./Forms/C. 2118.

Instructions regarding War Diaries and Intelligence Summaries are contained in F. S. Regs., Part II. and the Staff Manual respectively. Title Pages will be prepared in manuscript.

WAR DIARY
or
INTELLIGENCE SUMMARY
(Erase heading not required.)

Army Form C. 2118

Place	Date	Hour	Summary of Events and Information	Remarks and references to Appendices
MAROC	7-10-16		LIVERPOOL STREET and BANK SAP again shelled with rum jars At 9.30 pm patrol of 1 officer & 4 or reconnoitred enemy wire at M 10c.20.70 At 10 pm 2 officers & 2 or went across to enemy trenches and threw some Mills Bombs into his trenches Enemy retaliated later with 4 rifle grenades. Casualties : Nil	
MAROC	8-10-16		At 12 noon our own artillery fired at a Sniper's Post on the SOUTHERN CRASSIER with apparently good effect. Usual Trench Mortar activity on both sides. 1 officer & 2 or left Right Coy and reached M 9.D 60.10 and then returned. At 1.30 am 2/Lt BADHAM of the left Coy and 5 or left BANK SAP and patrolled craters at foot of CRASSIER. This party returned at 3.15 am reporting craters empty & no hostile parties seen. Orders received today for our relief tomorrow by the 13th Bn Rifle Brigade. "The right subsection, MAROC Section, will be handed over to the 111th Brigade on the 9th inst". Casualties : Wounded O.R. 4	APL
MAROC	9-10-16		The Battn was relieved in the right subsection MAROC by the 13th Bn Rifle Brigade. Relief completed at 11.30 am. The Battn then moved into billets in "D" Area LES BREBIS. Casualties : Nil.	APL
LES BREBIS	10-10-16		In Billets in LES BREBIS A draft of 25 or reported and were posted : 12 to 'D' Coy : 7 to 'A' Coy : 6 to 'C' Coy. Casualties : Nil	APL
LES BREBIS	11-10-16		In billets. Orders received for tomorrow's relief:- "The 112th Brigade will take over the new LOOS Section from BANK SAP at M 4c.5.6. to BOYAU 110 at M.6.b.4.6. both inclusive on 11th & 12th October. " Major D. APPLEBY left to proceed to England for a 2½ months course at Aldershot in the duties of a Commanding Officer. Capt C V LYNE acting 2nd in command. Casualties : Nil.	APL APL

1875 Wt. W593/826 1,000,000 4/15 J.B.C. & A. A.D.S.S./Forms/C. 2118.

Instructions regarding War Diaries and Intelligence Summaries are contained in F. S. Regs., Part II. and the Staff Manual respectively. Title Pages will be prepared in manuscript.

WAR DIARY
or
INTELLIGENCE SUMMARY
(Erase heading not required.)

Army Form C. 2118

Place	Date	Hour	Summary of Events and Information	Remarks and references to Appendices
LES BREBIS N. MAROC	12.10.16		Batt^n left LES BREBIS and relieved the 12th B^n Suffolk Regt in Brigade Reserve to new LOOS section in N. MAROC. Casualties :- Nil	APL
N. MAROC	13.10.16		In Reserve Billets. Battalion mostly employed on fatigues. Casualties :- Killed O.R. 2 Wounded O.R. 4 (on a fatigue to Tunnelling Coy).	APL
N. MAROC	14.10.16 15.10.16		In reserve Billets. Major E.B. POOLE 3rd DORSETS reported for a months attachment for instruction on 15th. Battalion on fatigue. Casualties :- Nil.	APL
N. MAROC NE. MAROC	16.10.16		Battalion relieved the 12th B^n SWB in Brigade Support in N.E. MAROC. Disposition of Companies 'A' Coy in O.G.1 'B' Coy finding garrison of TRAVERS KEEP, 'C' Coy finding garrison of ST JAMES KEEP — remainder of 'B' & 'C' Companies billeted in cellars in NE MAROC; 'D' Coy in DUKE STREET. Relief complete at 3.45 pm. At 4.23 pm a telegram received "TEST ATTACK — one round ~~Right~~ Left Batn, Right Brigade". By 4.30 pm whole Battalion was standing to arms. At 5.20 pm message received to resume normal conditions. Casualties :- Nil.	
NE. MAROC	17.10.16		In Brigade support. At 6am enemy artillery activity commenced and shelled billets in N & NE Maroc intermittently until 12 noon. The Keeps were shelled with Rum jars & minnies. Casualties :- Killed: 2/Lt K.P. LLOYD WILLIAMS (officer i/c ST JAMES KEEP) Wounded :- O.R. 1.	APL
N.E. MAROC	18.10.16		In Brigade Support. Col C.J. Wilkie (commanding officer) and Capt C.V. Lyne (acting second in command) were killed at about 3.45 pm. by a High Explosive Shell at the junction of SOUTH STREET and ST JAMES STREET whilst on a tour of the trenches occupied by this unit as Support Battalion. Capt H.P.B. Gough returned from the 119th Brigade Headquarters to assume duties of Commanding Officer ~~and~~ Capt W.P. Stratton (O.C. A Coy) took over duties of second in command. Casualties :- Killed :- Lt Col C.J. WILKIE, Capt C.V. LYNE.	APL

1875 Wt. W593/826 1,000,000 4/15 J.B.C. & A. A.D.S.S./Forms/C. 2118.

Instructions regarding War Diaries and Intelligence Summaries are contained in F. S. Regs., Part II. and the Staff Manual respectively. Title Pages will be prepared in manuscript.

WAR DIARY
or
INTELLIGENCE SUMMARY
(Erase heading not required.)

Army Form C. 2118

Place	Date	Hour	Summary of Events and Information	Remarks and references to Appendices
NE MAROC	19.10.16		In Brigade Support. Instructions received as to the relieving of the 40th Division in this sector. Casualties :- Nil.	[illegible]
NE MAROC RIGHT LOOS	20.10.16		Relieved the 18th (S) Bn the Welsh Regiment in the Right Loos Subsection (old Right Maroc) Disposition of Companies :- 'B' Coy on right; 'C' Coy on left; 'A' Coy right support and 'D' Coy left support. Double CRASSIER held by 2 officers and 60 bombers. Relief complete at 2.30 pm Casualties :- Nil	[illegible]
RIGHT LOOS	21.10.16		Usual TM activity. Between 3 & 4 pm several mines [illegible] fell on left of N. CRASSIER and also to the left of TRIANGLE CRATER. In the morning L/Cpl Allcock one of the bombers on the CRASSIER started a conversation with a German on the Southern CRASSIER. He then went across to the S. CRASSIER and was followed by L/Sergt Hobby and Sergt [illegible]. They found out that the Germans belonged to the 204th Reserve R. and also the 26th Bavarian Regt. Some 15 to 20 Germans were in this trench. These NCOs then returned unmolested to our own lines bringing back with them a button, pipe and cigars etc. A small officers patrol left Right Coy front at 1.10 am and returned later reporting no enemy patrols seen or heard Casualties :- Nil.	[illegible]
RIGHT LOOS	22.10.16		Major F. S. B. JOHNSON assumed the command of the Battalion at noon. Quiet day with the exception of the usual TM. activity. A small patrol out from Right Coy at 9.15 pm reported no enemy patrols seen. The work of wiring the front and improving the trenches (generally which suffered considerable damage from the strafe on Oct 17th) was carried on. Casualties :- Nil	[illegible]
RIGHT LOOS	23.10.16		TMs again active and dropping shells to N. of CRASSIER. An officer (2/Lt J.L. Hughes) and 6 or left BARRICADE SAP at 9 pm to reconnoitre enemy wire. Rain and darkness made it difficult to see and at 10.30 pm this patrol returned without having been able to discover any gaps in hostile wire Casualties :- Nil	[illegible]

1875 Wt. W593/826 1,000,000 4/15 J.B.C. & A. A.D.S.S./Forms/C. 2118.

Army Form C. 2118

Instructions regarding War Diaries and Intelligence Summaries are contained in F. S. Regs., Part II. and the Staff Manual respectively. Title Pages will be prepared in manuscript.

WAR DIARY
or
INTELLIGENCE SUMMARY
(Erase heading not required.)

Place	Date	Hour	Summary of Events and Information	Remarks and references to Appendices
RIGHT LOOS	24.10.16		Usual T.M activity. 2/Lt BADHAM and 6 or patrolled from 10.15 pm until 1.30 am for purpose of discovering gaps in enemy's wire. Owing to darkness of the night they were unsuccessful. Casualties Nil.	AM.
"	25-10-16		Quiet day. 2/Lt BADHAM and 6 or again patrolled No Mans Land but had to return to our own lines as a strong hostile covering party was protecting some enemy wirers. The Boche seemed to be firing some new kind of aerial dart which is fired similarly to our Stokes and with equal rapidity. Casualties:- Nil	AM
"	26.10.16		T.M. activity especially on the right near the Double Crassier. 2/Lt BADHAM again patrolled with intention of discovering gaps in enemy wire. He discovered a hostile wiring party out protected by a strong covering party. One of these returned to the Boche lines and sent off a Very light upon which a M.G. opened fire on our patrol, which took cover and returned safely to our trenches at 11.50 pm. Hostile aeroplane dropped 3 bombs on CARFAX Road & CORDIALE Avenue in the afternoon doing no damage. Casualties:- Killed or. 2 Wounded or. 3.	AM
"	27.10.16		Major F.J.B. JOHNSON left to take temporary command of the 20th Middlesex Regt and Major C.B. HOKE assumed the command of the Battn at 12 noon. 2/Lt HUGHES left D Coy with 7 or for purpose of discovering any gaps, and this attempt was also frustrated owing to the presence of a strong hostile covering party. Casualties; Nil	AM

1875 Wt. W593/826 1,000,000 4/15 J.B.C. & A. A.D.S.S./Forms/C. 2118.

Instructions regarding War Diaries and Intelligence Summaries are contained in F. S. Regs., Part II. and the Staff Manual respectively. Title Pages will be prepared in manuscript.

WAR DIARY
or
INTELLIGENCE SUMMARY
(Erase heading not required.)

Army Form C. 2118

Place	Date	Hour	Summary of Events and Information	Remarks and references to Appendices
RIGHT LOOS	28.10.16		The raid which was due to take place on the left of the line tonight was [illegible] cancelled and 2/Lt BADHAM and 12 OR went out at 5.45 pm with the intention of engaging the Bosche covering party which has been reported protecting the enemy wire for the past three nights. This fighting patrol waited out until 1 am but as no Bosche covering party put in an appearance they had to return to our own trenches without having accomplished anything. Casualties, Nil	[illegible]
RIGHT LOOS LES BREBIS	29.10.16		Battalion was relieved in the Right Loos Sector by the 7th NORTHANTS. Relief complete 1.45 pm. Battalion then moved into billets in B. Area LES BREBIS. Orders received for the move on the 31st. Casualties. Nil	[illegible]
LES BREBIS	30.10.16		In Billets. Battalion busily engaged in preparing for the move tomorrow to BRUAY. Casualties: Nil.	[illegible]
LES BREBIS BRUAY	31.10.16		Battalion moves to BRUAY	[illegible]

1875 Wt. W593/826 1,000,000 4/15 J.B.C. & A. A.D.S.S./Forms/C. 2118.

Instructions regarding War Diaries and Intelligence Summaries are contained in F. S. Regs., Part II. and the Staff Manual respectively. Title Pages will be prepared in manuscript.

WAR DIARY
or
INTELLIGENCE SUMMARY
(Erase heading not required.)

Army Form C. 2118

8 of 6

Place	Date	Hour	Summary of Events and Information	Remarks and references to Appendices
			CONFIDENTIAL WAR DIARY of 17th (S) Bn The Welsh Regiment from Nov 1st 1916 to Nov 30th 1916. (Volume 6)	6. D. 3 sheets

1875 Wt. W593/826 1,000,000 4/15 J.B.C. & A. A.D.S.S./Forms/C. 2118.

Instructions regarding War Diaries and Intelligence Summaries are contained in F. S. Regs., Part II. and the Staff Manual respectively. Title Pages will be prepared in manuscript.

WAR DIARY
or
INTELLIGENCE SUMMARY
(Erase heading not required.)

Army Form C. 2118

Place	Date	Hour	Summary of Events and Information	Remarks and references to Appendices
BRUAY LA THIEULOYE	1-11-16		Battalion marched from BRUAY to LA THIEULOYE.	APL
LA THIEULOYE TERNAS	2-11-16		Battalion marched from LA THIEULOYE To TERNAS	APL
TERNAS	3-11-16		Battalion resting in TERNAS	APL
TERNAS BONNIERES	4-11-16		Battalion marched from TERNAS to BONNIERES. Draft of 50 OR. arrived and were distributed:- 10 to 'A'; 10 to 'C' and 30 to 'D' Coy.	APL
BONNIERES	5-11-16		Battalion marched from BONNIERES to BOISBERGUES.	APL
BOISBERGUES	6-11-16 to 14-11-16		Battalion billeted in BOISBERGUES and training carried on.	APL
NOEUX	15-11-16		Battalion marched from BOISBERGUES to NOEUX.	APL
NOEUX ~~BARLY~~	16-11-16		Battalion carried out training in NOEUX	APL
BARLY	17-11-16		Battalion marched from NOEUX to BARLY. Leave reopened for the battalion.	APL
BREVILLERS	18-11-16		Battalion marched from BARLY to BREVILLERS. Major Gilbert reported for duty having completed his duties as Commandant First Army Rest Camp.	APL

1875 Wt. W593/826 1,000,000 4/15 J.B.C. & A. A.D.S.S./Forms/C. 2118.

Instructions regarding War Diaries and Intelligence Summaries are contained in F. S. Regs., Part II. and the Staff Manual respectively. Title Pages will be prepared in manuscript.

WAR DIARY

or

~~INTELLIGENCE SUMMARY~~

(Erase heading not required.)

Army Form C. 2118

Place	Date	Hour	Summary of Events and Information	Remarks and references to Appendices
BREVILERS	19-11-16 21-11-16		Battalion training in BREVILLERS.	APL
GEZAINCOURT	22.11-16		Battalion marched from BREVILLERS to GEZAINCOURT	APL
FRANQUEVILLE	23.11.16		Battalion marched from GEZAINCOURT to FRANQUEVILLE.	APL
VAUCHELLES LES QUESNOY	24.11.16		Battalion marched from FRANQUEVILLE to VAUCHELLES LES QUESNOY	APL
VAUCHELLES LES QUESNOY	25-11-16 to 30-11-16		Battalion training in VAUCHELLES LES QUESNOY.	APL

Instructions regarding War Diaries and Intelligence Summaries are contained in F. S. Regs., Part II. and the Staff Manual respectively. Title Pages will be prepared in manuscript.

WAR DIARY
or
INTELLIGENCE SUMMARY
(Erase heading not required.)

Army Form C. 2118

Vol 7

Place	Date	Hour	Summary of Events and Information	Remarks and references to Appendices
			CONFIDENTIAL WAR DIARY of The 17th (S) Bn The Welsh Regt for period Dec 1st to Dec 31st 1916	T.D. Gréhnt.

1875 Wt. W593/826 1,000,000 4/15 J.B.C. & A. A.D.S.S./Forms/C. 2118.

HQ 115 Inf Bde

Enclosed please find the War Diary of this unit for the month of December 1916

CB Hore Lt Col
Cmdg 17 Welsh Regt

31/XII/16

Instructions regarding War Diaries and Intelligence Summaries are contained in F. S. Regs., Part II. and the Staff Manual respectively. Title Pages will be prepared in manuscript.

WAR DIARY
or
INTELLIGENCE SUMMARY
(Erase heading not required.)

Army Form C. 2118

Place	Date	Hour	Summary of Events and Information	Remarks and references to Appendices
VAUCHELLES - LES - QUESNOY	Dec 1 – 9	–	Battalion training in VAUCHELLES LES QUESNOY	[initials]
CAMP 12 (BOIS CELESTINS)	10	–	Battalion marched from VAUCHELLES LES QUESNOY to PONT REMY and then entrained to EDGEHILL (near BUIRE SUR L'ANCRE) where it detrained and marched to Camp 12 (BOIS CELESTINS) near CHIPILLY, arriving in camp at about 7 p.m.	[initials]
Camp 12 (Bois CELESTINS)	11 – 25	–	Battalion in Camp 12. Training carried on and the camp which is in a bad state ~~[illegible]~~ improved by making paths, drains and horse shelters &c. On Dec 13th a draft of 160 o.r. reported and were distributed to Companies as shown: 47 o.r. to A Coy; 53 to 'B'; 30 to 'C'; 30 to 'D'. On Dec 18th Major E.H. St. G. Gilbert was appointed an Area Commandant to the XV Corps (CHIPILLY area). Christmas day passed very quietly and the men were given cigarettes &c.	[initials]
Camp 21	26		Battalion marched from Camp 12 to Camp 21 which is between SUZANNE and MARICOURT. Route taken – BRAY – SUZANNE – Camp 21. Camp 21 is also in a bad state and roads in the Camp are non-existent.	[initials]
TRENCHES S. of RANCOURT	27		Left Camp 21 to proceed to the trenches. Personnel carried as far as MAUREPAS in motor lorries and then marched via COMBLES to front line system of trenches SE of RANCOURT and opposite the German line on outskirts of BOIS ST. PIERRE VAAST. At 4.30 pm guides from the 1st MIDDLESEX whom ~~[illegible]~~ we relieved were met at LE PRIEZ FARM. Distribution of Companies: Right front sector – A Coy. Left front – C Coy; Support – D Coy. Reserve B Coy. Owing to the lack of trenches and appalling condition of the ground the Left Coy have	

1875 Wt. W593/826 1,000,000 4/15 J.B.C. & A. A.D.S.S./Forms/C. 2118.

Instructions regarding War Diaries and Intelligence Summaries are contained in F. S. Regs., Part II. and the Staff Manual respectively. Title Pages will be prepared in manuscript.

WAR DIARY
or
~~INTELLIGENCE SUMMARY~~
(Erase heading not required.)

Army Form C. 2118

Place	Date	Hour	Summary of Events and Information	Remarks and references to Appendices
			only two platoons in front line and the right Coy three. The remaining two platoons of 'C' and one of 'A' being with 2 platoons of 'D' Coy in Support and 'B' Coy in reserve having two platoons of 'D'. The relief between ourselves and the 1st MIDDLESEX was completed at 11.50 pm. Dec 27th and was carried out without casualties.	BM
TRENCHES	28.12.16		Activity confined to artillery fire on both sides. Machine guns, Trench Mortars, Rifle Grenades & Rifle fire – nil; The work carried out by every available man was that of improving the trenches. The reserve Coy carrying rations for the three other Companies. Owing to the non existence of communication trenches and that from Battn H.Q forward the whole system of our trenches is under German observation daylight communication with the front and support companies is impossible. Telephonic communication is only available to the Support Company. The Ration carrying party of 'A' Coy which was supplied by 'B' Coy failed to reach 'A' Coy with the days rations and left them with the Support Coy. In the evening a heavy mist came on and great difficulty experienced in getting over the ground owing to the ~~difficulty~~ large numbers of shell holes full of mud and water and the thick mist. Casualties :- Nil.	BM
TRENCHES	29.12.16		The ration parties of both 'C' & 'A' Coys. failed to reach their Companies early this morning on account of heavy mist and heavy going. In the afternoon 2/Lt L.A. WALTON succeeded in reaching 'A' Coy – which Coy has not received any rations since it took over the line on the night of the 27th – and took with him a jar of Rum. He went for most of the way "over the top" in broad daylight and was sniped at frequently. When he arrived at A Coy H.Q he was in a very exhausted condition and bare footed – having fallen into a shell-hole on his way and only extracted himself by leaving his thigh gum boots in the mud. He returned safely. Artillery active very pronounced on both sides throughout the day and Bn H.Q was shelled	

Instructions regarding War Diaries and Intelligence Summaries are contained in F. S. Regs., Part II. and the Staff Manual respectively. Title Pages will be prepared in manuscript.

WAR DIARY
or
INTELLIGENCE SUMMARY
(Erase heading not required.)

Army Form C. 2118

Place	Date	Hour	Summary of Events and Information	Remarks and references to Appendices
			between 12 noon and 1.30 pm. The enemy is also evidently suffering from the condition of the ground as a German was seen walking along enemy's front line and appeared to have difficulty in getting along on account of the mud. A party of the enemy was observed drilling in field below MOISLAINS WOOD. The work of improving the trenches is proceeding slowly. The rations tonight were taken up to the front line companies together with the two days rations of 'A' which were not delivered and the one days rations of "C". Casualties:- Wounded O.R. 1.	[illegible]
TRENCHES	30.XII.16		Artillery activity marked on both sides. Front and support lines and Battn HQ heavily shelled and his Machine guns were also active and occasioned three casualties. Fires & smoke seen rising from parts of BOIS ST. PIERRE VAAST. Two Germans were seen wandering this morning behind the lines on our right (held by the 14th Bn H.L.I.) Both appeared exhausted and disappeared frequently into shell holes. They were shelled by their own artillery and one seemed to have been hit. The H.L.I. were informed and a good look out maintained. The work of improvement continues. A Reconnoitring patrol was sent out from left Coy and found the enemy wire to be in a good condition. The gaps in our front line are patrolled at regular intervals during the night. The number of sick is increasing and 29 men were admitted to hospital today. Three of these were suffering from Trench feet and others had the complaint in its incipient stage. Casualties:- Wounded O.R. 4.	[illegible]
TRENCHES	31.XII.16		Hostile artillery again active in the morning and again paying attention to Bn HQ	

1875 Wt. W593/826 1,000,000 4/15 J.B.C. & A. A.D.S.S./Forms/C. 2118.

Instructions regarding War Diaries and Intelligence Summaries are contained in F. S. Regs., Part II. and the Staff Manual respectively. Title Pages will be prepared in manuscript.

WAR DIARY
or
~~INTELLIGENCE SUMMARY~~
(Erase heading not required.)

Army Form C. 2118

Place	Date	Hour	Summary of Events and Information	Remarks and references to Appendices
			The Battalion was relieved by the 19th Bn. Royal Welsh Fusiliers and relief was completed at 9 pm. The Battalion moved into support and occupied trenches vacated by the 18th Welsh Regt. Casualties:- Killed o.r. 2 Wounded o.r. 4.	AM

1875 Wt. W593/826 1,000,000 4/15 J.B.C. & A. A.D.S.S./Forms/C. 2118.

Army Form C. 2118

Instructions regarding War Diaries and Intelligence Summaries are contained in F. S. Regs., Part II. and the Staff Manual respectively. Title Pages will be prepared in manuscript.

WAR DIARY
or
INTELLIGENCE SUMMARY
(Erase heading not required.)

Place	Date	Hour	Summary of Events and Information	Remarks and references to Appendices

1875 Wt. W593/826 1,000,000 4/15 J.B.C. & A. A.D.S.S./Forms/C. 2118.

Instructions regarding War Diaries and Intelligence Summaries are contained in F. S. Regs., Part II. and the Staff Manual respectively. Title Pages will be prepared in manuscript.

WAR DIARY
or
~~INTELLIGENCE SUMMARY~~

(Erase heading not required.)

Army Form C. 2118

Place	Date	Hour	Summary of Events and Information	Remarks and references to Appendices
RANCOURT SECTOR	1.1.1917 to 4.1.1917		Battalion in Support. Whilst in support numerous cases of trench feet developed – 70 o.r. on Jan 1st; 74 on Jan 2nd; 11 on Jan 3rd and 10 on Jan 4th were evacuated to Hospital as suffering from trench feet. This makes a total of 113 for the complete tour of the trenches. Casualties: Wounded o.r. 1 (Jan 1st). 2/Lt H.H.M. Thomas struck off (sick to England 3.1.17)	APL
	4.1.1917		Relieved in Support Line by the 14th (S) Bn Argyle & Sutherland Highlanders. When relief was complete Battalion marched to Camp 21.	APL
Camp 21	5.1.17 to 8.1.17		Battalion in Brigade Reserve in Camp 21. Time devoted to cleaning up and making good generally. Capt E.W. Jeffreys struck off (sick to England) 3.1.17.	APL
	8.1.17		Lt Col. C.B. Hore O.C. 17th Bn Welsh Regt. was relieved of the command of his Battalion and Major B.F. Murphy (12th S.W.B) assumed command.	
Right Front BOUCHAVESNES N. Sector.	8.1.17		Battalion relieved the 13th (S) Bn Yorkshire Regiment in Right Subsector BOUCHAVESNES. N. Sector of trenches. On the Right are the French; on the left the 12th Bn S.W.B. Companies were distributed: 'B' on right; 'D' on left; 'C' in Support and 'A' in Reserve at ANDOVER. 400 o.r. taken into line and each Company left 30 o.r. with Reserve Coy for purposes of ration carrying &c. Casualties Wounded o.r. 1	APL
"	9.1.17		Battalion in front line. The Support Coy being in such a bad trench were relieved by the Reserve Coy. Artillery was active on both sides throughout day and night. Wire was put out in front of right Coy. and also in front of left. Trenches were improved and drained and duck boards put down to enable the men to have dry standings. Casualties Nil.	APL

1875 Wt. W593/826 1,000,000 4/15 J.B.C. & A. A.D.S.S./Forms/C. 2118.

Instructions regarding War Diaries and Intelligence Summaries are contained in F. S. Regs., Part II. and the Staff Manual respectively. Title Pages. will be prepared in manuscript.

WAR DIARY
or
INTELLIGENCE SUMMARY
(Erase heading not required.)

Army Form C. 2118

Place	Date	Hour	Summary of Events and Information	Remarks and references to Appendices
Right Sub Sector BOUCHAVESNES Nr Sector	10.1.17		Artillery fairly active on both sides. The improving of the trenches generally was carried on and patrols were sent out to keep in touch with the Battalion on our left and the French on the right. The Reserve Coy 'C' relieved 'D' Coy in the Left Front and 'A' Coy relieved 'B' Coy in Right Front. Major D APPLEBY reported for duty from the Senior Officers Course in England. Casualties Nil.	AML
"	11.1.17		At intervals during the day enemy artillery shelled selected points behind our front line. Work in front and support trenches carried on and wire put out in front of right and left companies. Casualties: Wounded O.R. 1	AML
"	12.1.17		At 5.30 pm a telephone message was received from the 119' Inf Bde to the effect that the French on our right had sent up a SOS rocket. The French liason corporal attached to our headquarters was immediately sent to the French Battalion Headquarters to make enquiries. Hostile artillery was active behind our front lines and our own artillery retaliated. When the French corporal returned it was found out that the signal the French sent ~~up~~ up was not the SOS signal but a signal showing that the British Artillery was firing short into their front line. At 10.30 the Battalion was relieved in this Sector by the 19' Bn RWF Casualties: Wounded O.R. 1.	AML
Reserve Line ASQUITH FLATS	13.1.17		Battalion in reserve in ASQUITH FLATS. It was originally intended that the Reserve Battalion should go into billets at Camp 23 but it was since discovered that the Support and Reserve Battalion could both stop in dug outs at ASQUITH FLATS. Casualties: Nil	AML
"	14.1.17		In Reserve. Lieut M.B GRAHAM (of the 1st Royal Irish Fusiliers) reported and commenced his duties as Adjutant.	AML.

1875 Wt. W593/826 1,000,000 4/15 J.B.C. & A. A.D.S.S./Forms/C. 2118.

Instructions regarding War Diaries and Intelligence Summaries are contained in F. S. Regs., Part II. and the Staff Manual respectively. Title Pages will be prepared in manuscript.

WAR DIARY
or
~~INTELLIGENCE SUMMARY~~
(Erase heading not required.)

Army Form C. 2118

Place	Date	Hour	Summary of Events and Information	Remarks and references to Appendices
Reserve ASQUITH FLATS	15.1.17		Battalion in Reserve. Lt. T. WALLACE reported from England and was taken on the strength of the Battalion. Casualties nil	APL
Right Front Sub. Sector BOUCHAVESNES	16.1.17		The Battalion relieved the 19th RWF in Right Sub Sector BOUCHAVESNES N. Sector The relief was complete at 10.30 pm. Disposition of Companies. Right 'B'; Left 'D'; Support 'A'. Reserve 'C' Casualties - Wounded 2/Lt H. N. O'DONNELL O.R. 1.	APL
"	17.1.17		In front trenches. Work of improvement carried on and wire put out. In the night 'C' Coy from reserve relieved 'A' Coy in Support. Casualties. wounded O.R. 1	APL
" Camp 21.	18.1.17		In front trenches. About 5 am a man was seen crawling towards a part of the right company from "No Mans Land". He entered our trenches and was found to be a deserter from the 1st Company No 6 Reserve Inf. Regt 9th Division (Bavarian) He was sent on to Bde HQ. The Battalion was relieved by the 11th Bn K.O.L.R. and marched to MAUREPAS Cm Roads - thence to Camp 21 by lorries. The relief was complete at 8.30 pm.	APL
Camp 21.	19.1.17 to 22.1.17		Battalion in Brigade Reserve in Camp 21.	
MAUREPAS RAVINE	22.1.17		Battalion relieved 13th Yorkshire Regiment in Reserve in MAUREPAS RAVINE and was accomodated in dug-outs and iron shelters. Lt Col. A. BRYANT (Gloucestershire Regiment) assumed the command of the Battalion. Casualties - Nil	APL

Instructions regarding War Diaries and Intelligence Summaries are contained in F. S. Regs., Part II. and the Staff Manual respectively. Title Pages will be prepared in manuscript.

WAR DIARY
or
INTELLIGENCE SUMMARY
(Erase heading not required.)

Army Form C. 2118

Place	Date	Hour	Summary of Events and Information	Remarks and references to Appendices
MAUREPAS RAVINE	23.1.17 to 25.1.17		Battalion in Brigade Reserve in MAUREPAS RAVINE. Casualties. Nil	APL
Right Sub Sector RANCOURT Sector	25.1.17		On night 25/26 Battalion relieved the 19th Bn Royal Welsh Fusiliers in right sub-sector of RANCOURT sector. During night our artillery fired steadily on enemy lines in ST PIERRE VAAST WOOD and continuous communication was maintained between the posts in front line and the Battalions on our right and left. Casualties :- Nil.	APL
ditto	26.1.17		Work carried on continuously on front line posts & improvement of support & reserve lines. Support lines were shelled by hostile artillery from 11.30 pm to midnight. Own artillery also active. Casualties :- Wounded OR 2	APL
ditto	27.1.17		Battalion in front line until 8 pm when it was relieved by 2nd Royal Berkshire Regiment. On completion of relief Battalion marched via COMBLES to MAUREPAS CROSS ROADS. Lorries conveyed personnel thence to Camp 124 (West) which is between SAILLY LORETTE and SAILLY LE SEC. On arrival in camp men were given hot soup, hot tea and rum.	APL
Camp 124 (West)	28.1.17 to 31.1.17		Battalion in Camp 124 (West). Time devoted to cleaning up, re-organization generally and squad drill. Major B.F. MURPHY (attached) evacuated sick to Hospital 30.1.17.	APL

1875 Wt. W593/826 1,000,000 4/15 J.B.C. & A. A.D.S.S./Forms/C. 2118.

Instructions regarding War Diaries and Intelligence Summaries are contained in F. S. Regs., Part II. and the Staff Manual respectively. Title Pages will be prepared in manuscript.

WAR DIARY
or
INTELLIGENCE SUMMARY
(Erase heading not required.)

Army Form C. 2118

Vol 9

Place	Date	Hour	Summary of Events and Information	Remarks and references to Appendices
			Confidential.	
			War Diary	
			of	
			17th (Service) Battalion The Welsh Regiment.	
			from 1-2-1917. To 28-2-1917.	
			(Volume)	9.D. 5 sheets

1875 Wt. W593/826 1,000,000 4/15 J.B.C. & A. A.D.S.S./Forms/C. 2118.

Army Form C. 2118.

Instructions regarding War Diaries and Intelligence Summaries are contained in F. S. Regs., Part II. and the Staff Manual respectively. Title pages will be prepared in manuscript.

WAR DIARY
or
~~INTELLIGENCE SUMMARY.~~

(*Erase heading not required.*)

Place	Date	Hour	Summary of Events and Information	Remarks and references to Appendices
CAMP 124 WEST.	1.2.17		Battalion Reserve training continued. 2/Lt S. C. L. DUKE 17/Lancers joined for duty posted to 'D' Coy.	M.B.
"	2.2.17		Reserve training continued.	M.B.
"	3.2.17		Reserve training continued.	M.B.
"	4.2.17		Sunday Church Parades.	M.B.
"	5.2.17		Training of fighting Platoons commenced. 2/Lt D. T. LEWIS B.I.O. went sick to Hospital. 2/Lt S. T. HENNELL appointed B.I.O. pro tem.	M.B.
"	6.2.17		Battalion Bathing, 'C' & 'D' Coys inoculated, Commanding Officer went to see a demonstration of the attack by the French.	M.B.
"	7.2.17		A & B Coys inoculated. No training carried on.	M.B.
"	8.2.17		Coys inspected by the C.O. Orders received to march by March Route to Camp 21. on 10th inst.	M.B.
"	9.2.17		Battalion busily engaged in preparing for the move tomorrow to Camp 21.	M.B.
CAMP. 21.	10.2.17		Battalion marched from Camp 124 (West) to Camp 21 which is between SUZANNE and MARICOURT route taken - BRAY - SUZANNE - Camp 21.	M.B.
RANCOURT SECTOR	11.2.17 16.2.17		The Battalion moved into Support 3 Coys at ALBANY 1 Coy at LE FOREST and occupied trenches vacated by the 2nd Rifle Brigade.	M.B.

2353 Wt. W2544/1454 700,000 5/15 D. D. & L. A.D.S.S./Forms/C. 2118.

Instructions regarding War Diaries and Intelligence Summaries are contained in F. S. Regs., Part II. and the Staff Manual respectively. Title pages will be prepared in manuscript.

WAR DIARY

or

~~INTELLIGENCE SUMMARY~~.

(*Erase heading not required.*)

Army Form C. 2118.

Place	Date	Hour	Summary of Events and Information	Remarks and references to Appendices
RANCOURT SECTOR	11-2-17 to 15.2.17		Whilst in support all available men were employed on R. E. fatigues. Casualties NIL.	M.B.
			Officially notified that on 4.2.17 2/Lt H. N. O'DONNELL died of wounds received in action on 16.1.17	M.B.
	15.2.17		Lieut F. T. WILLIAMS and 2/Lt. A. R. JONES reported from England were taken on the strength of the Battalion. 2/Lt E. HAMMOND rejoined for duty from Hospital 2/Lt Davis proceeded to join 4th Field Survey Coy.	M.B.
RIGHT subsector RANCOURT Sector.	15.2.17		On the night of 15/16th the Battalion relieved the 19th Bn. Royal Welsh Fusiliers in the Right Sub-sector of RANCOURT sector, relief was complete at 2-30 am. Disposition of Companies RIGHT 'D' Coy. LEFT 'B' Coy. SUPPORT 'C' Coy. RESERVE 'A' Coy. Casualties NIL.	M.B.
ditto	16.2.17		Our Artillery shelled steadly throughout the night ST. PIERRE VAAST WOOD. The enemy shelled with 4.2's our Right Coy. front line Support trenches between 8 am and 10 am. from the direction of MOISLANS WOOD no material damage was sustained. At 1pm a few whiz-bangs fell near H.Q. Support Coy. Casualties NIL.	M.B.
ditto	17.2.17		At 3 am enemy shelled Right Coy front line with 4.2 shells and large minenwerfer. shelling appeared to come from the EAST, but it was thought another Battery was also firing from N.E. Our Artillery was fairly active all day. Casualties NIL.	M.B.

2353 Wt. W2544/1454 700,000 5/15 D. D. & L. A.D.S.S./Forms/C. 2118.

Army Form C. 2118.

Instructions regarding War Diaries and Intelligence Summaries are contained in F. S. Regs., Part II. and the Staff Manual respectively. Title pages will be prepared in manuscript.

WAR DIARY
or
INTELLIGENCE SUMMARY.
(Erase heading not required.)

Place	Date	Hour	Summary of Events and Information	Remarks and references to Appendices
ditto	18.2.17		Enemy opened fire on our front line at 5.35 am. Our telephonic communication was cut in several places and trenches partially damaged. In response to our call for retaliation our artillery opened fire at 5.45 am on the enemys front & support line trenches with great effect. Trench boards were observed being blown up in their front line communication trenches. One of our men got sniped while endeavouring to connect up the telephone wires about 5.15 pm. Our communication was re-established at 6 pm. Casualties 1. O. R.	N.B.
"	19.2.17		Artillery on both sides was quiet all day owing to a very thick mist, at 5.10 pm two gas shells fell near H. Q. of our Right Coy. Battalion in front line until 8.30 pm when it was relieved by the 19th Bn Royal Welsh Fusiliers, on completion of relief Battalion marched via COMBLES to MAOREPAS RAVINE in Brigade Reserve, on arrival men were given Hot soup, tea, & rum. Casualties Nil.	N.B.
MAOREPAS RAVINE	20.2.17 to 21.2.17		Battalion in Brigade Reserve in MAOREPAS RAVINE. Casualties NIL The Battalion was relieved by the 21st Middlesex Regt at 4 pm & marched to Camp III. Via - SOZANNE - BRAY - Camp III.	N.B.

2353 Wt. W2544/1454 700,000 5/15 D. D. & L. A.D.S.S./Forms/C. 2118.

Instructions regarding War Diaries and Intelligence Summaries are contained in F. S. Regs., Part II. and the Staff Manual respectively. Title pages will be prepared in manuscript.

WAR DIARY
or
INTELLIGENCE SUMMARY.
(Erase heading not required.)

Army Form C. 2118.

Place	Date	Hour	Summary of Events and Information	Remarks and references to Appendices
Camp III.	22.2.17		Bn. in Camp III. Time devoted to cleaning up, re-organization generally. Lt Col A. Bryant assumed Temporary Command of the 119th Infy Bde. Major D. Appleby took over Temporary Command of the Battalion.	W.B.
"	23.2.17		Bn in Camp III. Lt. M. B. GRAHAM 1/Royal Irish Fusiliers was appointed Adjutant of the Bn.	W.B.
"	24.2.17		Bn in Camp III. 2/Lt D. T. LEWIS rejoined from Hospital.	W.B.
"	25.2.17		Bn in Camp III. Cleaning up, re-organization & drill continued.	W.B.
"	26.2.17		Sunday. Church parades not held, owing to having to find working parties.	W.B.
"	27.2.17		Battalion in Camp III. Training Continued.	W.B.
"	28.2.17		Battalion in Camp III. practically no training, owing to having to find Working Parties.	W.B.

2353 Wt. W2544/1454 700,000 5/15 D. D. & L. A.D.S.S./Forms/C. 2118.

17th (GLAM.) Bn.
31 MAR. 1917
No. 17/WR/344
THE WELSH REGT.

H.Q.

119th Infantry Brigade.

Herewith War Diary of the
Battalion under my Command
for the month of MARCH 1917.

Please acknowledge.

A. Bryant [signature]

Lieut. Colonel
Commanding 17th (S) Bn., The Welsh Regt.

31-3-1917

Instructions regarding War Diaries and Intelligence Summaries are contained in F. S. Regs., Part II. and the Staff Manual respectively. Title pages will be prepared in manuscript.

WAR DIARY
or
~~INTELLIGENCE SUMMARY.~~
(Erase heading not required.)

Army Form C. 2118.

17 Welsh Regt

Vol 10

Place	Date	Hour	Summary of Events and Information	Remarks and references to Appendices
CAMP III BELAIR	1.3.17		The Battalion in Reserve training, we celebrated St Davids Day by giving a Battalion Dinner to the men at 5 pm. followed by a Concert at 7 pm. which was thoroughly enjoyed by all ranks.	M.B.
do.	2.3.17		Reserve training continued, The Officers held a Regimental Dinner at 8 pm to celebrate St Davids Day. The dinner was a great success & was attended by the Brigade Staff.	M.B.
do	3.3.17		Reserve training practically impossible owing to large working parties.	M.B.
do	4.3.17		The Battalion had to find all available men for working parties.	M.B.
do	5.3.17		Reserve training continued.	M.B.
do.	6.3.17		The Battalion marched by march route to Camp 19. SUZANNE.	M.B.

10. (D.)

2353 Wt. W2544/1454 700,000 5/15 D. D. & L. A.D.S.S./Forms/C. 2118.

Instructions regarding War Diaries and Intelligence Summaries are contained in F. S. Regs., Part II. and the Staff Manual respectively. Title pages will be prepared in manuscript.

WAR DIARY

~~or~~

~~INTELLIGENCE SUMMARY.~~

(Erase heading not required.)

Army Form C. 2118.

Place	Date	Hour	Summary of Events and Information	Remarks and references to Appendices
From CAMP 19. SUZANNE into SUPPORT CLERY Sector.	7.3.17		Bn. H.Q. in [illegible] The Battalion marched by march route into Support in the CLERY SECTOR. disposition of Coys as follows. 'B' 'C' 1 2 platoons D Coy in MAUD AVENUE, two platoons D Coy in WURZEL AVENUE and CLERY CHATEAU, two platoons 'A' Coy at Bn. H.Q. MADELEINE left Bn. two platoons in MERLIN TRENCH. Casualties Nil.	[illegible]
From SUPPORT to Right Sub-sector of CLERY SECTOR.	8.3.17		Bn. H.Q. in [illegible] The Battalion relieved the 20th R. Fusiliers in the right Subsector of the CLERY SECTOR, disposition of Companies. 'A' Coy right 'B' Centre 'C' Left 'D' Support. Casualties 1. O.R.	[illegible]
RIGHT SUBSECTOR CLERY SECTOR	9.3.17		Our artillery shelled the enemy's back areas during the day and night. M.G.s and T.M.s silent. The enemy shelled our line with 77 m.m. shells at N.12.d 3.2. Enemy's T.M.s fired into our right and centre Companies at intervals during the night. Casualties 1. O.R.	[illegible]
do.	10.3.17		Our Artillery retaliated on enemy's H.T.M. on extreme right of our line with good effect at 10.30 a.m. Hostile Artillery was active during the day and night. Enemy's Machine guns very active at "Stand to" and occasional bursts throughout the night on centre Company front. Casualties 1. O.R.	[illegible]

Instructions regarding War Diaries and Intelligence Summaries are contained in F. S. Regs., Part II. and the Staff Manual respectively. Title pages will be prepared in manuscript.

WAR DIARY

~~or~~

~~INTELLIGENCE SUMMARY.~~

(Erase heading not required.)

Army Form C. 2118.

Place	Date	Hour	Summary of Events and Information	Remarks and references to Appendices
RIGHT SUBSECTOR CLERYSECTOR	11.3.17		Our Artillery was active throughout the day and night. Enemy shelled our left Coy H.Q. (I.7.a.8) during the morning. Hostile gas shells fell in vicinity of Right Coy H.Q. at 5pm. 10.30pm. and 1.30 am. Our Artillery effectively retaliated. Casualties 1 Officer (Capt W.P. STRATTON) 1 O.R.	N.B.
do	12.3.17		Enemy's Artillery was active during the day along our front. Our Artillery effectively retaliated on enemy's front and support lines at 6pm and 10.30pm. Our machine guns were very active during the night firing at openings in enemy wire. Casualties. 1 O.R. The Battalion relieved the 19th R.W.F in Brigade Support. Bn. H.Q. in P.C. MERTON.	N.B.
SUPPORT CLERYSECTOR	13.3.17 to 15.3.17		The Battalion in Support. Capt. A.E. GRANT and 2/Lt J.L. HUGHES rejoined from Hospital. 2/Lt C.S. THOMAS joined the Bn for duty and posted to A Coy. Casualties 2 O.R. Whilst in support all available men were employed on fatigue. The Battalion was relieved at 11.45pm 15/3/17 by the 12th Suffolk Regt. On completion of relief Battalion marched via FRISE – SUZANNE – to Camp 17. Casualties NIL.	N.B.
CAMP 17	16.3.17		The Battalion in Divisional Reserve. at 7pm the Battalion was ordered to move next day to Camp 162	N.B.

Instructions regarding War Diaries and Intelligence Summaries are contained in F. S. Regs., Part II. and the Staff Manual respectively. Title pages will be prepared in manuscript.

WAR DIARY

~~or~~

~~INTELLIGENCE SUMMARY.~~

(Erase heading not required.)

Army Form C. 2118.

Place	Date	Hour	Summary of Events and Information	Remarks and references to Appendices
LINGER	17.3.17		The Battalion proceeded by march route to LINGER CAMP (No 162)	[illegible]
CAMP. 164.	18.3.17		The Battalion employed in ~~[illegible]~~ preparing for G.O.C. inspection	[illegible]
do	19.3.17		The Battalion employed in cleaning up for G.O.C. inspection. The inspection was cancelled & orders were received to prepare for move to HAUT-ALLAINES the next day.	[illegible]
do	20.3.17		The Battalion proceeded by march route to HAUT-ALLAINES. The Bn. band played at intervals en route. We relieved the 13th East Surreys in outpost positions. Casualties NIL	[illegible]
HAUT-ALLAINES	21.3.17		Battalion occupying outpost positions (line of resistance) [illegible]. Orders received to the effect that this Battalion would form the Infantry Battalion of a mobile column, consisting in addition of the XV Corps Mounted Troops (Wilts Yeomanry), 4 guns (18 pdrs), Section Amm. Column, 1 platoon pioneers, the whole under command of [illegible]. Casualties Nil.	[illegible]
do	22.3.17		Battalion occupying outpost positions (line of resistance). C & D Companies in support. 'A' & 'B' Coys in front line. 'C' Company billeted in ALLAINES. 'D' Company in dugouts in trench from I.10.d.1.7.	[illegible]

Army Form C. 2118.

Instructions regarding War Diaries and Intelligence Summaries are contained in F. S. Regs., Part II. and the Staff Manual respectively. Title pages will be prepared in manuscript.

WAR DIARY

~~or~~

~~INTELLIGENCE SUMMARY.~~

(Erase heading not required.)

Place	Date	Hour	Summary of Events and Information	Remarks and references to Appendices
HAUT-ALLAINES	22/3/17 (cont.)		to I 10. d. 5.9. "A" Company on right of line from I 10 d 5.8 to I 11. c 5.9. "B" Company on left of line from I 11 c 9.8 to I 6. d. 10.4. Casualties NIL.	C.W.
do	23-3-17		Battalion holding line of resistance of ~~outpost~~ position. All available men engaged on new line of resistance, wiring & improving old German trenches and making strong points and L.G. emplacements. Our artillery was active about 3.15 p.m. Enemy lightly shelled DRIENCOURT with shrapnel at 10.45 a.m. Three enemy shrapnel shell burst high over AIZECOURT-LE-HAUT at 4.30 p.m. Two Germans were observed at J 6. c. 4.4; a look-out post is suspected at this point. Casualties NIL.	C.W.
do	24/3/17		Battalion in ~~outpost~~ (line of resistance) position. All available men	

2353 Wt. W2544/1454 700,000 5/15 D. D. & L. A.D.S.S./Forms/C. 2118.

Instructions regarding War Diaries and Intelligence Summaries are contained in F. S. Regs., Part II. and the Staff Manual respectively. Title pages will be prepared in manuscript.

WAR DIARY
~~or~~
~~INTELLIGENCE SUMMARY.~~
(*Erase heading not required.*)

Army Form C. 2118.

Place	Date	Hour	Summary of Events and Information	Remarks and references to Appendices
HAUT-ALLAINES	24/3/17		working on next line of resistance. Information received that the Mobile Column would cease to exist after 12 midnight, (tonight) and that the whole Brigade would be taken out of the line and employed on road work. The Battalion band played selections in HAUT-ALLAINES near Bn H.Q at 4 p.m. this afternoon. The first British band to play in the village, at least since the evacuation of it by the enemy. Casualties NIL	
do	25/3/17		Battalion was relieved by the [illegible] Battalion of the 143rd Bde. At 1.30 p.m. LIEUT & ADJT: M.B. GRAHAM ordered our Lewis Gun and team to open fire on a hostile aeroplane flying over the village. After the second burst of fire it was observed that the airman changed his course, making off in a N.N.E'ly direction. The Battalion proceeded by march route to billets	

Army Form C. 2118.

Instructions regarding War Diaries and Intelligence Summaries are contained in F. S. Regs., Part II. and the Staff Manual respectively. Title pages will be prepared in manuscript.

WAR DIARY

~~or~~

~~INTELLIGENCE SUMMARY.~~

(Erase heading not required.)

Place	Date	Hour	Summary of Events and Information	Remarks and references to Appendices
HAUT-ALLAINES	25-3-17		in BOUCHAVESNES (LANGTON Barracks). Capt. C.M. DUNN left for 10 days leave. Casualties NIL.	C.W.
BOUCHAVESNES	26-3-17		Battalion commenced work on BOUCHAVESNES - MOISLAINES road.	C.W.
do	27-3-17		Battalion repairing BOUCHAVESNES - MOISLAINS road. 2/Lt. H.P.A. BAILEY reported for duty & posted to "B" Coy. Lt. F. BADHAM reported from hospital & posted to "D" Coy for duty. LIEUT. & ADJT. GRAHAM left for 10 days leave.	C.W.
do	28-3-17		Battalion engaged repairing road BOUCHAVESNES - MOISLAINS.	C.W.
do	29-3-17		do —— do —— do	C.W.

Instructions regarding War Diaries and Intelligence Summaries are contained in F. S. Regs., Part II. and the Staff Manual respectively. Title pages will be prepared in manuscript.

WAR DIARY

~~or~~

~~INTELLIGENCE SUMMARY.~~

(Erase heading not required.)

Army Form C. 2118.

Place	Date	Hour	Summary of Events and Information	Remarks and references to Appendices
BOUCHAVESNES	30.3.17		Battalion occupied repairing HOLLANDS – BOUCHAVESNES road	E.W.
do	31.3.17		Battalion occupied repairing BOUCHAVESNES – CLERY road.	E.W.

31.3.17. [illegible] 17th Bn Welsh Regt

2353 Wt. W2544/1454 700,000 5/15 D. D. & L. A.D.S.S./Forms/C. 2118.

Instructions regarding War Diaries and Intelligence Summaries are contained in F. S. Regs., Part II. and the Staff Manual respectively. Title pages will be prepared in manuscript.

WAR DIARY
or
~~INTELLIGENCE SUMMARY.~~
(Erase heading not required.)

Army Form C. 2118.

Vol XI

Place	Date	Hour	Summary of Events and Information	Remarks and references to Appendices
			CONFIDENTIAL	
			WAR DIARY OF THE 17th (S) Bn THE WELSH REGIMENT from April 1st 1917 to April 30th 1917. Volume 11.	

11.D. 10 meets

2353 Wt. W2544/1454 700,000 5/15 D. D. & L. A.D.S.S./Forms/C. 2118.

119/40

Army Form C. 2118

17th Welch

Instructions regarding War Diaries and Intelligence Summaries are contained in F. S. Regs., Part II. and the Staff Manual respectively. Title Pages will be prepared in manuscript.

WAR DIARY

or

~~INTELLIGENCE SUMMARY~~

(Erase heading not required.)

Place	Date	Hour	Summary of Events and Information	Remarks and references to Appendices
BOUCHAVESNES	1-4-17		The Battalion engaged repairing BOUCHAVESNES – CLERY road.	C.H.
do	2-4-17		The Battalion occupied repairing MOISLAINS – BOUCHAVESNES road. A draft of 85 O.R. arrived and were allotted to Companies according to their strength. 2nd Lt M.M. WILLIAMS proceeded to ETRICOURT with 10 O.R. to prepare Battalion H.Q. and billets for the Battalion.	C.H.
do	3-4-17		The Battalion bathing by companies at CRANTMIERES & cleaning equipment & clothing.	C.H.
do	4-4-17		The Battalion cleaning up & drilling in close order by companies. All officers who could be spared reconnoitred new line of resistance to be held by us.	C.H.
do	5-4-17		Companies at the disposal of company commanders ~~[illegible]~~ carrying out instruction in outpost duties.	C.H.
do	6-4-17		Companies at the disposal of company commanders carrying out outpost drill & close order drill.	C.H.
do	7-4-17		The Battalion proceeded by march route to ETRICOURT and relieved a Battalion of the 121st Brigade in DIV: RESERVE.	C.H.
ETRICOURT	8-4-17		The Battalion engaged repairing MAMANCOURT – MOISLAINS road. Capt C.A. Davies returned from leave. Lieut A.B. Graham	C.H.

1875 Wt. W593/826 1,000,000 4/15 J.B.C. & A. A.D.S.S./Forms/C. 2118.

Instructions regarding War Diaries and Intelligence Summaries are contained in F. S. Regs., Part II. and the Staff Manual respectively. Title Pages will be prepared in manuscript.

WAR DIARY
or
~~INTELLIGENCE SUMMARY~~
(Erase heading not required.)

Army Form C. 2118

Place	Date	Hour	Summary of Events and Information	Remarks and references to Appendices
ETRICOURT	8.4.17		returned from leave. 2nd Lt A.P. LLOYD left for 10 days leave.	
"	9.4.17		Battalion working on MAMANCOURT - MOISLAINS road.	WRG
"	10.4.17		Battalion working on MAMANCOURT - MOISLAINS road.	WRG
	11.4.17		" " " " "	WRG
	12.4.17		" " " " "	WRG
	13.4.17		" " " " "	WRG
	14.4.17		" " " " "	WRG
	15.4.17		" " " " "	WRG
	16.4.17		" " " " " 2/Lt. C. WARING proceeded on 10 days leave.	WRG
	17.4.17		The Battalion marched by march route to FINS into Brigade Reserve. the following were the dispositions of the Battalion	WRG
	~~18.4.17~~		Bn H.Q. FINS 'B' & 'D' Coys in DESSART WOOD A & C Coys in FINS They relieved 2 Coys 13th Yorkshire Regt. and two Coys 21st Middlesex Regt respectively.	

1875 Wt. W593/826 1,000,000 4/15 J.B.C. & A. A.D.S.S./Forms/C. 2118.

Instructions regarding War Diaries and Intelligence Summaries are contained in F. S. Regs., Part II. and the Staff Manual respectively. Title Pages will be prepared in manuscript.

WAR DIARY
or
~~INTELLIGENCE SUMMARY~~
(Erase heading not required.)

Army Form C. 2118

Place	Date	Hour	Summary of Events and Information	Remarks and references to Appendices
FINS	18.4.17		The Battalion in Brigade Reserve in FINS. Training devoted to improving billets etc. MAJOR. R. J. ANDREWS. M.C. 2nd DEVON RGT, joined the Bn as Second-in-Command vice MAJOR D. APPLEBY.	C.W.
FINS	19.4.17		The Battalion in Brigade Reserve.	C.W.
FINS	20.4.17		The Bn in Brigade Reserve.	
		8 pm	The Battalion moved into support at QUEENS CROSS (REF. 57c S.E. 1/20,000 Q26 d. 4. 3) in main line of resistance relieving the 12th S.W.B.	C.W.
	21.4.17		The Battalion relieved the 12th S.W.B in their Outpost line and the dispositions of the Companies were as follows: "A" Coy on the right, "B" in the centre, "D" on the left & "C" Coy in support.	C.W.
	22.4.17		The Battalion held Outpost Line	C.W.
	23.4.17		The Battalion moved to ~~[illegible]~~ FIFTEEN RAVINE preparatory to the assault to be made on the morning of the 24th inst.	C.W.
	24.4.17	4.15 am	Our artillery commenced barrage on hostile trenches on high ground at R.14 c.8.0 & R.14 b.2.8 (REF. MAP. T.S. 5A 1/20,000)	C.W.
		3.45 am (ZERO 30 mins)	The Battalion was drawn out in column of platoons in following order "D" Coy on right, "B" on left, A Coy in support of D and C in support of B Coy. At 4.21 am the barrage crept forward at rate of 100x in 4 minutes according to plan. At 4.45 am the Company reported that they held road (R.14. b.1.8 to R 14 a. 9.4.) with two platoons [illegible] "D" Coy	C.W.

1875 Wt. W593/826 1,000,000 4/15 J.B.C. & A. A.D.S.S./Forms/C. 2118.

Instructions regarding War Diaries and Intelligence Summaries are contained in F. S. Regs., Part II. and the Staff Manual respectively. Title Pages will be prepared in manuscript.

WAR DIARY
or
~~INTELLIGENCE SUMMARY~~
(Erase heading not required.)

Army Form C. 2118

Place	Date	Hour	Summary of Events and Information	Remarks and references to Appendices
			to dig in forward of this road. At 6.5 a.m. "B" Company reported that the Battalion was held up by uncut wire this side of objective at R.14 central, this was confirmed by a message from "D" Company. ~~[illegible]~~ At this point they came under hostile rifle and machine gun fire which was vigorously replied to. The O.C. "D" Company then saw a gap in the wire on his left which was being utilized by "B" Company he thereupon followed B Company through & joined with them in bombing the trench from R.14 b 2.2 to R14 b 9.1. clear of the enemy. At 7.5 a.m. all objectives had been reached but there were a few of the enemy remaining in the trench running from R.14 b 5.1. to R15 a 2.1. These were speedily dealt with with bombs. At 9.40 a.m. it was reported to Bde H.Q that all objectives had been gained & that we were consolidating our new positions. ~~[illegible]~~ As the result of the attack the whole of the objectives (situated on high ground overlooking the HINDENBURG LINE and its strong points) were gained. By 12.30 p.m. the position was completely clear of the enemy & the companies settled down to dig themselves in. Total of prisoners captured, 1 officer 39 O.R. All ranks behaved with the utmost gallantry & dash & were splendidly led. The advance under the barrage was made cooly & steadily as on a parade ground. Below is a copy of the Special Order of the Day issued by the G.O.C. concerning the operations.	

1875 Wt. W593/826 1,000,000 4/15 J.B.C. & A. A.D.S.S./Forms/C. 2118.

Instructions regarding War Diaries and Intelligence Summaries are contained in F. S. Regs., Part II. and the Staff Manual respectively. Title Pages will be prepared in manuscript.

WAR DIARY

or

~~INTELLIGENCE SUMMARY~~

(Erase heading not required.)

Army Form C. 2118

Place	Date	Hour	Summary of Events and Information	Remarks and references to Appendices
			Copy	
			Special Order of the Day by Brigadier General F. P. Crozier D.S.O. Commanding 119th Inf. Bde. Wednesday, 25th April 1917.	
			G.O.C. 119th Infantry Brigade wishes to thank all ranks of the Brigade which he has the honour to command, on the success of their operations on the 21st & 24th April 1917 and to congratulate them on the valour displayed. The gaining of all the objectives & the retention of same throughout was only made possible by the infantry co-operation [illegible] & the support of the 8th Divisional Artillery. The manner in which the troops in every [illegible] was as steady as on a parade ground movement. The keeping up of communication ~~[illegible]~~ kept up working to the maximum throughout the operations.	
			(Signed) D. F. Hume Captain Staff Captain 119th Infantry Brigade	D.V.

1875 Wt. W593/826 1,000,000 4/15 J.B.C. & A. A.D.S.S./Forms/C. 2118.

Instructions regarding War Diaries and Intelligence Summaries are contained in F. S. Regs., Part II. and the Staff Manual respectively. Title Pages will be prepared in manuscript.

WAR DIARY
or
~~INTELLIGENCE SUMMARY~~
(Erase heading not required.)

Army Form C. 2118

Place	Date	Hour	Summary of Events and Information	Remarks and references to Appendices
R14 c. 8.0 to R. 14 b. 2.8 (REF. MAP T.S. 52 1/20,000)	25-4-17		All day the Battalion was occupied consolidating and improving trenches & establishing posts forward of new position. Hostile artillery very active day & night. During the night our line was advanced 50 yards and a loop made to join up with the advanced trenches thus forming a strong defensive flank on the right. Also, a considerable amount of wire was placed in front of our position.	C.W.
"	26-4-17		During the night the whole of the trenches were wired & deepened. A machine gun, located in vicinity of LA VACQUERIE, which had troubled us with enfilade fire was spotted & put out of action by our LEWIS GUNS. The summit of the hill marking our new position was marked with a board RHONDDA HILL.	C.W.
	27-4-17		The whole of our front was thoroughly patrolled during the night. A hostile working party observed at 2 a.m. were dispersed by our fire. Trenches were further deepened and improved. Further to the report of the hostile M.G. which was "scissored" by our Lewis Guns last night, Lt F.T. WILLIAMS & six men proceeded to reconnoitre the position. They found a trench 1½ to 2' deep untraversed & showing no signs of	C.W.

1875 Wt. W593/826 1,000,000 4/15 J.B.C. & A. A.D.S.S./Forms/C. 2118.

Instructions regarding War Diaries and Intelligence Summaries are contained in F. S. Regs., Part II. and the Staff Manual respectively. Title pages will be prepared in manuscript.

WAR DIARY
or
~~INTELLIGENCE SUMMARY.~~
(Erase heading not required.)

Army Form C. 2118.

Place	Date	Hour	Summary of Events and Information	Remarks and references to Appendices
			[illegible]	
	20-7		[illegible]	

A7092 Wt. W12S 9/M1293 750,000. 1/17. D. D. & L. Ltd. Forms C2118/14.

Instructions regarding War Diaries and Intelligence Summaries are contained in F. S. Regs., Part II. and the Staff Manual respectively. Title pages will be prepared in manuscript.

WAR DIARY
or
~~INTELLIGENCE SUMMARY~~.

(*Erase heading not required.*)

Army Form C. 2118.

Place	Date	Hour	Summary of Events and Information	Remarks and references to Appendices
			with satisfactory results + valuable information was obtained.	
			Battalion holding position on RHONDDA HILL.	
	29-4-17		The ground N + N.E of our position and in direction of LA VACQUERIE was regularly patrolled from 8.50 to 10.0 p.m but it was impossible to get close to enemy wire owing to burning very lights. No enemy patrols were seen.	
			After remaining 6 consecutive days in the position captured by us, we were relieved by the 19th R.W.F. The relief was completed by 11.40 p.m without incident.	C.W.
GOUZEAUCOURT	30-4-17		The Battalion in Brigade reserve on the old line of resistance. Battalion relieved at midnight by the 19th R.W.F. + then marched into Brigade Reserve in billets in EQUANCOURT.	H.B.
			Casualties Killed O.R. 1. Wounded O.R. 1.	

1/5/17 [illegible] Major
Comdg 17th [illegible] Regt

A7092 Wt. W128 9/M1293. 750,000. 1/17. D. D & L. Ltd. Forms/C2118/14.

Instructions regarding War Diaries and Intelligence Summaries are contained in F. S. Regs., Part II. and the Staff Manual respectively. Title pages will be prepared in manuscript.

WAR DIARY

or

INTELLIGENCE SUMMARY.

(Erase heading not required.)

Army Form C. 2118.

Place	Date	Hour	Summary of Events and Information	Remarks and references to Appendices
	[illegible]		[illegible]	
			[illegible]	
			[illegible] Capt [illegible]	
			Lieut R. [illegible]	
			[illegible]	
			[illegible]	
			[illegible] 58.	

A7092 Wt. W128 9/M1293 750,000. 1/17. D. D & L. Ltd. Forms/C2118/14.

Instructions regarding War Diaries and Intelligence Summaries are contained in F. S. Regs., Part II. and the Staff Manual respectively. Title pages will be prepared in manuscript.

WAR DIARY
~~or~~
~~INTELLIGENCE~~ SUMMARY.
(Erase heading not required.)

Army Form C. 2118.

Vol 12

Place	Date	Hour	Summary of Events and Information	Remarks and references to Appendices
			Confidential.	
			WAR DIARY	
			of	
			17th (S) Bn the Welsh Regiment.	
			From 1. 5. 17 to 31. 5. 17.	

12. D.
11 sheets.

A7092 Wt. W128 9/M1293 750,000. 1/17. D. D & I. Ltd. Forms/C2118/14.

Instructions regarding War Diaries and Intelligence Summaries are contained in F. S. Regs., Part II. and the Staff Manual respectively. Title pages will be prepared in manuscript.

WAR DIARY
~~or~~
~~INTELLIGENCE SUMMARY.~~
(Erase heading not required.)

Army Form C. 2118.

7th [illegible] MAY 1917

Place	Date	Hour	Summary of Events and Information	Remarks and references to Appendices
EQUANCOURT	1-5-1917		[illegible]	
do	2-5-17		do	
do	3-5-17		do [illegible]	
			[illegible]	
do	4-5-17		[illegible]	
			[illegible] ESSART [illegible] FINS	
FINS	[illegible]		[illegible]	
			[illegible]	

A7092 Wt. W128 9/M1293 750,000. 1/17. D. D. & L. Ltd. Forms/C2118/14.

Instructions regarding War Diaries and Intelligence Summaries are contained in F. S. Regs., Part II. and the Staff Manual respectively. Title pages will be prepared in manuscript.

17th Bn. WELSH REGT. **WAR DIARY** ~~or~~ ~~**INTELLIGENCE**~~ **SUMMARY.** MAY. 1917.

(*Erase heading not required.*)

Army Form C. 2118.

Place	Date	Hour	Summary of Events and Information	Remarks and references to Appendices
			REF. MAP. 57c S.E 1/20000	
Night of LA VACQUERIE	5/6 May		a few shells fell short thus causing a few casualties to our men. The hostile barrage in reply was good – chiefly H.E. and intense from 11-15 – 11-30 pm in area R.21 d central – R.21 a. central	HPaB
			The assaulting companies 'C' – 'A' forced their way in good style through the village, in spite of very thick wire and obstacles, and a good deal of hostile opposition. All objectives were gained & the trenches in R.16c. cleared of the enemy. 'A' company then sent out a patrol under 2/Lt Waring which proceeded along the road by the church in a N.E. direction & endeavoured to gain touch with the Battalion on our left, but finding no signs of this battn the patrol withdrew owing to intense M.G + rifle fire – one prisoner was captured by this patrol. Numerous Very lights + coloured rockets were sent up by the enemy who fired many aerial darts into the village throughout the operations.	HPaB
			Many casualties were inflicted on the enemy; five prisoners were taken (2 wounded) and several wounded Germans, including a mortally wounded German officer, were left behind. The prisoners belonged to the 8th Coy 459th Inf. Regt.	
			The withdrawal of the attacking party through the support company 'B' was effected in splendid order, at 1 A.M. and all our casualties evacuated – a difficult task in view of the darkness + uncut wire.	HPaB
			Major Andrews, the Intelligence Officer, together with a party of signallers + runners followed the raiding party and established a post at R.21 b 6.5. Here a wire was run back to Battle H.Q. – at point R.26 b 9.9 in the sunken road and communication	

H.P.Bailey

A7092 Wt. W128 9/M1293 750,000. 1/17. D. D & L. Ltd. Forms/C2118/14.

Army Form C. 2118.

Instructions regarding War Diaries and Intelligence Summaries are contained in F. S. Regs., Part II. and the Staff Manual respectively. Title pages will be prepared in manuscript.

WAR DIARY
or
INTELLIGENCE SUMMARY.
(Erase heading not required.)

Place	Date	Hour	Summary of Events and Information	Remarks and references to Appendices
[illegible]	5/6	[illegible]	[illegible]	
			[illegible]	
			[illegible]	
			[illegible]	
			[illegible] 2.30 a[illegible]	
			[illegible]	
			[illegible]	
			[illegible]	
			[illegible] 1.Of[illegible] 2 [illegible]	
			2 [illegible]	
			1 [illegible]	
			3 [illegible]	
			27	

A7092 Wt. W128 9/M1293 750,000. 1/17. D. D. & L. Ltd. Forms/C2118/14.

Instructions regarding War Diaries and Intelligence Summaries are contained in F. S. Regs., Part II. and the Staff Manual respectively. Title pages will be prepared in manuscript.

WAR DIARY
~~or~~
~~INTELLIGENCE SUMMARY.~~
(Erase heading not required.)

17th Bn WELSH REGT. MAY. 1917.

Army Form C. 2118.

Place	Date	Hour	MAP REF. SHEET 57c S.E 1/20,000 Summary of Events and Information	Remarks and references to Appendices
GOUZEAUCOURT	6/5/17		After the operations in LA VACQUERIE, the Battalion assembled in Quarry in R.25d for the Roll Call & then marched back to DESSART WOOD arriving about 7 a.m. The remainder of the day was spent in resting and cleaning up. At 8.30 p.m. the Battalion again moved forward to GOUZEAUCOURT to take up position in Brigade close support in the old main line of resistance and the disposition of the battalion was as follows:– 'A' Coy in sunken road at Q.30 b 5.2 'C' – Quarry in R.25d 'B' } in Fifteen Ravine R.19.d. 'B' Company on left with 'D' on the right 'D' } B.H.Q. in N. end of GOUZEAUCOURT at Q.30 D. 9.8	H.a.B.
			Casualties { Major R.J. ANDREWS M.C. and 2Lt D.J. MOULD slightly wounded and at duty }	
do	7/5/17		Battalion in close support. During night C Coy furnished a working party for digging front line trenches under R.E. supervision	H.a.B.
do	8/5/17		Battalion in close support. Battalion employed in draining and improving billets. During night 'A' & 'B' furnished working parties for digging Front Line trenches under R.E.'s Captain P. WILLIAMS 19th R.W.F. left battalion & proceeded on a course at the 4th Army School at FLEXICOURT	H.a.B.

H.a. Bailey

2353 Wt. W2544/1454 700,000 5/15 D. D. & L. A.D.S.S. Forms/C. 2118.

Instructions regarding War Diaries and Intelligence Summaries are contained in F. S. Regs., Part II. and the Staff Manual respectively. Title pages will be prepared in manuscript.

7th Bn. WELSH REGT.

WAR DIARY
or
INTELLIGENCE SUMMARY.
(Erase heading not required.)

MAY 1917.

Army Form C. 2118.

Place	Date	Hour	MAP REF Sheet 57c S.E. 1/20,000 — Summary of Events and Information	Remarks and references to Appendices
GOUZEAUCOURT	9/5/17.		Battalion in Brigade Close Support. Men employed in erecting shelters and improving billets. "C" & "D" companies furnished working parties at night for digging front line trenches under R.E. supervision.	H.R.B.
-do-	10/5		Battalion in Brigade Close Support. "A" & "B" coys. employed on working parties for digging front line trenches under R.E. supervision at night.	H.R.B.
-do-	11/5		Battalion in Brigade close Support. All four companies - A.B.C.&D. - employed at night in working on the front line system of trenches under R.E. supervision. Experimental Rockets were fired at 9.30 pm from the front line trenches and this battalion rendered a report as to visibility, which was good. Major ANDREWS left the Battalion to take over the temporary command of the 19th R.W.F. in DESSART WOOD.	H.R.B.
-do-	12/5		Battalion in Brigade Close Support. All four companies again employed at night on the front line trenches under R.E. supervision.	H.R.B.
-do-	13/5		Battalion in Brigade Close Support. All four companies again employed at night on the front line under R.E. supervision.	H.R.B.
-do-	14/5		The Battalion relieved the 18th Welsh at night in the front line and the disposition of the companies was as follows:—	H.R.B.

2353 Wt. W2544/1454 700,000 5/15 D. D. & L. A.D.S.S. Forms/C. 2118.

Instructions regarding War Diaries and Intelligence Summaries are contained in F. S. Regs., Part II. and the Staff Manual respectively. Title pages will be prepared in manuscript.

WAR DIARY
or
~~INTELLIGENCE~~ SUMMARY.

(*Erase heading not required.*)

17th Bn WELSH REGT. MAY 1917.

Army Form C. 2118.

Place	Date	Hour	Summary of Events and Information MAP REF. 57c S.E. 1/10000	Remarks and references to Appendices
GOUZEAUCOURT FRONT LINE	14/5 ctd.		Disposition of the companies was as follows :— 'B' took over the right sector of the Battalion front and 'D' the left sector. 'C' company occupied the support trenches in R.26.c. and 'A' company moved up into FIFTEEN RAVINE as reserve company. Strong officer patrols were sent out at night from each company in the front line to keep touch with the enemy and to prevent him from repairing gaps in his wire. Patrols remained out from dusk until dawn.	H.C.B.
-do-	15/5		Battalion in front line. Strong officer patrols again sent out from the 2 front line companies.	H.C.B.
-do-	16/5		— " — — " — — " —	H.C.B.
-do-	17/5		— " — — " — — " —	
-do-	18/5		— " — A strong patrol consisting of 3 officers and 30 O.R., under command of Capt H.P.B. Gough, went out from the right company front at 9.30 pm with the object of securing identifications and examining THE BARRACKS R.21.d, and enemy wire and trenches between S.E. corner of LA VACQUERIE and the main CAMBRAI ROAD. At 9.55 pm — after a 5 minutes barrage as arranged, our artillery lifted off the trench referred to above and the patrol dashed forward through the gaps in the wire in 3 parties. The right and left parties entered the trench and bombed inwards whilst the centre party remained on the parapet. About R.22.a.1.1 a look-out post held by a machine gun and small infantry detachment was encountered. 2 unwounded men, both belonging	H.C.B.

[illegible] Baker

Instructions regarding War Diaries and Intelligence Summaries are contained in F. S. Regs., Part II. and the Staff Manual respectively. Title pages will be prepared in manuscript.

WAR DIARY
or
INTELLIGENCE SUMMARY.
(Erase heading not required.)

Army Form C. 2118.

7th Bn WELSH REGT. MAY 1917.

Place	Date	Hour	Summary of Events and Information (REF MAP 57c S.E. 1/20000)	Remarks and references to Appendices
GOUZEAUCOURT FRONT LINE	18/5	contd.	of the 11th Coy 3rd Bn 82nd Res. Inf. Regt., 22nd Division, and the machine gun were captured. The remainder of the hostile post were either killed or wounded. The rest of the trench was found to be unoccupied. A party, specially detailed, under 2/LT BAILEY thoroughly searched the SAPHEAD which was found to be unoccupied. The patrol then withdrew at 10.15 pm bringing back the captured Machine Gun and prisoners. No casualties were sustained. The flanks of the raiding party were protected as follows:– Right flank by a Lewis Gun team from 'C' Company which remained in a trench at R.21.d.4.5. Left flank by an officer's patrol and a Lewis Gun team which established itself about R.21.b.3.3. The officers who led the assaulting parties were 2/LT A.R. JONES and 2/LT C. WARING. All arrangements worked admirably and the success of the enterprise was due to the dash and discipline of the men engaged who obeyed their instructions to the letter. The whole party finally reached our lines at 10.25 pm. The ~~[illegible]~~ battalion front continued to be patrolled after the raid and withdrawn in case of retaliation, but none resulted. After the raid the following Inter Battalion relief took place:– 'A' company relieved 'D' in the front line and 'C' company relieved 'B'. H.A. Bailey	

2353 Wt. W2544/1454 700,000 5/15 D. D. & L. A.D.S.S. Forms/C 2118.

Army Form C. 2118.

Instructions regarding War Diaries and Intelligence Summaries are contained in F. S. Regs., Part II. and the Staff Manual respectively. Title pages will be prepared in manuscript.

17th Bn Welsh Regt

WAR DIARY
or
~~INTELLIGENCE SUMMARY.~~
(Erase heading not required.)

May. 1917

Place	Date	Hour	Summary of Events and Information	Remarks and references to Appendices
			REF MAP 57c S.E. 1/10000	
GOUZEAUCOURT FRONT LINE	19/5		Batt. in Front Line – An officer's patrol was sent out from each front line company at dusk (9.45pm) and remained out until daybreak (3.15am) with the object of keeping touch with the enemy and in order to prevent him from working on his wire.	HLB
–do–	20/5		Batt in Front Line – An officer's patrol was again sent out from each front line company at dusk (9.45pm) and remained out until dawn (3.15am) to reconnoitre ground and enemy's wire	HLB
–do– –do–	21/5 22/5		Batt in Front Line – A raid was carried out with artillery cooperation on the night of 21/22nd with object of clearing up the situation at SONNET FARM and obtaining identifications. The raiding party consisted of 2 officers and 30 O.R under the direction of LIEUT. TREVOR-JONES The party was lined up about 100 yds N of the CAMBRAI RD. and about 20 yds from enemy wire at 1.55am (22nd) with SERGT. OWEN and 9 O.R immediately behind to act as a "mopping up" party. The assaulting troops were divided into 3 groups. The right group under LIEUT F.S. HIGSON were to clear trench S. of SONNET FARM, the centre group under 2LT. A.J. ELMITT were to deal with the FARM, and the left group under SERGT REES were to work round the FARM. The barrage fell at ZERO – 2am on the trench N of the CAMBRAI Rd. about R.22.c.1.8 – about 50 yds in advance of the party & consisted of H.E. but at 2.5 am. it slowed	

HLeBailey

Instructions regarding War Diaries and Intelligence Summaries are contained in F. S. Regs., Part II. and the Staff Manual respectively. Title pages will be prepared in manuscript.

WAR DIARY
or
INTELLIGENCE SUMMARY.
(Erase heading not required.)

Army Form C. 2118.

Place	Date	Hour	Summary of Events and Information	Remarks and references to Appendices

A7092 Wt. W125 9/M1293 750,000. 1/17. D. D. & L. Ltd. Forms/C2118/14.

Army Form C. 2118.

Instructions regarding War Diaries and Intelligence Summaries are contained in F. S. Regs., Part II. and the Staff Manual respectively. Title pages will be prepared in manuscript.

17th Bn Welsh Regt

WAR DIARY
~~or~~
~~INTELLIGENCE SUMMARY.~~
(*Erase heading not required.*)

MAY. 1917

Place	Date	Hour	Summary of Events and Information	Remarks and references to Appendices
			REF. MAP 57c S.E. 1/10,000	
FINS	23/5		Battalion in Brigade Reserve – Battalion moved to EQUANCOURT at 6.30 pm	R.B.P.
EQUANCOURT	24/5		——— do ———	
"	25		Battalion in Bde Reserve, Re-organization & cleaning carried out.	
"	26		–"– Battalion Training continued.	R.B.P.
"	27		–"– –"–	
"	28		–"– –"–	
"	29		–"– –"–	R.B.P.
SOREL-LE-GRAND	30		Battalion in Bde Reserve, the Battalion marched into Camp at SOREL-LE-GRAND.	R.B.P.
–"–	31		The Battalion working on roads.	

R.J. Manning Major.
Commdg. 17th Welsh Regt.

A7092 Wt. W128.9/M1293. 750,000. 1/17. D. D & L. Ltd. Forms/C2118/14.

Confidential

17th (S) Bn. The Welsh Regt.

War Diary

From 1st June 1917

To 30th June 1917.

Vol 13

Amyot
B. 21

Instructions regarding War Diaries and Intelligence Summaries are contained in F. S. Regs., Part II. and the Staff Manual respectively. Title pages will be prepared in manuscript.

17th (S) Bn. The Welsh Regt. **WAR DIARY** ~~or~~ ~~**INTELLIGENCE SUMMARY.**~~

(Erase heading not required.)

JUNE. 1917

Army Form C. 2118.

Place	Date	Hour	Summary of Events and Information — Ref. Map. 57c S.E. 1/10.000	Remarks and references to Appendices
SOREL-LE-GRAND	1/6/17		Battalion in Brigade Reserve, working on roads	HaB
do	2/6		—do— —do—	
GOUZEAUCOURT	3/6		Batt. went into Bde. Support relieving 12th SUFFOLKS (121st Inf. Bde.) and the disposition of the Coys was as follows:—	HaB
			C. Coy in Sunken Road Q 30 b 7.1 with B.H.Q. A, B, + D. companies in FIFTEEN RAVINE	HaB
—do—	4/6		Batt. in Bde. Support: all companies engaged in making "gooseberries" and working on the Front Line at night.	
—do—	5/6		—do— —do—	
—do—	6/6		—do— —do— 2/LT. A.H.B. DUDLEY reported for duty + was posted to "A" Coy	HaB
—do—	7/6		—do— —do—	
—do—	8/6		—do—. 2 small officers patrols were attached to the 18th Welsh in the Front Line with the object of learning the front and the nature of the enemy defences – One patrol ~~—~~ went out from the right company front and one from the left company front	HaB
—do—	9/6		Batt in Bde. Support – all companies working on Front Line at night and making gooseberries by day. Three small officers patrols went out at night to learn nature of NO MAN'S LAND. Two patrols were attached to the 18th Welsh and 1 patrol to the 12th S.W.B. The patrol which was attached to the 12th S.W.B. came into contact with the enemy and 2 O.R. were wounded	HaB HaB
—do—	10/6		Batt. in Bde. Support – all companies working on the Front Line at night and making "gooseberries" by day. 2/LT. T. T. DAVIES reported for duty + was posted to "B" Coy.	HaB

A7092 Wt. W12S 9/M1293 750,000. 1/17. D. D & I. Ltd. Forms/C2118/14.

Instructions regarding War Diaries and Intelligence Summaries are contained in F. S. Regs., Part II. and the Staff Manual respectively. Title pages will be prepared in manuscript.

Army Form C. 2118.

WAR DIARY
or
~~INTELLIGENCE~~ SUMMARY.
(*Erase heading not required.*)

17th (S.) Bn The Welsh Regt. JUNE 1917.

Place	Date	Hour	MAP REF. 57c S.E. 1/10000 — Summary of Events and Information	Remarks and references to Appendices
GOUZEAUCOURT	11/6		Batt in Bde Support. On the night 11/12th June the Batt relieved the 18th WELSH [illegible] LEFT SUBSECTOR of the VILLERS PLOUICH section of the LINE. The disposition [illegible] as follows:–	[illegible]
LEFT SUBSECTOR VILLERS PLOUICH	12/6		A. Coy on the right with D. Coy in support B – – left – C – – –. BHQ [illegible] FIFTEEN RAVINE	[illegible]
— do —	13/6		Battalion in Front Line. Officers patrols went out at [illegible] with the object of reconnoitring NO MANS LAND and the enemy wire.	[illegible]
— do —	14/6		Batt in Front Line – Officers patrols went out again at night from each coy [illegible] the patrol from the Left Company came into contact with the enemy on the night 14/15th [illegible] 2 O.R. were wounded and were safely brought back.	[illegible]
— do —	15/6		The following Inter-Company relief took place at night. "C" Coy relieved "B" in the Front Line on the Left and "D" Coy relieved "A" Coy on the right.	[illegible]
— do —	16/6		Batt in Front Line. Officers patrols out as usual from each Coy. front.	[illegible]
— do —	17/6		Batt in Front Line [illegible] patrolling as usual [illegible]	[illegible]

Instructions regarding War Diaries and Intelligence Summaries are contained in F. S. Regs., Part II, and the Staff Manual respectively. Title pages will be prepared in manuscript.

17TH BATT. THE WELSH REGT. **WAR DIARY** ~~or~~ ~~INTELLIGENCE~~ **SUMMARY.** JUNE. 1917.

(*Erase heading not required.*)

Army Form C. 2118.

Place	Date	Hour	Summary of Events and Information MAP. 57c S.E. 1/10000	Remarks and references to Appendices
LEFT SUBSECTOR VILLERS-PLOUICH	18/6		Batt. in Front Line. On night 17/18th June a raiding party consisting of 3 officers – LT. TREVOR-JONES 2/LT. W.J. GRIFFITHS & 2/LT. A.J. ELMITT + 40 O.R. the whole under the direction of CAPT. W.R. STRATTON left our Right Coy. front at C' ravine (R 8c 7.5) about 12.45 am. and proceeded towards FARM TRENCH. The party carried 2 Bangalore torpedoes intending to blow a gap in the enemy's wire & then enter hostile trench. 2/LT. ELMITT led the party detailed to carry the torpedoes which were safely placed in position under the wire. The fuses were then fired but failed to explode the torpedoes which were withdrawn & taken back to our lines. The party then endeavoured to find a gap in the hostile wire but without success. As the raiding party were returning to our lines sounds of bombing were heard coming from the direction of B' ravine and shortly after a strong hostile patrol was seen making off rapidly towards the sunken road on the right of the Battalion front. 2/LT. GRIFFITHS immediately detached a few men from our party & endeavoured to cut off the hostile raiders & succeeded in forcing them to abandon one of our wounded who was being carried away as a prisoner. It was found that an enemy patrol had entered our lines near B' ravine & had bombed a L.G. post causing 5 O.R. casualties wounded.	[illegible]
—do—	19/6		Batt. in Front Line. A raiding party left C' Ravine on night 18/19 June at 1.30 am. consisting of the same officers & men as on previous night and endeavoured to raid FARM TRENCH. The party again carried 2 Bangalore torpedoes & was accompanied by L/Cpl MELLORS of 224 F. Coy. R.E. specially detailed to fire the torpedoes. However, on arriving some 20 yards from hostile wire heavy rifle fire was opened on the party from the enemy's trenches causing several casualties. The party was forced to withdraw. Many gallant acts occurred during the withdrawal but all our casualties were safely brought in. Casualties 2 O.R. killed 1 officer, LT. A. TREVOR JONES badly wounded and 5 O.R. wounded.	[illegible]

A7092 Wt. W128.9/M1293 750,000. 1/17. D. D. & L. Ltd. Forms/C2118/14.

Instructions regarding War Diaries and Intelligence Summaries are contained in F. S. Regs., Part II. and the Staff Manual respectively. Title pages will be prepared in manuscript.

WAR DIARY
~~or~~
INTELLIGENCE SUMMARY.

(Erase heading not required.)

Army Form C. 2118.

June

Place	Date	Hour	Summary of Events and Information	Remarks and references to Appendices
[illegible]	[illegible]		[illegible]	
Villers-Plouich	[illegible]		[illegible]	
Dessart Wood	[illegible]		[illegible]	
— do —	[illegible]		[illegible]	
— do —	[illegible]		— do — [illegible]	
— do —	4/6		— do — [illegible]	
— do —	5/6		— do — [illegible]	
— do —	6/6		— do — [illegible]	
— do —	7/6		— do — [illegible]	[illegible]
			A Coy in Tents at W 10 c 8 4. "B" Coy in trenches at X 1 a "C" Coy + B H Q in sunken road at W. 6 d 7.2 "D" Coy in trenches at Quentin Mill in R 31 d	
Gonnelieu Sector.	28/6		Batt in Brigade Reserve. All companies working (ying?) on front line [illegible]	[illegible]
— do —	29/6		" "	[illegible]
— do —	30/6		" "	

[illegible] Major

A7092 Wt. W128 9/M1293 750,000. 1/17. D. D & L Ltd. Forms/C2118/14.

Instructions regarding War Diaries and Intelligence Summaries are contained in F. S. Regs., Part II. and the Staff Manual respectively. Title pages will be prepared in manuscript.

17th Welsh Regt.

WAR DIARY
~~or~~
~~INTELLIGENCE SUMMARY.~~

(Erase heading not required.)

June 1917.

Army Form C. 2118.

Place	Date	Hour	Summary of Events and Information			Remarks and references to Appendices
			LIST OF HONOURS AND AWARDS - Officers [redacted]			
			OFFICERS	AWARDED		
LA VACQUERIE	May 5/6		MAJOR R.J. ANDREWS M.C.	D.S.O.	In charge of forward operations in raid on LAVACQUERIE, night of May 5/6 - successfully superintended withdrawal of raiding parties.	
DO	do		LIEUT. F.S. Higson	M.C.	Coolness and gallantry in LAVACQUERIE raid, night 5/6th May	
	24 April		Capt. H.P.B. Gough	M.C.	Coolness and skilful leadership during advance on WELSH RIDGE (RHONDDA HILL)	
	24 April		2/LT. L. WALTON	~~M.C.~~ D.S.O. CROIX de GUERRE	Dash and gallantry displayed during advance on WELSH RIDGE	
LA VACQUERIE	18th MAY		2/LT. A.R. JONES 2/LT. C. WARING	M.C. M.C.	Dash and skilful leadership during raid on enemy trench, resulting in the capture of 2 prisoners and a machine gun, without a single casualty to the raiding party.	
			CAPT. C.M. DUNN CAPT. W.P. STRATTON	Mentioned in Despatches	Birthday Honours	
			2/LT. L. WALTON	M.C.	Birthday Honours	

Instructions regarding War Diaries and Intelligence Summaries are contained in F. S. Regs., Part II. and the Staff Manual respectively. Title pages will be prepared in manuscript.

Army Form C. 2118.

~~WAR DIARY~~ or INTELLIGENCE SUMMARY.

(Erase heading not required.)

June 1917.

17th Bn The Welsh Regt. List of Ho[illegible] NCOs and Men

~~Place~~ NAME	Regtl. ~~Date~~ No.	~~Hour~~ RANK	COY.	AWARD	Summary of ~~Events and Information~~	Remarks and references to Appendices
FLACK G	26146	L/Cpl	D.	M.M.	Displayed great dash and gallantry during [illegible] April 24th 1917.	[illegible]
BROWN W.J.	27096	Pte.	A.	"		
STANGHAM G	36394	–	–	"	——— do ———	
DAVIES M	46604	L/Cpl	C.	"		
PHILLIPS P.J.	25966	Pte.	A.	" {Croix de Guerre		
LARCOMBE S.A.	26068	–	A.	M.M.		
HUGHES J.D.	26040	Sergt	A.	"	Displayed great dash and courage during raid on [illegible]	
JONES J.H	25992	Pte.	A.	"		
SULLIVAN D.R	25576	L/Cpl	A.	"	——— do ———	
LEWIS J.	25666	Pte	A.	"		
TONKIN T.J	25226	L/Sergt	B.	"	Displayed great dash and courage during raid on enemy [illegible] on night of 18th May 1917	
WOODMAN E.G	58524	Pte.	B	"		
HIGGINS H.	25343	L/Cpl	A	"		
PIZEY A.E.	26257	Pte	B	D.C.M.	BIRTH DAY Honours	
HOBBY T.	21909	Sergt	C	{Mentioned in Despatches	——— " ———	[illegible]
REES-JONES D	25046	Sergt	C	M.M.	Set a fine example of courage [illegible] under fire [illegible] raid on enemy [illegible] on night of 18/19 June	
ISAAC E	26020	Corpl	D	M.M.	Set a fine example of courage [illegible] duty during raids on enemy trenches on nights of 17/18th and 18/19th June	
PLUES R	33626	Pte.	C	M.M.	Displayed great gallantry and initiative during raids on enemy trenches on nights of 17/18th and 18/19th June.	

A7092 Wt. W125 9/M1293 750,000 1/17. D. D & L. Ltd. Forms/C2118/14.

Army Form C. 2118.

Instructions regarding War Diaries and Intelligence Summaries are contained in F. S. Regs., Part II. and the Staff Manual respectively. Title pages will be prepared in manuscript.

17th Bn The Welsh Regt.

WAR DIARY
or
~~**INTELLIGENCE SUMMARY**~~.
(Erase heading not required.)

July. 1917

Place	Date	Hour	Summary of Events and Information — Map reference 57c S.E. 1/20,000	Remarks and references to Appendices
GONNELIEU SECTOR	1/7		Battalion in Brigade Reserve. Battalion working at night on Front Line System. Major R.J. ANDREWS D.S.O. M.C. returned from leave and took over command of the Batt. vice Major D. APPLEBY	HPaB
	2/7		Battalion in Brigade Reserve – working at night on Front Line System	HPaB
	3/7		—— do —— —— do ——	
	4/7		—— do —— —— do —— Captain & Adjt. M. B. GRAHAM evacuated sick to FINS. 2/Lieut. H.P.A. BAILEY took over duties as Acting Adjutant.	HPaB
GONNELIEU RIGHT SUB-SECTOR	5/7		On night 5/6th July the Battalion relieved the 18th Welsh in the Right subsector of the GONNELIEU SECTOR. The dispositions of the companies were as follows:–	HPaB
	6/7		A. Coy in Right Subsector D Coy in support of A Coy on the right B " Left " C " " " B " " left.	HPaB
	7/7		Battalion in Front Line. No man's Land patrolled nightly from each coy. front	HPaB
	8/7		—— do —— —— do ——	
	9/7		—— do —— Inter Company Relief on night 9/10th D Coy relieved A Coy, C " " B " Patrolling as usual	HPaB
	10/7		—— do —— On night 10/11th LIEUT. T. WALLACE, while in charge of a patrol from the Right company front was struck by a hostile bomb and seriously wounded. Total casualties suffered by our patrol were 1 officer wounded, and 2 O.R. slightly wounded	HPaB

HPaBailey

2353 Wt. W2544/1454 700,000 5/15 D. D. & L. A.D.S.S. Forms/C. 2118.

Instructions regarding War Diaries and Intelligence Summaries are contained in F. S. Regs., Part II. and the Staff Manual respectively. Title pages will be prepared in manuscript.

17th (S) Bn the Welsh Regt

WAR DIARY
~~or~~
INTELLIGENCE SUMMARY.

(Erase heading not required.)

July 1917

Army Form C. 2118.

Place	Date	Hour	Summary of Events and Information Ref. Pl. 57c S.E. 1/20000	Remarks and references to Appendices
GONNELIEU Right Subsector	11 July		Battalion in front line. On night 11/12th a raiding party consisting of 2 Offrs LIEUT D.R. WALTERS and 2/Lt. R.L. JONES and 44 O.Rs – the whole under the command of a/CAPT. F.T. WILLIAMS. An attempt was made to blow gaps in hostile wire with 2 Bangalore torpedoes but the fuses failed to explode. The party then endeavoured to cut gaps in wire with wire-cutters but it was found to be too thick. No other gaps could be discovered & the party was forced to withdraw about 3 a.m. without attaining its object.	[illegible]
do	12 July		Battalion in front line. Patrols sent out at night from both coy. front to keep No man's Land clear of the enemy or to reconnoitre hostile defences.	[illegible]
do	13 July		Battalion in front line. The Battalion was relieved on night 13/14th by the 18th Welsh, who suffered some casualties from hostile shelling during relief. On completion of the relief the Battalion took over the billets vacated by the 12th S.W.B. and the disposition of the Companies was as follows:–	
			A coy in dugouts & trenches in R.31.b.6.2	
			B – – – R.26.d.2.1	(in Brigade Support) [illegible]
			C – – – R.26.a.7.5	
			D – – – R.32.a.9.9	
			BHQ in dugouts & shelters in R.31.c.1.1	

A7092 Wt. W128 9/M1293 750,000. 1/17. D. D. & L. Ltd. Forms/C2118/14.

Instructions regarding War Diaries and Intelligence Summaries are contained in F. S. Regs., Part II. and the Staff Manual respectively. Title pages will be prepared in manuscript.

17th Bn The Welsh Regt

WAR DIARY
or
~~INTELLIGENCE SUMMARY.~~

~~(Erase heading not required.)~~

July 1917.

Army Form C. 2118.

~~Place~~ NAME	~~Date~~ No	~~Hour~~ Coy	HONOUR	Summary of Events and Information	Remarks and references to Appendices
				List of Honours and Awards – 17th Bn The Welsh Regt	
Sergeant THOMAS THOMAS	25071	D	M.M	On the night 10/11th July 1917. Sergt THOMAS, L/Cpl DAVIES and Private FURLONG were members of a patrol sent out to examine enemys wire and defences. The patrol was attacked by four separate hostile parties and the officer in charge wounded. In the sharp fighting which ensued these three men showed great gallantry and brought in the wounded officer.	
L/Cpl. ARTHUR JOHN DAVIES	25931	A.	M.M		
Private. WALTER FURLONG	18529	D	M.M.		

A7092 Wt. W128 9/M1293 750,000. 1/17. D. D & L. Ltd. Forms/C2118/14.

Instructions regarding War Diaries and Intelligence Summaries are contained in F. S. Regs., Part II. and the Staff Manual respectively. Title pages will be prepared in manuscript.

17 Welsh Regt.

WAR DIARY
or
INTELLIGENCE SUMMARY.
(Erase heading not required.)

July. 1917

Army Form C. 2118.

Place	Date	Hour	Map ref. 57c S.E. 1/20000 — Summary of Events and Information	Remarks and references to Appendices
GONNELIEU Right Subsector	14/7		Battalion in Brigade Support – furnished working parties [illegible]	[illegible]
— do —	15/7		—— do —— —— do ——	
— do —	16/7		—— do —— —— do ——	
— do —	17/7		—— do —— [illegible] working [illegible] bombarded [illegible] Casualties (1 OR killed 2 [illegible] [illegible])	
— do —	18/7		Battalion in Brigade Support engaged in working in front line at night	[illegible]
— do —	19/7		—— do —— —— do ——	[illegible]
— do —	20/7		—— do —— —— do ——	[illegible]
— do —	21/7		Battalion relieved the 18th Welsh in front Line Right subsector GONNELIEU [illegible] night of 21/22 July. The dispositions of the Companies were as follows. A coy. on the Right with D Coy in Support. B — — Left with C —— Support. A patrol from the Left Coy. consisting of 1 officer and [illegible] OR came into contact with 2 strong hostile parties and we suffered 1 officer – 2/Lieut R.M. EVANS and 7 OR wounded and 4 OR missing	[illegible]

17th Bn The Welsh Regt. **WAR DIARY** *or* **INTELLIGENCE SUMMARY.** July 1917 Army Form C. 2118.

Instructions regarding War Diaries and Intelligence Summaries are contained in F. S. Regs., Part II. and the Staff Manual respectively. Title pages will be prepared in manuscript.

(Erase heading not required.)

Place	Date	Hour	Summary of Events and Information	Remarks and references to Appendices
			Ref. Map 57c S.E. 1/20000	
GONNELIEU Right Subsector	22/7		Battalion in Front Line. Both coy. fronts patrolled at night. A search party was sent out from Left Coy. front to endeavour to find the missing men of previous night's patrol, but without success	HPaB.
	23/7		Battalion in Front Line. NO MANS LAND patrolled at night and hostile wire examined	HPaB
	24/7		Battalion in Front Line. During night 24/25 the enemy heavily bombarded our Right Coy. front - about 1am - with rifle grenades & aerial darts for about 5 minutes - followed by 3 minutes intense bombardment with gas shells, H.E. & rifles grenades & aerial darts. Casualties 2 officers - LIEUT. D.K. WALTERS and 2/Lt R.S.R. DAVID and 11 O.R. were slightly gassed. 1 O.R. killed and 1 O.R. wounded	HPaB
	25/7		Battalion in Front Line - Inter Company relief, night of 25/26th D Coy. relieved A on the right and C coy relieved B Coy on the Left. Patrolling at night as usual	HPaB
	26/7		Battalion in Front Line. Patrolling whole Battalion front as usual at night	HPaB
	27/7		— do — — do —	HPaB
	28/7		— do — — do —	HPaB
	29/7		Battalion in Front Line. about 6pm. a prisoner was captured about R 27b.5.1 by L/Cl Rogers No 26388 of C. Coy. The prisoner was a signaller - L/Corpl - who had mistaken our line for his own. On night 29/30 July the Battalion was relieved by the 18th Welsh, and on completion of relief moved back into Brigade Reserve, taking over billets from the 12th S.W.B. The dispositions of the companies was as follows: —	HPaB

HPaBarling

Instructions regarding War Diaries and Intelligence Summaries are contained in F. S. Regs., Part II. and the Staff Manual respectively. Title pages will be prepared in manuscript.

17th Bn The Welsh Regt.

WAR DIARY ~~or INTELLIGENCE SUMMARY.~~

(Erase heading not required.)

July. 1917.

Army Form C. 2118.

Place	Date	Hour	Summary of Events and Information — map reference. 57c S.E. 1/20000	Remarks and references to Appendices
GONNELIEU RIGHT SUBSECTOR	29/7	(contd)	Dispositions of the companies:—	
			A coy. in trenches at X. 1. b	
			B " " " R. 31 d. QUENTIN MILL	
			C " " " " " "	
			D " and B.H.Q. at W. 6. d. 6.2. in Sunken Road (GRANTHAM) in dugouts and [illegible]	M.B
	30/7		Battalion in Brigade Reserve. 3 companies working by night and 1 company by day on the Front Line system — Lt-Col A. BRYANT D.S.O. returned from the 120th Brigade + resumed command of the Battalion vice Major ANDREWS D.S.O. M.C	
	31/7		Battalion in Brigade Reserve. 2 Companies bathed in GOUZEAUCOURT – (C + B Coys). musketry practised on range in W. 6 d. 6.2. working parties as usual on front line	M.B

A Bryant Lieut-Colonel
Cdg. 17 Welsh Regt
31 July 1917.

2353 Wt. W2514/1454 700,000 5/15 D. D. & L. A.D.S.S. Forms/C. 2118.

Instructions regarding War Diaries and Intelligence Summaries are contained in F. S. Regs., Part II. and the Staff Manual respectively. Title pages will be prepared in manuscript.

17 Welsh Regt

WAR DIARY or ~~INTELLIGENCE SUMMARY.~~

(Erase heading not required.)

July. 1917.

Army Form C. 2118.

Vol 14

Place	Date	Hour	Summary of Events and Information	Remarks and references to Appendices
Honours and Awards			17th Bn. The Welsh Regt. – List of Honours and Awards	
Military Cross			T/2nd LT. AUSTIN JOHN ELMITT. On the nights 17/18 June and 18/19th June 1917, on the occasion of 2 successive raids on enemy's trenches, he set an example of coolness and contempt for danger beyond all praise. He handled his party with great skill. He had previously shewn gallant behaviour on the occasion of the attack on hostile positions on April 24th 1917.	Signed with D.R.O. 10/7/17
Military Cross			T/2nd LT. WILLIAM JOHN GRIFFITHS. On the occasion of 2 successive raids on hostile trenches on nights of 17/18 and 18/19 June 1917, he behaved most gallantly & set a fine example to his men. During the withdrawal to our lines a hostile party was met. With a couple of men he attacked this party and rescued one of our wounded who was being carried off a prisoner	
D.C.M.			No 26892 Pte. HENRY HOLMAN. On the night 18/19 June 1917, on the occasion of a raid on the enemy's trenches Pte. Holman realizing the necessity of getting all casualties back to our lines and also organized parties for their removal. His gallantry was extraordinary.	

A7092 Wt. W128 9/M1293 750,000. 1/17. D. D & L. Ltd. Forms/C2118/14.

H.D.
7 sheets

Vol 15

War Diary

17th (S) Bn The Welsh Regt.

August 1917.

15 D.
8 sheets

Instructions regarding War Diaries and Intelligence Summaries are contained in F. S. Regs., Part II. and the Staff Manual respectively. Title pages will be prepared in manuscript.

17th Bn The Welsh Regt

WAR DIARY or ~~INTELLIGENCE SUMMARY.~~

August 1917.

(Erase heading not required.)

Army Form C. 2118.

Place	Date	Hour	Summary of Events and Information Map 57c S.E. 1/20000	Remarks and references to Appendices
GONNELIEU Right SubSector	1/8		Battalion in Brigade Reserve. Musketry practices carried out by the companies.	HPaB.
LEFT SubSector VILLERS PLOUICH	2/8		On the night 2/3rd August the Battalion relieved the 14th Argyle & Suth. Hrs. in the Right subsector of the VILLERS PLOUICH Sector, and the dispositions of the companies were:— D. Coy in Right Subsector, with A coy in Right Support B " " Left " " C " " Left " On relief taking place information was passed that the enemy artillery had cut 2 gaps in our wire in R. 14 on the Right coy front. In consequence the gaps were repaired and listening posts established at these points. At 2.30 am. the enemy attempted to raid one of these posts and a loud explosion was heard. L. Gunfire was at once opened on them. In answer to a rocket which burst into 3 yellow balls the enemy put down a heavy T.M., H.E. & M.G. barrage on our line but nothing further developed & the enemy never got beyond our wire. Our artillery was prompt & effective and enemy fire soon ceased. Search parties were sent out immediately to secure identification and 2 large unexploded Bangalore torpedoes were brought in. On the following night over 500 bombs and a large number of German rifles were found in No MAN'S LAND	HPaB

HPaBailey - 4Lt

Instructions regarding War Diaries and Intelligence Summaries are contained in F. S. Regs., Part II. and the Staff Manual respectively. Title pages will be prepared in manuscript.

WAR DIARY
or
INTELLIGENCE ~~SUMMARY~~.
(Erase heading not required.)

Army Form C. 2118.

17th Bn. [illegible] Regt.

Place	Date	Hour	Summary of Events and Information — Map. Ref. 57c [illegible] 20000	Remarks and references to Appendices
LEFT SUBSECTOR VILLERS PLOUICH	3/8		Battalion in [illegible]. On the night 3rd August the Battalion [illegible]	
			welsh and [illegible] Back [illegible]	[illegible]
	4/8		Battalion in [illegible] [illegible] [illegible] carried out by the [illegible]	[illegible]
	5/8		Battalion in Brigade [illegible] " " " "	[illegible]
	6/8		Battalion in Brigade Reserve " " " "	[illegible]
	7/8		On night of 7/8th August the Battalion relieved the 18th Welsh in the [illegible]	
			of the VILLERS PLOUICH SECTOR and the dispositions [illegible]	
			D Coy in Right front Subsector with A Coy in Support	[illegible]
			B " " Left " " " C " " "	
	8/8		Battalion in Front line. Each company [illegible] patrols at night	[illegible]
	9/8		—— do —— —— do ——	[illegible]
	10/8		—— do —— —— do ——	[illegible]
	11/8		—— do —— —— do —— [illegible] Battalion [illegible]. A Coy relieved	[illegible]
			D Coy in right front and C Coy relieved B Coy in left front.	
	11/8		The following officers reported for duty from the Base & were posted as follows	
			2/Lieut. A. EVANS A Coy, Captain MORGAN-GRIFFITHS B Coy, 2/Lt. L. PHILLIPS C Coy, and	
			2/Lt D.M. DAVIES D Coy.	

W.H. [illegible] 2/Lt

2353 Wt. W2544/1454 700,000 5/15 D. D. & L. A.D.S.S. Forms/C. 2118.

Instructions regarding War Diaries and Intelligence Summaries are contained in F. S. Regs., Part II. and the Staff Manual respectively. Title pages will be prepared in manuscript.

17th (S) Bn The Welsh Regt.

WAR DIARY
or
~~INTELLIGENCE SUMMARY.~~

(Erase heading not required.)

August. 1917

Army Form C. 2118.

Place	Date	Hour	Summary of Events and Information — Map Ref 57c S.E. 1/20000	Remarks and references to Appendices
VILLERS PLOUICH LEFT SUBSECTOR	12/8		Battalion in Front Line. Major R.J. ANDREWS DSO. MC. took over temporary command of the Battalion vice Lieut-Colonel A. BRYANT D.S.O. who proceeded to England on leave (14/8)	HPaB
	13/8		Battalion in Front Line. No MANS LAND patrolled at night as usual	HPaB
	14/8		—— do —— —— do ——	HPaB
GOUZEAUCOURT	15/8		On the night 15/16th August the Battalion was relieved by the 18th Welsh. On completion of relief the Battalion moved back into Brigade Reserve and occupied its former reserve billets. A Coy in GOUZEAUCOURT-TRESCAULT RD, B Coy and C Coy near QUENTIN MILL, D Coy + B.H.Q at GRANTHAM W.6.d. 6.2	HPaB
	16/8		Battalion in Brigade Reserve. Day spent in cleaning up	HPaB
	17/8		—— do —— Training under coy. arrangements. 3 coys working at night on Front Line.	HPaB
	18/8		Battalion in Brigade Reserve Musketry training. 3 coys working at night on Front Line	HPaB
	19/8		—— do —— —— " —— —— " ——	HPaB
	20/8		—— do —— —— " —— —— " ——	HPaB
	21/8		—— do —— —— " —— —— " ——	HPaB
	22/8		—— do —— —— " —— —— " ——	HPaB

HPaBailey 2/Lieut

Army Form C. 2118.

Instructions regarding War Diaries and Intelligence Summaries are contained in F. S. Regs., Part II. and the Staff Manual respectively. Title pages will be prepared in manuscript.

WAR DIARY
or
INTELLIGENCE SUMMARY.
(Erase heading not required.)

10th (S) Bn. The Welsh Regt. August 1917.

Place	Date	Hour	Summary of Events and Information — Map reference GOUZEAUCOURT Ed 1B 1/20000	Remarks and references to Appendices
GOUZEAUCOURT	23/8		Battalion in Brigade Reserve. On the night 23/24th the Battalion relieved the 13th Welsh in the Left Subsector VILLERS PLOUICH and the dispositions of the companies were as follows	
LEFT SUBSECTOR VILLERS PLOUICH			A Coy Right front with D Coy in support. C Coy Left front with B Coy in support. 2/Lt F.P.M. PEERS and 2/Lt TREVOR DAVIES rejoined battalion from Base. 2/Lt Peers was posted to B Coy. 2/Lt T Davies to D Coy.	
	24/8		Battalion in front Line. Patrols sent out nightly from both company fronts.	H.A.B.
	25/8		—— do —— —— do ——	H.A.B.
	26/8		—— do —— Lt Colonel A BRYANT DSO arrived back from leave and took over command of the Battalion vice Major R.J. ANDREWS DSO, MC.	H.A.B.
	27/8		Battalion in Front Line. Inter Batt relief D Coy relieved A Coy in Right Subsector and B Coy relieved C Coy in Left Subsector. Patrolling at night as usual.	H.A.B.
	28/8		Battalion in Front Line. A strong fighting patrol composed of 2 officers (2/Lt R.L. JONES and 2/Lt D.M. DAVIES) and 30 O.R. — the whole under the control of Captain F.S. HIGSON searched the area around the CEMETERY but no trace of the enemy was found.	H.A.B.
	29/8		Battalion in Front Line. Patrolling at night as usual	H.A.B.

H.A. Bullen 2/Lt

2353 Wt. W2544/1454 700,000 5/15 D. D. & L. A.D.S.S. Forms/C 2118.

Instructions regarding War Diaries and Intelligence Summaries are contained in F. S. Regs., Part II. and the Staff Manual respectively. Title pages will be prepared in manuscript.

Army Form C. 2118.

WAR DIARY or ~~INTELLIGENCE SUMMARY~~.

17th (S) Bn. The Welsh Regt. August 1917.

(Erase heading not required.)

Place	Date	Hour	Summary of Events and Information	Remarks and references to Appendices
			Map Ref. Gouzeaucourt 1/20000	
VILLERS PLOUICH LEFT SUBSECTOR	30/8		Battalion in front Line. On the night 30/31st August a strong raiding patrol consisting of 2 officers (2/Lt T.T. DAVIES and 2/Lt J. REDROBE) and 30 O.R. - the whole under command of Capt. C.M. DUNN attempted to enter FARM TRENCH by the aid of a Bangalore Torpedo - The party was accompanied by 2/Lt. E.F. BORRIE R.E. - the officer specially detailed to fire the torpedo. 2 thick belts of wire - over 30 yds apart prevented the success of the enterprise and the party withdrew about 4 am without firing the torpedo - no hostile patrols were encountered. Casualties 1 O.R. wounded	HaB
	31/8		Battalion in front Line. On the night 31st August/1st Sept. a raiding party consisting of 2 officers (a/Capt F.S. HIGSON M.C. + 2/Lt T.T. DAVIES) and 30 O.R. - the whole under command of Capt. C.M. DUNN again attempted to raid FARM TRENCH by the aid of a Bangalore Torpedo - The party was again accompanied by 2/Lt E.F. BORRIE, the R.E. officer specially detailed to fire the torpedo. The party left our advanced trenches on the Left Coy front at 9 pm and reached the enemy wire at point R.9.c.20.00 about 10.50 pm. The wire was found to be too wide for the Bangalore and Capt. HIGSON M.C. commenced to cut a gap. The gap in the outer wire was almost completed and the Bangalore inserted when the raiding party was discovered by a large hostile working party. The raiders at once opened rapid fire and inflicted several casualties on the enemy. Very heavy rifle and M.G. fire was opened on the raiding party in reply and Capt. F.S. HIGSON M.C. ordered a withdrawal. This was being	HaB

HaBailey 2/Lt

Instructions regarding War Diaries and Intelligence Summaries are contained in F. S. Regs., Part II. and the Staff Manual respectively. Title pages will be prepared in manuscript.

17th (S) Bn The Welsh Regt.

WAR DIARY
~~INTELLIGENCE SUMMARY.~~

(*Erase heading not required.*)

August 1917

Army Form C. 2118.

Place	Date	Hour	Summary of Events and Information	Remarks and references to Appendices
			Map Ref. 5/A Sheet GOUZEAUCOURT 1/20000	
VILLERS-PLOUICH LEFT SUBSECTOR			successfully carried out when the party came under heavy M.G. from the right which wounded Capt. HIGSON in the hand. He continued to direct the withdrawal until he fell mortally wounded. The whole of the party returned safely and all casualties were brought in.	
	31/8		Casualties 1 Officer Captain F.S. HIGSON M.C. killed - 1 O.R. killed. 1 O.R. wounded.	HRC
			On night 31st August/1st Sept. the Battalion was relieved by the 18th Welsh, and on completion of relief moved into Brigade Reserve. The disposition of the companies was as follows:	
			A Coy + B.H.Q. in GOUZEAUCOURT-TRESCAULT Rd. Q30d 5.8	
			C + B Coys near QUENTIN MILL R.31d	
			D Coy. in sunken road in Q29d.	
			The following officers reported for duty and were posted as follows:	
			2/Lieut P HAY A Coy, 2/Lieut F S J M LEWIS B Coy, 2/Lieut J.O. HILL D Coy.	
			1/9/17. A N Bryant, Lieut. Colonel Cdg 17th (S) Bn The Welsh Regt.	

2353 Wt. W2534/1454 700,000 5/15 D. D. & L. A.D.S.S. Forms/C 2118.

HPakdin 7/4.

Instructions regarding War Diaries and Intelligence Summaries are contained in F. S. Regs., Part II. and the Staff Manual respectively. Title pages will be prepared in manuscript.

17th (S) Bn The Welsh Regt

WAR DIARY

~~or~~

~~INTELLIGENCE SUMMARY.~~

(Erase heading not required.)

August 1917.

Army Form C. 2118.

Place	Date	Hour	Summary of Events and Information	Remarks and references to Appendices
			List of Honours and Awards.	
Honours	Coy	Regtl No		
Bar to M.M.	D	26020	Sergeant E. ISAAC. M.M. On night 2/3rd August 1917, on the occasion of an attempted hostile raid on our trenches, Sergt. ISAAC displayed great gallantry.	
M.M.	D	39129	Pte. E. DUNFORD. On night 2/3rd August 1917, on the occasion of an attempted hostile raid on our trenches, Pte DUNFORD displayed great gallantry and skill in handling his L.G.	
M.M.	C	26388	L/Cpl F. ROGERS. In daylight on the afternoon of 29th July 1917 L/Cpl F. ROGERS seeing a German soldier in No MANS LAND about 300 yds. away from our Lines, left our trenches alone, stalked and captured the German who tried twice to escape.	
M.M.	A	46252 25142 48130 54062	Pte A. LEACH - W. ALDERMAN - F. DAGGER - W.F. DAVIES For gallant conduct and devotion to duty during an enemy gas shell bombardment on night 24/25th July 1917. These four S. Bearers showed great courage and initiative in entering the gas-shelled area, in carrying away the wounded and in adjusting respirators on wounded men.	
M.C.			T/Lieutenant T. WALLACE. For gallant conduct and good leadership on night 10/11th July 1917 when in command of a patrol. Although attacked by 3 or 4 hostile parties, by skilful handling of his men, Lieut. WALLACE drove off the enemy and prevented them from raiding our trenches.	

H.G. Bailey - 2/Lieut

Vol 16

War Diary

17th (S) Bn The Welsh Regiment

September 1917

Instructions regarding War Diaries and Intelligence Summaries are contained in F. S. Regs., Part II. and the Staff Manual respectively. Title pages will be prepared in manuscript.

17th (S.) Bn. The Welsh Regt.

WAR DIARY
or
INTELLIGENCE SUMMARY.
(Erase heading not required.)

September 1917

Army Form C. 2118.

Place	Date	Hour	Map Ref. GOUZEAUCOURT SHEET 1A 1/20000 Summary of Events and Information	Remarks and references to Appendices
VILLERS-PLOUICH LEFT SUBSECTOR	1/9		Battalion in Brigade Reserve. Day spent in resting and cleaning up. Captain J.N. GILBEY - 2nd Welsh Regt - reported for duty and took over duties as a/Adjt vice 2/Lieut H.P.A. BAILEY	HaB
	2/9		Battalion in Brigade Reserve. Battalion working under R.E.s on front line system: 1 Coy by day and 3 Coys by night.	HaB
	3/9		Battalion in Brigade Reserve - working on front line system - 1 Coy by day and 3 Coys by night. A Coy bathed at HEUDICOURT. B+C Coys carried out musketry practice on range near QUENTIN MILL in R 31 d.	HaB
	4/9		Battalion in Brigade Reserve - working on front line system as usual - B Coy bathed at HEUDICOURT.	HaB
	5/9		Battalion in Brigade Reserve - working on front line system as usual. - C Coy bathed at HEUDICOURT. About 4pm a shell fell on a shelter in B Coy's billets near QUENTIN MILL killing 10 O.R. and wounding 3 O.R.	HaB.
	6/9		Battalion in Brigade Reserve - working on front line system as usual - D Coy bathed at HEUDICOURT.	HaB
	7/9		Battalion in Brigade Reserve.	HaB
	8/9		Battalion in Brigade Reserve. Battalion relieved the 18th Welsh in the Front Line and the dispositions of the companies were as follows :-	HaB

H.a. Bailey 2/Lieut.

D/15[illegible] the [illegible] Regt. [illegible]

WAR DIARY
~~or~~
~~INTELLIGENCE~~ SUMMARY.

(Erase heading not required.)

Army Form C. 2118.

Instructions regarding War Diaries and Intelligence Summaries are contained in F. S. Regs., Part II. and the Staff Manual respectively. Title pages will be prepared in manuscript.

Place	Date	Hour	Map Ref [illegible] Sheet [illegible] 1/20000 Summary of Events and Information	Remarks and references to Appendices
VILLERS PLOUICH LEFT SUBSECTOR	8/9	[illegible])	A Coy Right Front with D Coy in support C " Left Front " B " "	[illegible]
	9/9		Battalion in Front line. Patrols sent out nightly from both company fronts	[illegible]
			do	
	10/9		do	
	11/9		do	
			Patrol from right Coy searched area around R21a.8.9 & found that a piece of trench shown on map ([illegible]) [illegible]	[illegible]
	12/9		Battalion in front line. Patrols sent out from both Company fronts. A Patrol consisting of 1 Off. ([illegible]) & [illegible] made a reconnaissance of the Enemy's wire between R15.c.5.8 & R9c.0.1 previous to a [illegible]	[illegible]
	13/9		Battalion in front line. Inter battalion relief. D Coy relieved A Coy in right front subsector & B Coy relieved C Coy in left [illegible] [illegible] sent out a fighting patrol consisting of 2 offs ([illegible]) & [illegible] with a view to effecting an entry into the enemy trenches at a point between R15.c.5.8 & R9.c.0.1 to obtain an identification. A bangalore party ([illegible]) accompanied our patrol with the object of blowing a gap in the (contd)	[illegible]

A7092 Wt. W128 9/M1293 750,000. 1/17. D. D & L Ltd. Forms/C2118/14.

Instructions regarding War Diaries and Intelligence Summaries are contained in F. S. Regs., Part II. and the Staff Manual respectively. Title pages will be prepared in manuscript.

WAR DIARY
or
~~INTELLIGENCE SUMMARY.~~
(Erase heading not required.)

Army Form C. 2118.

17th (S) Battn The Welsh Regt — September 1917.

Map Ref Spl Sheet GOUZEAUCOURT 1/20000

Place	Date	Hour	Summary of Events and Information	Remarks and references to Appendices
VILLERS PLOUICH LEFT SUBSECTOR	13/9	(Contd)	second belt of hostile wire. A large hostile wiring party was seen & our patrol withdrew to our advanced trenches. Our M.Gs fired on & dispersed the enemy wiring party. At 2 AM our party again went out with the same objective. The enemy was very alert & when our patrol was within 40 yds of the hostile wire the enemy opened up a heavy M.G barrage & rifle grenaded NO MANS LAND in front of his wire. Our party was under these circumstances forced to withdraw under protection of our M.Gs & Artillery barrage. The enemy wire was found to consist of two stout belts of knife rests & behind these three rows of thick barbed trip wire heavily anchored down. Our party returned to our lines at 5-30 AM. Casualties:- 1 Officer (2/Lt. F.S. Lewis) very slightly wounded. 2/Lt D R Morgan reported for duty & was posted temporarily to D Coy.	[illegible]
	14/9		Battalion in front line Patrolling at night as usual	[illegible]
	do		— do —	
	16/9		Major R J Andrews DSO MC takes over Command of the Battalion vice Lieut-Col A Bryant D.S.O. who proceeded to Div H Qrs for duty. 2/Lt M M Davies reported back from a Course. Capt. A E Granted reported back from Hospital. Capt W P Strachan took over duties as Second in Command	[illegible]

[illegible]

A7092 Wt. W1128 9/M1293. 750,000. 1/17. D. D & L. Ltd. Forms/C2118/14.

13th (S) Batt. The Welsh Regt.

Instructions regarding War Diaries and Intelligence Summaries are contained in F. S. Regs., Part II. and the Staff Manual respectively. Title pages will be prepared in manuscript.

WAR DIARY
~~or~~
~~INTELLIGENCE~~ SUMMARY.
(Erase heading not required.)

Army Form C. 2118.

Place	Date	Hour	Summary of Events and Information	Remarks and references to Appendices
			Map of Sht. GOUZEAUCOURT [illegible]	
VILLERS PLOUICH LEFT Subsector.	16/9		Battalion in front line [illegible] the [illegible] the [illegible] was relieved by the 18th Welsh Regt. and [illegible] position [illegible] relief moved into Brigade Reserve. The [illegible] position [illegible] was as follows — 1 A [illegible] B [illegible] R.R. [illegible] C & B [illegible] D Company [illegible] from Musketry course.	
	17/9		[illegible]	
	18/9		[illegible]	
	19/9		[illegible]	
	20/9		—— do —— —— do ——	
	21/9		—— do —— —— do ——	
	22/9		—— do —— —— do ——	
	23/9		—— do —— —— do ——	

[illegible] Lieutenant

A7092 Wt. W128 9/M1293 750,000. 1/17. D. D & L. Ltd. Forms/C2118/14.

Instructions regarding War Diaries and Intelligence Summaries are contained in F. S. Regs., Part II. and the Staff Manual respectively. Title pages will be prepared in manuscript.

17th (S) Bn. The Welsh Regt.

WAR DIARY

~~or~~

~~INTELLIGENCE SUMMARY.~~

(Erase heading not required.)

September 1917

Army Form C. 2118.

Place	Date	Hour	Summary of Events and Information — Map ref. Special Sheet GOUZEAUCOURT. 1/20000	Remarks and references to Appendices
VILLERS PLOUICH LEFT SUBSECTOR	24/9		On the night 24/25th the Battalion relieved the 18th Welsh in the Front Line and the dispositions of the companies was as follows: A Coy Right Front with D Coy in support C " Left Front with B " " "	HaB
	25/9		Battalion in Front Line. At 7.30pm, on commencement of minor operation by the 121 Brigade on our right, the enemy put down a heavy H.E. barrage on our wire, front & support trenches. This bombardment lasted until 8.15pm. Owing to careful precautions being taken only 2 casualties resulted – 1 O.R. killed + 1 O.R. shocked. The Battalion front carefully patrolled at night by patrols from each front line company	HaB HaB
	26/9		Battalion in Front Line – Both company fronts thoroughly patrolled at night	
	27/9		Battalion in Front Line. Patrolling at night as usual. Nothing unusual occurred	HaB
	28/9		— do — Inter. Company relief D Coy relieving A Coy in right front, B " " C " " left front	HaB
	29/9		— do — Patrolling at night as usual – nothing unusual occurred	HaB
	30/9		— do — — do — — do.	

HaBailey
2/Lieut.
17 Welsh R.

R. J. Andrews
Major
Cdg. 17th Welsh Regt

A7092 Wt. W128 9/M1293 750,000. 1/17. D. D & L. Ltd. Forms/C2118/14.

Instructions regarding War Diaries and Intelligence Summaries are contained in F. S. Regs., Part II. and the Staff Manual respectively. Title pages will be prepared in manuscript.

WAR DIARY
or
INTELLIGENCE SUMMARY.

(Erase heading not required.)

Army Form C. 2118.

Vol 17

Place	Date	Hour	Summary of Events and Information	Remarks and references to Appendices
			War Diary 17th (S) Bn. The Welsh Regt. October 1917.	17/D. 20 pages

A7092). Wt. W12839/M1293 750,000. 1/17. D. D & L., Ltd. Forms/C2118/14.

17th (S) Bn Welsh Regt.

Army Form C. 2118.

Instructions regarding War Diaries and Intelligence Summaries are contained in F. S. Regs., Part II. and the Staff Manual respectively. Title pages will be prepared in manuscript.

WAR DIARY
or
INTELLIGENCE SUMMARY.

(Erase heading not required.)

October 1917

Place	Date	Hour	Summary of Events and Information (map refce. Gouzeaucourt 1/20000)	Remarks and references to Appendices
VILLERS PLOUICH LEFT SUBSECTOR	1/10		Battalion in front line. Patrolling at night as usual.	WaB
	2/10		On night 2/3 October the Battalion was relieved by the 18th Welsh and on completion of relief moved into the reserve billets vacated by the 18th Welsh. The disposition of the companies was as follows: A Coy + B.H.Q. in the GOUZEAUCOURT–TRESCAULT RD. B + C companies at QUENTIN MILL. D Coy in Sunken Rd in Q.29.d.	WaB
	3/10		Battalion in Brigade Reserve.	WaB
	4/10		—— " ——	WaB
	5/10		—— " ——	WaB
	6/10		—— " ——	WaB
SORREL LE GRAND	7/10		On the night 7/8th the Battalion was relieved by the 11th K.R.R. (20th Division) + moved into huts in SORREL-LE-GRAND	WaB
DOINGT	8/10		The Battalion left SORREL-LE-GRAND + proceeded by motor bus to DOINGT, near PERONNE	WaB
"	9/10		119th Inf. Bde. paraded at PERONNE for inspection by Corps Commander (Genl Pulteney), who presented decorations. 21 decorations were presented to officers and men of this Battalion.	WaB

A7092 Wt. W128 9/M1293 750,000. 1/17. D. D & I. Ltd. Forms/C2118/14.

Army Form C. 2118.

Instructions regarding War Diaries and Intelligence Summaries are contained in F. S. Regs., Part II. and the Staff Manual respectively. Title pages will be prepared in manuscript.

WAR DIARY
or
INTELLIGENCE SUMMARY.
(Erase heading not required.)

Place	Date	Hour	Summary of Events and Information	Remarks and references to Appendices
			Reference Map 'LENS' 1/100 000	
[illegible]	[illegible]		[illegible]	
			PER[illegible] BEA[illegible]	
			[illegible]	
SIMENCOURT	[illegible]		[illegible]	
			BARN[illegible]	
			[illegible]	
	12-10-17		[illegible]	
			[illegible]	
	13-10-17		[illegible]	
	14-10-17		[illegible]	
	15-10-17		Battalion [illegible]	
	16-10-17		Do [illegible]	
	17-10-17		Do Do	
	18-10-17		Do Do	
	19-10-17		Do Do	
	20-10-17		Do Do	

A7092 Wt. W12859/M1293 750,000. 1/17. D. D. & L. Ltd. Forms/C2118/14.

Instructions regarding War Diaries and Intelligence Summaries are contained in F. S. Regs., Part II. and the Staff Manual respectively. Title pages will be prepared in manuscript.

WAR DIARY
or
INTELLIGENCE SUMMARY.
(Erase heading not required.)

Army Form C. 2118.

14th (S) Batt Welsh Regt

October 1917

Place	Date	Hour	Summary of Events and Information — Reference Map "Lens" 1/100,000	Remarks and references to Appendices
SIMENCOURT.	21st	10/17	Church parades. Games in afternoon	W.P.S.
	22.		Battalion training. Capt J. N. Gelby appointed Adjutant	W.P.S.
	23.		Attack practice by 119th inf Bde.	W.P.S.
	24		Inspection of 119th Bde by G.O.C. Division.	W.P.S.
	25.		Battalion training. Won challenge cup — Bde. transport competition.	W.P.S.
	26.		Do Do.	W.P.S.
	27		Do Do.	W.P.S.
	28		Do Do.	W.P.S.
COULLEMOUNT	29		Battalion proceeded by route march to COULLEMOUNT.	W.P.S.
	30		Battalion training	W.P.S.
	31		Do Do	W.P.S.

R. J. Andrews
Lt Col
Comdg 14th (S) Batt
Welsh Regt

W.P. [illegible] Capt
14th Welsh

A7092 Wt. W128 9/M1293 750,000. 1/17. D. D & I. Ltd. Forms/C2118/14.

17th. (Service) Battalion The Welsh Regt.

Training Programme for Wednesday October 31st. 1917

Battalion and location of Unit.	Description of Training.	Time.	Remarks.
Coullemont.	Physical Training (Running)	7.15 - 7.45 AM.	
Oct. 31st. 1917.	Battalion Drill. U.3.1.S.R.	9 - 9.45 am	Bn to parade as strong as possible. Dress Fighting order.
	Bombing.		
	Company in the attack.	10 - 10.45 AM	"A" Company.
	Bombing.	10 - 10.45 am	"B", "C" & "D" Companies.
	Extended Order Drill	11 - 11.45 AM	"B" Company
	Musketry.	11 - 11.45 AM	"A", "C" & "D" Companies.
		12.30 PM	
	Point to Point Run by Platoons.	2 - 4 PM.	"A" & "B" Companies. Strict March Discipline to be observed. Dress Fighting order. Starting point in each case Bn Orderly Room. Route "A" Company. SOMBRIEN - WARLUZEL - Back to Starting point. ROUTE "B" Company. WARLUZEL - SOMBRIEN Back to Starting point.

Training Programme (Contd)

Battalion & Location of unit.	Description of Training.	Time	Remarks
Coullemont Oct. 31st 1917.	Bombing. Bombing Musketry. Musketry.	2 – 3 PM 3 - 4 pm 3 - 4 pm 2 - 3 pm.	"C" Company. "D" Company. "C" Company. "D" Company.

Lieut. Colonel
Commanding 17th (S) Bn. The Welsh Regt.
30th Oct. 1917

The B[illegible] [illegible] collected [illegible] ([illegible])

17th (Service) Battalion. The Welsh Regiment

Training Programme for Week Ending 27th October 1917.

Bn & Location of H.Q.	Description of Training	Time.	Remarks.
17th Welsh Regt.	Physical Training	7.15am - 7.45am	
	Bn Route March.	9.15am.	ROUTE. SIMENCOURT. - WANQUENTIN. - WARLUS - + Rds R I C 9 b. - BERNEVILLE - SIMENCOURT. Order of March. Band. C. D. A. B. Coys
SIMENCOURT.	Bayonet Fighting	2pm - 2.45pm	
Thurs 25.	Gas Drill	3pm - 4pm	The Battn range is allotted to C Coy in the afternoon.
Friday 26th.			The Brigade Range is allotted to D Coy. (45 men)
	Physical Training	7.15am - 7.45am	
	Musketry	9am - 9.45pm	
	Company Drill	10am - 10.45am	The Bn range is allotted to B. Coy.
	Training in the handling and throwing of Bombs & rifle grenades.	11am - 12	
	Gas Drill	12 - 12.30pm	
	Musketry	2pm - 2.45 "	
	Coy. Drill.	3 " 4.0 "	
Sat. 27th.	Physical Training	7am - 7.45am	
	Company Drill	9 " 9.45 "	
	Gas Drill	10 " - 10.45 "	
	Musketry.	11 " - 11.45 "	
	Visual Training	12 " - 12.30pm	
	Games.	2 —	

[signature]

Captain
Adjutant
17th Welsh Regt.

17th Bn. The Welsh Regiment Copy No........

Order No. 20

1. The Battalion will leave SOREL on October 8th at an hour to be notified later, and will proceed to DOINGT either by lorries or by Decauville.

2. BILLETING PARTY.

Billeting Party consisting of Capt? Stratton and 1 N.C.O. from B.H.Q. and 1 N.C.O. per Company will report to the Town Major at DOINGT at 9.0am on October 8th to take over billets the above party will proceed to PERONNE by the Decauville leaving FINS at 10.0pm on the night of the 7th October and will report to the O.C. Rest Camp PERONNE for accomodation for the night of 7/8th October.

3. The Transport of Units of 119th Infantry Brigade together with all mounted cyclists will move into the PERONNE Area under the orders of the 119th Infantry Brigade Transport Officer at an hour to be notified later.

4. Every man will carry a rolled blanket when proceeding by rail or Lorry to DOINGT.

5. Officers Valises, Baggage, and mess property will be loaded on the Baggage wagons at SOREL one hour before the Battalion moves off. This time will be notified later.

6. Acknowledge.

Captain.
& Adjutant.
17th Bn. The Welsh Regiment.

Copies 1 Q.M.
" 2 Capt. Stratton.
3 to 6 O.C. Companies.
7 R.S.M.
8 Office.
9 Transport Officer.

119th Inf.Bde.No.36/264/G.L.

1 Cpy & Or Mr.

O.C.

17th Welsh

17th (GLAM.) Bn. WELSH R.
5 OCT.1917
No. 646

With reference to the move of the 119th Infantry Brigade.Group.

1. The following is the allotment of Sub-areas in the PERONNE Area from October 8th to 10th.

Group (a).

119th Brigade H.Q. 19th R.W.Fusiliers. 12th S.W.Borderers. 17th Welsh Regiment. 229th Field Coy. R.E. & 120th Brigade Works Coy. No.2 Coy. A.S.C.	DOINGT.

Group (b).

18th Welsh Regiment. 119th M.G.Company. 119th T.M.Battery. 136th Field Ambulance.	PERONNE.

The Transport Lines of Group (b) are at I.21.d.1.5. Map.62c.

2. Billeting Officers from each Unit with a N.C.O. for Unit H.Q. each Company and each Transport Lines will report to the Town Majors of DOINGT and PERONNE at 9 a.m. on October 9th for taking over billets.

1 N.C.O. [illegible]

3. The No. 2 Coy. A.S.C., the 136th Field Ambulance and the Transport of the 229th Field Company R.E. will move independently into the PERONNE Area.

4. The Transport of Units of the 119th Infantry Brigade together with all mounted cyclists will move into the PERONNE Area under the orders of the 119th Infantry Brigade Transport Officer at an hour to be notified later.

5. The remaining personnel of all Units and baggage will be taken to PERONNE by Lorry and Decauville from HEUDICOURT, SOREL and FINS. Exact times and places to be notified later.

6. If the surplus baggage of Units is not excessive it is hoped that all of it will be conveyed by Rail instead of being left at the Town Major, FINS.

[illegible]

7. Everyman is to carry a rolled blanket when proceeding by Rail or Lorry to PERONNE.

8. A G.S.Wagon will report to O.C. 119th T.M.Battery, HEUDECOURT from the S.A.A.Section, Divisional Ammunition Column at 9 a.m. on October 8th to load up the 8 Trench Mortars and any surplus kit not required on the journey. One man from the 119th T.M. Battery will be detailed as baggage guard and will proceed with and be rationed by the Divisional Ammunition Column. After loading up the wagon will return to the Divisional Ammunition Column.

J. Harr[illegible]

Captain.
Staff Captain.
119th Infantry Brigade.

5th Octr 1917.

119th Inf. Bde. No. 36/264/G.L.

O.C.

With reference to the move of the 119th Infantry Brigade Group.

1. The following is the allotment of Sub-areas in the PERONNE Area from October 8th to 10th.

   Group (a).

119th Brigade H.Q. 19th R.W. Fusiliers. 12th S.W. Borderers. 17th Welsh Regiment. 229th Field Coy. R.E. & 120th Brigade Works Coy. No. 2 Coy. A.S.C.	DOINGT.

   Group (b).

18th Welsh Regiment. 119th M.G. Company. 119th T.M. Battery. 136th Field Ambulance.	PERONNE.

   The Transport Lines of Group (b) are at I.21.d.1.5. Map.62c.

2. Billeting Officers from each Unit with a N.C.O. for Unit H.Q. each Company and each Transport Lines will report to the Town Majors of DOINGT and PERONNE at 9 a.m. on October 8th for taking over billets.

3. The No. 2 Coy. A.S.C., the 136th Field Ambulance and the Transport of the 229th Field Company R.E. will move independently into the PERONNE Area.

4. The Transport of Units of the 119th Infantry Brigade together with all mounted cyclists will move into the PERONNE Area under the orders of the 119th Infantry Brigade Transport Officer at an hour to be notified later.

5. The remaining personnel of all Units and baggage will be taken to PERONNE by Lorry and Decauville from HEUDICOURT, SOREL and FINS. Exact times and places to be notified later.

6. If the surplus baggage of Units is not excessive it is hoped that all of it will be conveyed by Rail instead of being left at the Town Major, FINS.

7. Everyman is to carry a rolled blanket when proceeding by Rail or Lorry to PERONNE.

8. A G.S. Wagon will report to O.C. 119th T.M. Battery, HEUDECOURT from the S.A.A. Section, Divisional Ammunition Column at 9 a.m. on October 8th to load up the 8 Trench Mortars and any surplus kit not required on the journey. One man from the 119th T.M. Battery will be detailed as baggage guard and will proceed with and be rationed by the Divisional Ammunition Column. After loading up the wagon will return to the Divisional Ammunition Column.

[signature]

Captain.
Staff Captain.
119th Infantry Brigade.

5th Octr 1917.

119th Inf.Bde.No.36/265/G.L.

O.C.

With reference to the move of the 119th Infantry Brigade into Army Reserve on October 10th.

1. Time and place of Entrainment will be notified later.

2. Billeting parties consisting of all Interpreters of Units 1 Billeting Officer and 1 O.R. per Unit will report to the Staff Captain at the 120th Brigade Entrainment Railhead on October 8th at time and place to be notified later, and will proceed to BEAUMETZ taking rations with them up to and including October 10th.

3. Billeting sub-areas will be as follows :-

UNIT.	LOCATION.	Billeting Parties to report to.
19th R.W.F. 17th Welsh Regt.	SIMENCOURT	Town Major WARLUS.
Brigade H.Q. and rest of Brigade Group.	GOUY-EN-ARTOIS	Sub-Area Commandant BARLY.

4. Appendices A and B shew particulars of Entraining on October 10th and Transport Proceeding by March Route.

5. Detraining Railhead is BEAUMETZ.

6. (a) All transport as shown in Appendix 'A' proceeding by March Route will come under the orders of O.C.40th Divisional Train on October 10th.

   (b) Major C.C.DOWDING,M.C., 18th Bn Welsh Regiment will be in charge of 1st Line Transport of Units of 119th Infantry Brigade proceeding by March Route on October 10th.

   (c) O.C. 19th Bn R.W.Fusiliers will detail a Mounted Officer who understands Transport Duties to report to Major C.C. DOWDING on the morning of October 10th.

   (d) M A R C H   T A B L E

Date.	From.	To.
October 10th	PERONNE	BAPAUME
" 11th	BAPAUME	NEW AREA.

7. Baggage Dumps may be established on October 9th at place of Entrainment

8. Sufficient cord should be provided to secure bicycles to wagons after the wagons have been put on the flats.

9. (a) The Brigade Transport Officer will supervise the entraining of both Omnibus Trains and the detraining of the Second Omnibus Train.

   (b) The Transport Officer of the 12th Bn South Wales Borderers will supervise the detraining of the First Omnibus Train.

10. Lt-Col.W.KENNEDY,M.C.) will be in Command of the
Commanding 18th Welsh Rgt.) 1st Coaching Train.

Lt-Col.J.F.PLUNKETT.M.C.) will be in Command of the
Commanding 19th R.W.Fus.) 2nd Coaching Train.

Lt-Col.M.E.ROWAN ROBINSON.) will be in Command of the
Commanding 136th Fd.Amblce.) 1st Omnibus Train.

Captain A.B.RAYNER.) will be in Command of the
Commanding 229th Fd.Coy.R.E.) 2nd Omnibus Train.

11. A party of 1 Officer and 30 O.R. is to be detailed on detrainment to clean each Train, as follows :-

First Coaching Train	18th Welsh Regt.
Second Coaching Train	19th R.W.Fusiliers.
First Omnibus Train.	136th Field Ambulance.
Second Omnibus Train.	119th T.M.Battery.

The R.T.O. will provide brooms on application.

12. A billeting party from the 121st Infantry Brigade will proceed by the 1st Coaching Train. The Party will report to O.C.the Train for accommodation on the Train.

13. All details attached by Division will proceed by the Second Coaching Train.

14. Lorries for conveyance of blankets, rolled in bundles of ten, will meet trains on arrival at BEAUMETZ.

15. Entrainment for Coaching Trains is to begin one hour before the hour of departure and for the Omnibus Trains 2 hours.

B. Home.

Captain.
Staff Captain.
119th Infantry Brigade.

5th October 1917.

APPENDIX "A"

FIRST OMNIBUS TRAIN. (1 Coach, 30 Covered Wagons, 17 Flats)

UNIT	RAIL: Flats	RAIL: WAGONS. Baggage	RAIL: WAGONS. Horses	RAIL: WAGONS. Personnel	RAIL: Officers	RAIL: Other Ranks.	RAIL: Cookers.	RAIL: Water Carts	RAIL: Mess Carts	RAIL: Maltese	RAIL: G.S.L.	ROAD: G.S.L.	ROAD: Carts.	ROAD: Wagons	RAIL: Riders	RAIL: L.D.	RAIL: H.D.	RAIL: Pack.	ROAD: Riders	ROAD: L.D.	ROAD: H.D.	ROAD: Pack.	Total Animals.	ROAD: Officers	ROAD: Other Ranks.	REMARKS
119th Bde.H.Q.	1	)1	2½	2	2	31					1		1	2	10	2			2	10			24		10	The 119th M.G.Coy. will find loading and unloading party of 90 men. There there are not 4 axles for each flat, the flat may also be used for baggage.
119th Sig.Secn	1	)			1	53				1	1				2	4							6			
18th Welsh.	6		6	1	1	45	4	2	1	1	6	4			10	19	8	7	1	11	1		57	1	15	
12th S.W.B.	6		6	1	1	45	4	2	1	1	6	4			10	19	8	7	1	9	1		55		13	
119th M.G.Coy.	1	1	)	2	5	90					2	3			6	4			1	7			18		9	
136th Fd.Amb.	1	1	)2	4	5	170					2	2	4	9		4			8	13	20		45	1	68	
229th Fd. Coy.RE	1		½		1	5					1	7	4	4		2			14	53		4	73	1	57	
	17	3	17	10	16	439																		3	172	

SECOND OMNIBUS TRAIN. (1 Coach, 30 Covered Wagons, 17 Flats)

UNIT	RAIL: Flats	RAIL: WAGONS. Baggage	RAIL: WAGONS. Horses	RAIL: WAGONS. Personnel	RAIL: Officers	RAIL: Other Ranks.	RAIL: Cookers.	RAIL: Water Carts	RAIL: Mess Carts	RAIL: Maltese	RAIL: G.S.L.	ROAD: G.S.L.	ROAD: Carts.	ROAD: Wagons	RAIL: Riders	RAIL: L.D.	RAIL: H.D.	RAIL: Pack.	ROAD: Riders	ROAD: L.D.	ROAD: H.D.	ROAD: Pack.	Total Animals.	ROAD: Officers	ROAD: Other Ranks.	REMARKS
119th M.G.Coy.	5		5	2	4	70		1	1		8					36							36			The 229th Field Coy. R.E. will find loading and unloading party of 100 men. There there are not 4 axles for each flat the flat may also be used for baggage.
19th R.W.F.	6		6	1	1	45	4	2	1	1	6	4			10	19	8	7	1	9	1		55	1	13	
17th Welsh.	6		6	1	1	45	4	2	1	1	6	4			10	19	8	7	1	9	1		55		13	
229th Fd.Coy.RE.		)			5	140																				
		)1		7																						
120th Works Coy		)			2	160																				
119th T.M.B.				1	4	44								1							2		2		3	
	17	1	17	12	17	504																		1	27	

APPENDIX 'B'

FIRST COACHING TRAIN

18th Welsh Regiment.	(a)	22	3rd Class Coaches	(40 men each in marching order)
		1	1st Class Coach	Officers.
		1	Covered Wagon.	Baggage.
12th S.W.Borderers.	(b)	22	3rd Class Coaches	(40 men each in marching order)
		1	1st Class Coach.	Officers.
		1	Covered Wagon.	Baggage.

- - - - - - - - - - - - - -

SECOND COACHING TRAIN

19th R.W.Fusiliers.	(a)	22	3rd Class Coaches	(40 men each in marching order)
		1	1st Class Coach.	Officers.
		1	Covered Wagon.	Baggage.
17th Welsh Regiment.	(b)	22	3rd Class Coaches	(40 men each in marhing order)
		1	1st Class Coach.	Officers.
		1	Covered Wagon.	Baggage.

- - - - - - - - - - - - - -

SECRET. COPY NO. 3

119TH INFANTRY BRIGADE ORDER NO.120

1. The move of the 119th Infantry Brigade Group will be carried out in accordance with the attached Time Table.

2. Officers will be detailed, as under, to superintend each Group embussing and debussing.

GROUP.	BY.
A.	O.C. 17th Welsh Regiment.
B.	O.C. 12th S.W.Borderers.
C.	O.C. 19th R.W.Fusiliers.
D.	O.C. 18th Welsh Regiment.

3. If possible supervising Officers of Groups A, B, and C will arrange for the last two vehicles of their Group to be Lorries in preference to Busses.

4. Time of departure will be wired when known.

5. Acknowledge.

Captain.
Brigade Major.
119th Infantry Brigade.

7th October 1917.

Copy No. 1 19th R.W.F.
2 12th S.W.B.
3 17th Welsh.
4 18th Welsh.
5 119th M.G.Coy.
6 119th T.M.B.
7 119th Signals.
8 119th Transport Officer
9 229th Field Company R.E.
10 120th Works Company.
11 130th Field Ambulance.
12 40th Division (G)
13 40th Division (Q)
14 40th Division A.P.M.
15 No. 2 Coy. A.S.C.
16 War Diary.
17 Brigade Major.
18 Staff Captain.
19 O.O. for G.O.C.
20 Office.

TIME TABLE TO ACCOMPANY 119TH INFANTRY BRIGADE ORDER NO.120

Movement of the 119th Infantry Brigade Group by BUS and DECAUVILLE on 8th October 1917.

Group	Unit	Embussing Points	DESTINATION	No. of Busses or Trucks available.	REMARKS
A	119th Bde. H.Q.	Head of A Group W.13.b.3.9.	DOINGT.	3 Busses	Men to be drawn up in groups of 25 and remainder of lorries for baggage.
	17th Welsh Regt	-do-	-do-	31 "	
B	229th Field Coy,RE & 120th Works Coy.	Head of B Group W.14.b.2.4.	-do-	14 "	Groups of 25 to start from W.13.b.
	12th S.W.Bors.	-do-	-do-	20 "	
C	Remainder of 12th S.W.Bors.	Head of C Group W.15.c.9.8.	-do-	12 "	
	19th R.W.Fus.	-do-	-do-	22 "	
I	Remainder of 19th R.W.Fus.	RAILTON W.16.c.9.9.	ST DENIS.	6 Trucks Train No 5	5 Trains of 8 Trucks, 28 men in a truck. 2 Baggage Trucks on last Train 1 for 18th Welsh & 119th M.G.C. 1 for 19th R.W.F.& 119th T.M.B. Trains leave at 5 minutes intervals.
	18th Welsh Rgt	-do-	-do-	Trains Nos.1,2 & 3 and 1½ trucks Train No.4	
	119th M.G.Coy.	-do-	-do-	4½ Trucks Train No.4.	
	119th T.M.B.	-do-	-do-	2 Trucks Train No.4.	

NOTES.

1. All vehicles and trains to be filled.
2. All men proceeding by train or bus to carry their blankets.
3. All parties to be formed up on the Right-hand side of the Raod at about 20 paces interval, half-an-hour before time of departure.
4. The Divisional Machine Gun Officer will superintend the whole operation and also the debussing.
5. 2 Lorries will meet last Train at ST DENIS to carry baggage.

Copy No ______

SECRET.

17th (Service) Battalion the Welsh Regiment.
Order No. 52.

---

1. The move of the 119th Infantry Brigade group will be carried out in accordance with the attached time table.
2. O.C. "A" Company will detail one Officer to suprintend the embussing and debussing of the Battalion and Brigade Headquarters which will be called group "A".

3. If possible the supervising Officer of group "A" will arrange for the last two vehicles of his group to be lorries in preference to busses.

4. Companies will march off from billets in SOREL in the following Order :-

Headquarters.	- -	9.15am.
"A" Company.	- -	9.20am.
"B" Company.	- -	9.25am.
"C" Company.	- -	9.30am.
"D" Company.	- -	9.35am.

5. Men will be drawn up in groups of 25 and the remainder of the lorries will be used for baggage. Groups of 25 men to start from W.13.b.

6. NOTES.
   (a) All vehicles will be filled.
   (b) All men proceeding by Bus will carry their blankets, rolled on top of the pack
   (c) All parties to be formed up on the right hand side of the road at about 20 paces interval, half an hour before time of departure.

7. Brigade Transport will be clear of camps by 10.30am and will march to PERONNE via LIERAMONT .

8. Acknowledge.

Captain.
& Adjutant.
17th Bn. The Welsh Regiment.

October 7th 1917.

Copies to 1 to 4 O.C.Companies.
5 Q.Master.
6 R.S.M.
7 Office.
8 T. Officer.

- - - - - - - - - - - -

Time Table to Accompany ~~Order~~ No. 52. Brigade Order No. 120

Movement of the 119th Infantry Brigade Group by Bus or Decauville on 8th Oct. 1917.

Group	Unit	Embussing Points	Destination	No of Busses or Trucks Available	
A.	119th Bde. HQ.	Head of A. Group W.13. b.3.9.	DOINGT	3. Busses	
	17th Welsh Regt.	- do -	- do -	31 - do -	

Copy No....

17th (Ser.) Battalion The Welsh Regiment.
Order No. 51.

- - - - - - - - - - - - - - - -

1. On the 10th October 1917 the Battalion will move to BEAUMETZ by rail.
Time and place of entrainment will be notified later.

2. BILLETING PARTIES
Lieut. Mould and Sergt Oliver "A" Company will report to the Staff Captain 119th Infantry Brigade at the 120th Brigade Entrainment Railhead on October 8th, time and place to be notified later. They will take rations with the up to and including 10th October.

3. Billeting sub areas will be as follows:-

UNIT.	LOCATION.	BILLETING PARTY. TO REPORT TO.
17th Welsh	SIMENCOURT	Town Major WARLUS.

4. TRANSPORT.

The following Transport will proceed by rail.

4 Field Kitchens.
2 Water Carts.
1 Officers Mess Cart.
1 Maltese Cart.
6 G.S. Limbers.
7 Pack Horses.

ANIMALS.

10 Riders.
17 L.D Horses.
8 H.D. Horses.

PERSONNEL.

1 Officer (Lieut. Hammond)
46. Other Ranks.

(b) The remainder of Transport comprising

4 G.S. Limbers.

ANIMALS.

1 Rider.
9 L.D. Horses.
1 H.D. Horse

PERSONNEL.

15 Other Ranks.

~~Above~~ is i/c of the Transport Sergeant.
The above underheading 4 (b) will proceed by march route as part of a Brigade Convoy under the Command of Major C.C.Dowling .M.C. 18th Welsh Regiment.

5. BLANKETS.
Lorries for conveyance of Blankets Rolled in bundles of 10 will meet trains on arrival at BEAUMETZ.

6. Acknowledge.

Captain.
& Adjutant.
17th Bn. The Welsh Regiment.

Copies 1 to Q.M.
2 " T.O
" 3 to 6 O.C. Coys.
" 7 R.S.M.
" 8 FILE.

A

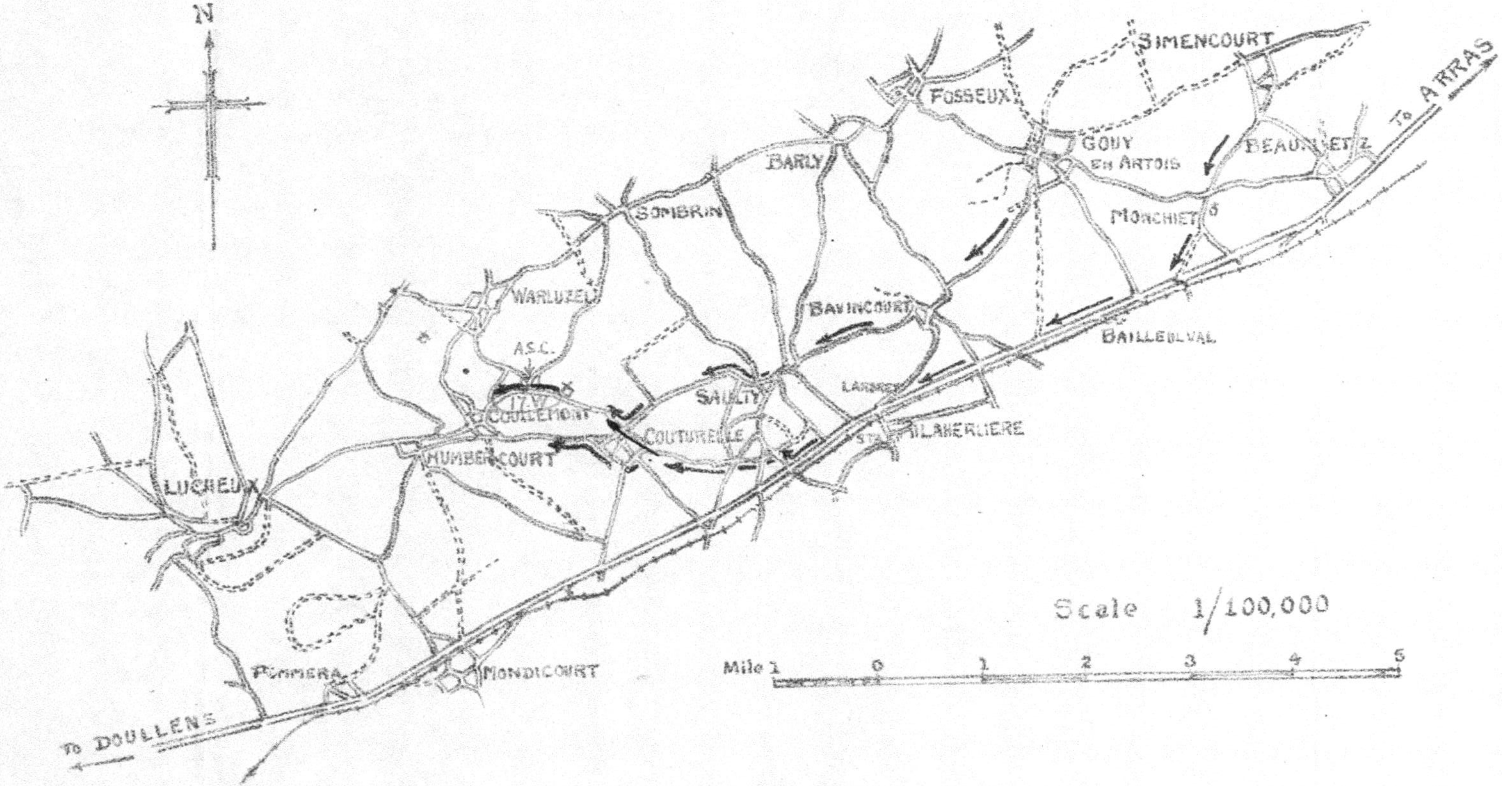
N
SIMENCOURT
FOSSEUX
GOUY
EN ARTOIS
To ARRAS
BARLY
SOMBRIN
MONCHIET
WARLUZEL
BAVINCOURT
BAILLEULVAL
A.S.C.
17.V
COULLEMONT
SAULTY
COUTURELLE
HUMBERCOURT
LUCHEUX
MONDICOURT
To DOULLENS
Scale 1/100,000
Mile 1 0 1 2 3 4 5

Secret   17 Welsh Regt. Order No.

Ref map: LENS 11 1/100,000
and 51 C 1/40,000

1. The 119 Inf Bde group will march on the 29 Oct 1917 to the LUCHEUX – COUTURELLE area.
Map of Route and Billeting area 'A' ~~are~~ issued to
(a) O.C. A Coy (leading company)
(b) Billeting Officer Lieut Mould.
(c) Transport Officer
(d) Bn. H.Q.

2. The Battn will parade and be ready to march off at 7.30 am to-morrow 29th.
Order of march ~~[illegible]~~, Bn. H.Q, Band, A. B. C. D Coys.
Starting point SIMENCOURT CHURCH at 7.30 am.
An interval of 200 yards will be maintained between companies and transport.
Route SIMENCOURT – MONCHIET – Q 33 A & 2.5. ARRAS – DOULLENS Rd. – thence through U 18 to COUTURELLE and COULLEMONT.

3. Lieut Wynne Full marching order
~~Lieut Mould~~ and 1 Billeting N.C.O per Coy will move off 2 hours ahead of the Battalion to take over billets from Lieut Basley. This party will report to Lieut [illegible] at 5.25 am 29/10/17 at Bn. H.Q.

4. Lieut C.S. Thomas D Coy will remain behind with 1 NCO + 10 men from the Coy on duty (D Coy) to clean up all billets and obtain necessary certificates as per orders issued out separately to this office.
The 1 N.C.O + 10 men will report to Lieut Thomas at Orderly Room at 7.30 am 29/10/17.

5. Officers valises will be dumped under arch leading to Q M Stores by 6.45 am.
Mens Blankets rolled in bundles of 10 will be dumped in the Guard room by 7.0 am.
All ranks will carry their leather jerkins ~~[illegible]~~ with their waterproof sheets under the flap of the pack.
Mess baskets will be dumped at Bn. H.Q. by 7.0 am.
Reveille 5.30 am
~~[illegible]~~ Breakfasts 6.15 am

6. Acknowledge

[illegible signature]

S E C R E T.

COPY NO. 3 ......

119TH INFANTRY BRIGADE ORDER NO.121

Reference Maps.
LENS 11, 1/100,000
and 51c. 1/40,000

1. The 119th Infantry Brigade Group will march on the 29th October 1917 to the LUCHEUX - COUTURELLE Area.
Map of Route and Billeting Area "A" and March Table "B" attached.

2. Refilling point COULLEMONT.

3. (a) Lorries will make two trips and will report at 1.30 p.m. as follows :-

LORRIES	PLACE	For UNIT.
1	GOUY CHURCH.	119th Brigade H.Q.) 120th Works Coy.)
1	do	12th S.W.Borderers.
1	do	18th Welsh Regt.
1	SIMENCOURT CHURCH	19th R.W.Fusiliers.
1	do	17th Welsh Regt.
1	do	119th M.G.Coy, &) 119th T.M.B.)

(b) Lorries are to be loaded and off-loaded without delay.

4. (a) The Officer detailed by each Unit for settling civilian claims and obtaining certificate of cleanliness from the Town Major, will, if possible, rejoin his Unit by the lorry on its second journey after handing in the required certificates to Major D.APPLEBY, 17th Welsh Regiment.

(b) Major APPLEBY will rejoin with his Interpreter as soon as he has collected all the certificates and has satisfied himself that all claims have been settled.

5. Billeting N.C.O's for Companies, under an Officer, will be sent two hours ahead of the Battalion to take over Billets from their Billeting Officer who has proceeded to the new area today.

6. Halts will be made for 10 minutes in each hour at 10 minutes before each clock hour.

7. Intervals of 200 yards will be maintained between all Units and between Companies and Transport.

8. 119th Infantry Brigade Headquarters will close at GOUY at 9 a.m. and open at COUTURELLE at the same hour.

9. Acknowledge.

Issued at 8 p.m.

28th Octr 1916.

Captain.A/Brigade Major
119th Infantry Brigade.

Copy No. 1. 19th R.W.F.
2. 12th S.W.B.
3. 17th Welsh.
4. 18th Welsh.
5. 119th M.G.Coy.
6. 119th T.M.B.
7. 119th Brigade Signals.
8. 229th Field Coy. R.E.
9. 136th Field Ambulance.
10. 120th Brigade Works Company.
11. No. 2 Coy. A.S.C.
12. 25th Divl. Supply Col.
13. 55th A.S.P. S.A.A.Section.
14. 40th Division (G)
15. 40th Division (Q)
16. 40th Division A.P.M.
17. War Diary.
18. Brigade Major.
19. Staff Captain.
20. Office.
21. Major D.APPLEBY.
22. H.Q. 120th Infantry Brigade.
23. H.Q. 121st Infantry Brigade.
24. C.R.E. 40th Division.

MARCH TABLE "B" TO ACCOMPANY 119TH INFANTRY BRIGADE ORDER NO.121

UNIT	STARTING POINT		DESTINATION	ROUTE
	TIME	PLACE		
No. 2 Coy. A.S.C.	9.10 a.m.	BAVINCOURT Cross Roads P.28.d.9.3.	COULLEMONT	Road passing through North of BAVINCOURT - SAULTY - COUTURELLE - COULLEMONT.
18th Welsh Regt.	9.14 a.m.	ditto	LUCHEUX	ditto
120th Works Coy.	9.30 a.m.	ditto	do	ditto
12th S.W. Borderers.	9.33 a.m.	ditto	HUMBERCOURT	ditto
119th Brigade H.Q.	9.49 a.m.	ditto	COUTURELLE	ditto
136th Field Ambulance	10. 1 a.m.	ditto	LUCHEUX	ditto
119th M.G.Coy and) 119th T.M.B. Attached)	8.25 a.m.	Fork Roads, Q.33.a.2.0.	HUMBERCOURT	ARRAS - DOULLENS Road thence through U.18 to COUTURELLE and COULLEMONT.
17th Welsh Regt.	8.30 a.m.	ditto.	COULLEMONT	ditto
19th R.W.Fusiliers	8.46 a.m.	ditto	COUTURELLE	ditto

War Diary

With Reference to 17th. Welsh Order No. dated October 22nd. 1917

---

1. The Battalion will parade on the Battalion Parade Ground at 9.15 a.m. to-morrow the 23rd. inst.

2. Officers will wear Kit similar to that worn by the men. No Sticks are to be carried by officers.

3. The barrage will be represented by 2 N.C.Os. and 6 men with 6 green and white flags.

4. Pill Boxes wi l be denoted by the waving of red flags, Lewis Gun Strong Points by the waving of blue signal flags, and a Light Machine Gun and rifle garrisons by the waving of white Signal flags with blue stripes.

5. The signal for opening fire will be given by a bugle sounding a "G" except in the actual lines B-B, C-C, D-D.

6. (a) 1 Bugler and 1 man per company will report at 9.30 a.m. on the 19th. R.W.F parade ground on October 23rd. to the Brigade Intelligence Officer.
The above party will report to the R.S.M. at Battalion Headquarters at 8.45 a.m. to-morrow October 23rd.

(b) 2 men per company will report to Major Gough M.C. as orderlies on the Battalion Parade Ground at 9.15 a.m. to-morrow October 23rd.
The above under headings (a) and (b) will wear caps.
They will not carry rifles or packs.

7 Three Very Lights will be fired for S.O.S. signal.

8. The 12th. S.W.B. and 18th. Welsh will wear white arm bands.

9. The Transport Officer will arrange for 6 pack animals to be on parade. 2 for Bn. H.Q. and 1 per company.

10. O.Cs. Companies will bear in mind the importance of previously arranging for all eventuallities which may arise.
e.g. necessity of throwing out a defensive flank.
Importance of quickly exploiting success, rapid consolidation of positions gained etc., the possibility of a counter attack.

11. No verbal messages are to be accepted. Messages sent out will invariably be put in envelopes.

12. 4 Lewis Guns will be kept at Bn. H.Qrs. the remainder to go with their platoons under arrangement made by O.Cs. Companies.

13. O.C. Snipers will arrange to organise his men. At the outset the Snipers will remain and be under the orders of Bn. H. Qrs.

14. 2/Lt. C.S. Thomas will report to the adjutant on parade at 9.15 a.m. to-morrow October 23rd.
He will be Officer in charge of dumps.

15. O.Cs. Companies will ensure that they are in possession of their complement of wire cutters, and men carrying these should if possible have some distinctive mark.

[signature]
Captain and Adjutant.
22nd. October 1917. 17th. Battn. The Welsh Regiment.

War Diary

SECRET. Copy No.

17th. Welsh Regiment Order No. 52

Reference map 51c. S.E. 1/40,000

1. The 40th. Division on the Right and the 92nd. Division on the left will attack and occupy the enemy lines on 23rd. October 1917 from Q.6.a.0.0. to fork roads (inclusive) at K.28.C.2.5.

2. The 120th. Infantry Brigade will attack on the right of the 119th. Infantry Brigade and the 227th. Infantry Brigade on the Left.

3. The boundary with the Right Brigade will be a line drawn between Q.4.d.2.9. and K.35.d.5.0. and with the left Brigade Q.4.a.6.8. and K.35 central.

4. (a) Each Battalion will attack on a 200 yards front.

(b) The 19th. R.W. Fusiliers will attack and capture the first objective on the right and the 17th. Welsh Regt. on the left.

(c) The 12th. S.W. Borderers will attack and capture the final objective on the right and the 18th. Welsh on the left.

5. The dividing line between Battalions will be a line drawn between Q.4.a.8.2. and K.35.d.2.5.

6. (a) The first objective is shown on accompanying sketch plan marked C-C (Q.5.a.B3.3.-K.34.d.7.2.) and the final objective is marked D-D (K.35;q. 5.0. - K.35 central)

ZZ. (b) Zero hour will be notified later.

7. Artillery Barrages will be as follows:-

	Minutes. From		Minutes. To
On Enemy Front Line B-B	Zero		2.
Creeping at 100 yards in 3 minutes from B-B to C-C	plus 2	plus	14.
On first objective C-C	" 14.	"	16.
Creeping at 100 yards in 3 minutes to 240 yards beyond C-C.	" 16	"	23.
Remaining on above.	" 23	"	33.
Creeping to final objective D-D	" 33	"	43.
Remaining on D-D	" 43	"	46.
Creeping to 300 yards beyond D-D	" 46	"	55.
Remaining on above	" 55	"	85.

8. The Battalion will find it's own moppers up.
The Moppers up will follow immediately behind the first wave and will be composed of the weakest platoon of each Company. They will be employed in mopping up the German Front Line B-B.
Moppers up will wear their caps.

9. The Battalion will form up A-A and B-B (marked by lettered Notice Boards) on a four company frontage in lines of column of platoons and will move up as near as safety will allow, and at Zero plus 2 will advance behind the barrage at 25 paces between lines and 50 paces between waves, with the exception of Moppers-up who will keep a distance of 20 paces between them and the leading wave.
The Battalion will form up in the following order:-
Left to Right. A.D.C.B. Companies.

10. (a) The 12th. S.W.B. and 18th. Welsh will form up behind the 19th. R.W.F and 17th. Welsh respectively, each on a four company frontage, in artillery snake formation, and at Zero plus 2 will move forward on to the ground vacated by the 19th. R.W.F and 17th. Welsh.
(b) At Zero plus 12 they will advance, passing through the 19th. R.W.F and 17th. Welsh in B-B and C-C and catching up to the Barrage at Zero plus 33. Extended formation will be adopted as soon as the situation demands it.
(c) Immediately the objective D-D is reached protective and reconnaissance patrols will be pushed out 250 yards behind the barrage.

11. Red Flares will be lighted by the most advanced troops when called upon by contact aeroplane.

12. The Battalion will carry (imaginary) grenades (2 per man) Sandbags (2 per man) Flares (2 per man)

~~11.~~ Dress; Fighting Order filled water bottles and Iron Rations Every man will be in possession of 120 rounds S.A.A Pi cks and shovels for consolidation will be carried by the rear wave of each company.

The Quartermaster will arrange to allot 20 picks and 25 shovels to each Company and the necessary number of tools for the rear platoon will be drawn to-morrow, October 23rd. 1917 before 8.30 and under Company arrangements

13. Watches will be synchronised at 9.45 a.m. to-morrow the 23rd. inst. ~~(a)~~

14. (a) The 119th. Machine Gun Company will first be employed on the barrage and indirect fire. Later, one section will be employed in Brigade Reserve in the line A-A. The remaining three section, under orders from Brigade Headquarters will be sent forward (as soon as the objective have been taken) to support the Infantry in positions immediately behind the Line held.

(b) O;Cs. Companies will detail a carrying party for the 119th. Machine Company as under:-

"A"	6 O.R.	"B"	6 O.R.
"C"	6 O.R.	"D"	7 O;R.

Further orders as to place of reporting will be detailed later.

15. (a) The 119th. T.M. Battery will assist the first assault with barrage fire from zero to plus 2.

(b) At plus 2 4 Trench Mortars will remain in the line A-A and four Trench Mortars will be moved forward in the German Front lineB-B, one of each to be at the disposal of each Battalion Commander.

(c)O.Cs. Companies will detail a carrying party for the 119th. T.M. Battery as under:-

"A" Company	6 O.R.	"B" Company	5 O.R.
"C" "	6 O.R.	"D" "	5 O.R.

16. the Strong points will be constructed about 200 yards in rear of the Final objective under the direction of O.C. 229th. Field Company R.E. in crucifix pattern.

17. Battle Headquarters will be located as under.

Brigade Headquarters.	Q.3.d.5.9.
19th. R.W.F and 12th S.W.B.	Q.4.a.5.0.
17th. Welsh and 18th. Welsh	Q.4.a.3.2.
119th. M.G/ Coy. and 119th. T.M.B.	Q.4. a.1.1.

18. Acknowledge.

Captain and Adjutant.
17th. (S) Bn. The Welsh Regt.

22nd October 1917.

Issued at

1 - 4 O.C. Coys.
5 Lewis Gun Officer.
6 O.C. Sniping Officer.
7 ~~Transport Officer.~~ Quartermaster.
8 Transport Officer.
9. O.C. Signallers.
10. Medical Officer.
11. Major Gough.
12 - 14 File.

Army Form C. 2118.

119 Bde

Instructions regarding War Diaries and Intelligence Summaries are contained in F. S. Regs., Part II. and the Staff Manual respectively. Title pages will be prepared in manuscript.

WAR DIARY
or
INTELLIGENCE SUMMARY.
(Erase heading not required.)

Vol 18

Place	Date	Hour	Summary of Events and Information	Remarks and references to Appendices
			119/40	
			War Diary	
			17th (S) Bn. The Welsh Regiment	
			November 1917	

18 D

29 [illegible]

A5834 Wt. W4973/M687 750,000 8/16 D. D. & L. Ltd. Forms/C.2118/13.

Army Form C. 2118.

WAR DIARY
or
INTELLIGENCE SUMMARY.
(Erase heading not required.)

Instructions regarding War Diaries and Intelligence Summaries are contained in F. S. Regs., Part II. and the Staff Manual respectively. Title pages will be prepared in manuscript. Ref Map "LENS" 1/100.000.

17th (S) Batt. Welch Regt. November 1917

Place	Date	Hour	Summary of Events and Information	Remarks and references to Appendices
	Nov			
COULLEMONT	1		Battalion training. Training Programme attached.	[illegible]
	2		do. do Capt. WARING M.C. proceeded to ENGLAND	[illegible]
	3		do do Lt. A.P. LLOYD takes command of A Co. " A.J. ELMIT " " D Co.	[illegible]
			2nd Lt. G.E. MORGAN reported for duty from ENGLAND.	[illegible]
	4		Divine Service Games in afternoon.	[illegible]
	5		Battalion Training.	[illegible]
				[illegible]
	6		" "	[illegible]
	7		" "	
	8		" "	[illegible]
	9		" " Brigade Scheme.	
	10		" " Capt. A.E. GRANT proceeded to 4th ARMY SCHOOL FLIXICOURT.	[illegible]
	11		Divine Service. Games in afternoon.	[illegible]

H.J. [illegible] Major

Instructions regarding War Diaries and Intelligence Summaries are contained in F. S. Regs., Part II. and the Staff Manual respectively. Title pages will be prepared in manuscript.

WAR DIARY
or
INTELLIGENCE SUMMARY.
(Erase heading not required.)

Army Form C. 2118.

17th (S) Batt. Welsh Regt. November 1917

Place	Date	Hour	Summary of Events and Information	Remarks and references to Appendices
			Ref Map "LENS"	
	Nov.			
COULLEMONT	12.		Battalion training	WPS.
	13		do do Capt. W P MORGAN GRIFFITHS proceeded to 4th ARMY musketry school.	WPS
	14		do do	WPS
	15		do do	WPS
SIMENCOURT	16		Battalion proceeded by route march to SIMENCOURT.	WPS
SOMMICOURT	17		Battalion proceeded by night march to SOMMICOURT.	WPS
	18		Battalion at SOMMICOURT. Lt. A. R. LLOYD to be acting capt. whilst 40th Div. no. 2 ILA.	WPS
BARASTRE	19		Battalion proceeded by route march to BARASTRE	WPS
	20		Battalion at BARASTRE. Lt. A. L. ELMITT M.C. appointed acting captain.	WPS
	21		" proceeded by route march to DOIGNIES	WPS
GRAINCOURT	22		" proceeded by night march to GRAINCOURT to assemble for attack on morning of 23rd.	WPS
	23.		119th Brigade attack on BOURLON WOOD. See Appendix	WPS

H. P. B. Emery? Major

A7092 Wt. W125 9/M1293 750,000. 1/17. D. D & L. Ltd. Forms/C2118/14.

Instructions regarding War Diaries and Intelligence Summaries are contained in F. S. Regs., Part II. and the Staff Manual respectively. Title pages will be prepared in manuscript.

WAR DIARY
or
INTELLIGENCE SUMMARY.
(Erase heading not required.)

Army Form C. 2118.

17th (S) Batt. Welsh Regt. November 1917

Place	Date	Hour	Summary of Events and Information	Remarks and references to Appendices
			Ref Map MOEUVRES 1/20000	
	Nov			
BOURLON WOOD	24		2nd day of attack in BOURLON WOOD.	H.B.
	25		3rd " " "	H.B.
			119th Inf Bde relieved at night by units from 62nd Div.	
			17th Welsh Casualties 18 officers 301 OR	
			Night of 25th spent at HINDENBURG LINE. N of HAVRINCOURT.	H.B.
			Major H.P.B. Gough MC in command.	
	26		Battalion marched to LECHELLE for the night.	H.B.
POMMIER.	27		" proceeded by train to BAUMETZ and marched to POMMIER	H.B.
	28		" in billets at POMMIER. Time spent in reorganisation.	
	29		" " " "	
	30		" " " "	

H.P.B. Gough Major

A7092 Wt. W128 9/M1293 750,000. 1/17. D. D & L Ltd. Forms/C2118/14.

War Diary

17TH. (SERVICE) BATTALION THE WELSH REGT.

TRAINING PROGRAMME FOR FRIDAY NOVEMBER 2ND. 1917.

BATTALION AND LOCATION OF UNIT.	DESCRIPTION OF TRAINING.	TIME.	REMARKS.
COULLEMONT. NOVEMBER 1ST 1917	PHYSICAL TRAINING.	7.15 - 7.45 A.M.	
	BATTALION DRILL.	9.30 - 10.30 A.M.	BATTALION TO PARADE AS STRONG AS POSSIBLE. DRESS - DRILL ORDER.
	COMPANY IN THE ATTACK.	10.45 - 11.45 A.M.	"A", "B" "C" & "D" Coys.
	MUSKETRY.	12.0 - 12.30 P.M.	"A", "B" "C" & "D" Coys.
	BOMBING	2.0 - 3.0 P.M.	"A" & "D" Coys.
	BAYONET FIGHTING.	2.0 - 3.0 P.M.	"B" & "C" Coys.
	INSPECTION AND BOX RESPIRATOR DRILL.	3.0 - 3.30 P.M.	"A", "B", "C" & "D" Coys.
	VISUAL TRAINING AND JUDGING DISTANCE	3.30 - 4.0 P.M.	"A" "B" "C". & "D" Coys.

[signature]
CAPTAIN.
& ADJUTANT.
17TH (S) BN. THE WELSH REGT.

To All Concerned.

Reference the attached Brigade Scheme.

The Battalion will proceed by Route March to H.33.c. Central (approximately).

Starting Point. Opposite Battalion Headquarter Guard Room at 7.30 a.m.

Order of March. Headquarters, "C", "B", "A", "D" Companies.

Dress. Battle Order. (Steel Helmets will be worn) Waterproof Sheets will be carried under Flap of haversack. Jerkins carried rolled on Belt.

Dinners will be on return to Billets.

Officers will wear the same kit as the Men, e.g. Battle Order.

Captain
& Adjutant.

11th. November 1917. 17th. (S) Battalion The Welsh Regt.

Copy No 9.

SECRET

17th Bn The Welsh Regt

Order No 54.

1. The 119th Infantry Brigade will move early on the 16th inst to its previous billets in the FOSSEUX area

2. Baggage waggons will report to Bn H.Q. at 9.0am Nov 15th

3. Refilling Point on 16th Nov will be GOUY-EN-ARTOIS.

4. ~~Refilling~~ 2/Lieut C.S. THOMAS and Corpl. B. HARRIS, "A" Coy & Sergt E. ISAAC "D" Coy are detailed as Battalion billeting party.
These 2 NCOS will report to 2Lieut THOMAS at Bn H Qrs at 9.0am tomorrow Nov 15th
This party will proceed to SIMENCOURT by bicycle where they will arrive before 12 NOON.
The Battalion Signalling Officer will arrange that 3 bicycles are available.
H.Qrs & Companies will occupy the same billets in SIMENCOURT as they previously vacated.

Tours.

5. All units requiring to make up their establishment will send a limber to draw SAA and Grenades from Brigade H. Qrs at 10 am Nov 15th

6. Detailed orders will be issued tomorrow Nov 15th.

Captain
Adjutant
17th Welsh Regt

11.55 pm
14/11/17

Copies to
1 – 4 Coys
5, 6, 7, 8. Q.M. T.O. Sig Officer Lt Thomas
9 War Diary
10 File

436

To O.C. Companies.
Transport Officer.
Quartermaster.
Signalling Officer.
Medical Officer.
R.S.M.
War Diary.
File.

Reference Brigade Scheme for to-morrow November 9th. 1917.

Reference Map 1/40,000, Sheet 51c.

1. INFORMATION

(a) The German Line which runs approximately FREVENT - NEUVILLETTE - [illegible] VISSE has been broken through between [illegible] VISSE and FREVENT and further to the North.

The Germans have been taken by surprise.

(b) The 119th. Infantry Brigade are ordered to clear that portion of the FORET de LUCHEUX lying in N.

The 120th. Infantry Brigade are operating immediately South in T.

"X" Division have been ordered to deal with IVERGNY.

The Brigade has arrived by Route March.

2. INSTRUCTIONS.

The Battalion will proceed by Route March to N. 32. Central.

Starting Point. Opposite Battalion Headquarter Guard Room at 7.30 a.m.

Order of March. Headquarters, Band, "B", "C", "D", "A" Companies.

Route. [illegible] - LUCHEUX - Junction of roads in T.15. b. 5. 5.

Dress. Battle Order. (Steel Helmets will be worn) Waterproof Sheets carried under flap of haversack, Jerkins carried rolled on Belt. A Haversack Ration will be taken. Dinners will be on return to Billets.

Lewis Gun Limbers and 2 Tool Carts will accompany the Battalion, and will march in rear of the Battalion.

A Wood Fighting Scheme will be carried out.

Further Orders will be issued on the Ground.

The 119th. T.M.B. will act as enemy, and will carry flags for this purpose.

Captain
& Adjutant.

8th. November 1917. 17th. (S) Battn. The Welsh Regt.

Herewith one copy of BRIGADE SCHEME for to-morrow, November 12th 1917.

Further instructions will be issued on the ground.

It is expected the Battalion will be back in billets by 2 p.m. but haversack rations will be taken.

for Captain
Adjutant.
17th (S) Battalion The Welsh Regiment.

11thNovr. 1917.

Army Form C. 2118.

Instructions regarding War Diaries and Intelligence Summaries are contained in F. S. Regs., Part II. and the Staff Manual respectively. Title pages will be prepared in manuscript.

WAR DIARY
or
INTELLIGENCE SUMMARY.
(Erase heading not required.)

Vol 19

Place	Date	Hour	Summary of Events and Information	Remarks and references to Appendices
			War Diary. 17th (S) Bn. The Welsh Regiment. Dec 1917.	

A7092). Wt. W12839/M1293. 750,000. 1/17. D. D & L., Ltd. Forms/C2118/14.

Instructions regarding War Diaries and Intelligence Summaries are contained in F. S. Regs., Part II. and the Staff Manual respectively. Title pages will be prepared in manuscript.

WAR DIARY
or
INTELLIGENCE SUMMARY.

(Erase heading not required.)

Army Form C. 2118.

14th Battn Welsh Regt

Place	Date	Hour	Summary of Events and Information	Remarks and references to Appendices
			Ref: Maps Hendecourt Ed 5 Special Sheet parts of 51B S.W. S.E. & 57C N.W. & N.E. Scale 1/20,000 ; Lens 1/100,000	
POMMIER	Dec 1		at POMMIER 4 organisation	WG
POMMIER	2		Battalion left billets at POMMIER and embussed at BAILLEULMONT VILLAGE for ERVILLERS. In the evening Bn moved into the Trenches U 14. d & U 20. b (TUNNEL TRENCH) relieving THE ROYAL IRISH REGIMENT.	WG
CROISILLES	3		Battalion in the LEFT SUB-SECTOR of the RIGHT SECTOR	
do	4		—— do —— do —— 2/LIEUT L PHILLIPS rejoined Bn from DOIGNIES	WG
do	5		—— do —— do ——	WG
do	6		—— do —— do —— The following officers were attached to this Bn. 2nd LIEUT L.C. PLACE of the 11th K.O.R.L. 2nd " G.G. WALKER " 14th ARGYLE & SUTHERLAND HIGHLANDERS 2nd " B. BOCKING " 12th YORKS BN. The following rejoined the Bn. Capt MORGAN-GRIFFITHS from COURSE. LIEUT REDROBE " " 2nd LIEUT D.R MORGAN " HOSPITAL	WG
do	7		Bn in the same Sector of Trenches. 2nd Lieut D.M. DAVIES evacuated to C.C.S.	WG
do	8		The Bn were relieved by the 18th WELSH on the night of the 8/9th and went into Support at RAILWAY. RESERVE	WG
"	9		Bn in Support working on GOLLYWOG TRENCH, TUNNEL TRENCH, and in RAILWAY RESERVE	WG
do	10		—— do —— do ——	WG
				WG

WAR DIARY
or
INTELLIGENCE SUMMARY.
(Erase heading not required.)

Army Form C. 2118.

Place	Date	Hour	Summary of Events and Information	Remarks and references to Appendices
			Ry map Hendecourt Special Sheet Ed 5.	
CROISILLES	11		Bn in Support working Parties on GOLLYWOG TRENCH, TUNNEL TRENCH & RAILWAY RESERVE The following Officers were attached to this Bn LIEUT H.E. COOKE. " H.A. CHRISTY 2nd " W.G. NORRIS	W.H.
do	12		Bn doing similar work as they did on the 11th Major H.P.B. Gough M.C. to be A/Lieut Colonel. Captain W.P. Stratton " " A/Major.	W.H.
do	13		The Bn working on GOLLYWOG TRENCH, TUNNEL TRENCH & RAILWAY RESERVE The following Officers were attached to this Bn 2nd LIEUT H.W. GAMMON from the 6th BN South WALES BORDERERS. 2nd " H.T. DALE " " 6th " " " The following Officers were evacuated as Gas Casualties LIEUT REDROBE 2nd LIEUT G.E. MORGAN	W.H.
do	14		The Bn moved from Support position into the Front Line Trenches in the ~~Left~~ subsector of the Right Sector of the Brigade thus relieving the 18th Bn The Welsh Regt. Capt MORGAN GRIFFITHS was evacuated as a Gas casualty.	W.H.

A7092 Wt. W128 9/M1293 750,000. 1/17. D. D & L. Ltd. Forms/C2118/14.

Army Form C. 2118.

WAR DIARY
or
INTELLIGENCE SUMMARY.
(Erase heading not required.)

Instructions regarding War Diaries and Intelligence Summaries are contained in F. S. Regs., Part II. and the Staff Manual respectively. Title pages will be prepared in manuscript.

Place	Date	Hour	Ref map Hendecourt Ed 5 Special Sheet. Summary of Events and Information	Remarks and references to Appendices
CROISILLES	15		Bn in the Front Line Trenches (Left subsector Right sector of Brigade)	
do	16		do do	
			The following Officers were attached to this Bn.	
			2nd LIEUT ABBOTT. from the 18th Bn THE WELSH REGt	W.H
			2nd " MacDONALD " " " "	
			2nd " ARMSTRONG " " " "	
			2nd " McGILLEY " " " "	
do	17th		Bn in Front Line Trenches	
			The following Officers left this Bn & rejoined their respective Units	W.H
			2nd LIEUT L.C. PLACE. 11th Bn K.O.R.L.	
			2nd " G G WALKER 14th " ARGYLE & SUTHERLAND HIGHrs	
			The following Officers rejoined this unit.	
			Capt A E GRANT from course	
			2nd " F. T. WILLIAMS " Sanity	
			2nd LIEUT D.M. DAVIES " HOSPITAL	
			The following officers were attached to the Bn	
			2nd LIEUT A.R SMEATHERS from the 5th Bn S.W.B's	
			2nd LIEUT W.G JONES " " " "	
			2nd LIEUT G.T. GREER	
			2nd " H.E. WILSON " " 18th " THE WELSH REGt	
			2nd " PROCTOR " " " " "	

A7092 Wt. W128 9/M1293 750,000. 1/17. D. D & L. Ltd. Forms/C2118/14.

Army Form C. 2118.

Instructions regarding War Diaries and Intelligence Summaries are contained in F. S. Regs., Part II. and the Staff Manual respectively. Title pages will be prepared in manuscript.

WAR DIARY
or
INTELLIGENCE SUMMARY.
(Erase heading not required.)

Place	Date	Hour	Summary of Events and Information (Ref map Hendecourt Ed 5 Special Sheet)	Remarks and references to Appendices
CROISILLERS	18		The Bn in the Front Line Trenches 2nd LIEUT H.E. WILSON rejoined his UNIT from this BN.	WH
do	19		The Bn in the Front Line Trenches The following Officers attached to this Bn 2nd LIEUT D.P. JONES from the 9th Bn THE ROYAL WELSH FUSILIERS 2nd " R.W.G. JONES " " 9th " " " The following Officers rejoined their UNIT from this BN 2nd LIEUT B. BOCKING 2nd " ABBOTT 2nd " ARMSTRONG 2nd " PROCTOR	WH
do	20		Bn in the Front Line Trenches In the evening this BN was relieved by the 18th BN WELSH REG after the relief had been completed this BN proceeded to INISKILLING CAMP near ERVILLERS	WH
ERVILLERS	21		Bn in Brigade Reserve and at work making barbed wire concertinas for use in front of the Front Line of Trenches	WH

A7092 Wt. W125 9/M1293 750,000. 1/17. D. D & I. Ltd. Forms/C2118/14.

Instructions regarding War Diaries and Intelligence Summaries are contained in F. S. Regs., Part II. and the Staff Manual respectively. Title pages will be prepared in manuscript.

WAR DIARY
or
INTELLIGENCE SUMMARY.
(Erase heading not required.)

Army Form C. 2118.

17th (S) Battn. The Welsh Regt
December 1917

Place	Date	Hour	Ref Map Hendecourt 51B S.E. Special Sheet — Summary of Events and Information	Remarks and references to Appendices
Inniskilling Camp	22		Bn in Brigade Reserve and at work making barbed wire concertinas for use in front of the front line of trenches.	I.D.G.
"	23		-ditto- Divine service in morning.	I.D.G.
"	24		Major F.E. BRADSHAW D.S.O. Notts & Derby Regt. appointed to command the battalion.	
			Battalion inspected by Brig Genl CROZIER	
			LIEUT COOKE appointed battalion signalling officer.	
			The following officer joined the battalion	
			2/LIEUT. WILLIAMS, R.W.M.	I.D.G.
"	25		Church services in the morning.	I.D.G.
"	26		In the evening the battalion relieved the 18th Welsh in the front line trenches. Relief completed 8.30 p.m.	I.D.G.
CROISILLES	27		Battalion in front line Trenches. At night a patrol went out, and reported on new enemy works, result of Artillery fire and position of ARGUS pill box, etc.	I.D.G.

A7092 Wt. W128.9/M1293 750,000. 1/17. D. D & L. Ltd. Forms/C2118/14.

WAR DIARY
or
INTELLIGENCE SUMMARY.
(Erase heading not required.)

Army Form C. 2118.

Instructions regarding War Diaries and Intelligence Summaries are contained in F. S. Regs., Part II. and the Staff Manual respectively. Title pages will be prepared in manuscript.

17th (S) Bn. The Welsh Regt
December 1917

Place	Date	Hour	Refmap HANDECOURT Ed. 5 Special Sheet — Summary of Events and Information	Remarks and references to Appendices
CROISILLERS	28		Battalion in the front line trenches.	
			The following officers joined from England –	
			2/LIEUT. GRAY R.A. — 2/LIEUT. EDWARDS D.J.	
			" JONES, V.T. — " WILLIAMS, T.	
			" GOODSON, A.C. — " GREEN, J.D.	
			" TUGBY L.A. — " HOPE-EVANS, J.I.	
			" GRAY S.J. — " GRIFFITHS L.O.	
			" GRAHAM, S. — " ROBERTS C.	
			" HURDIDGE A.W. — " LEWIS, A.J.	
			" FRANKLIN, A.J. — " STRONGMAN, J.	
			2/LIEUT TAYLOR F.C.	
			In the evening a patrol went out and visited the ruins of VULCAN pill box. R.E's destroyed ARGUS pill box. Another patrol proceeded along FAG ALLEY. There was nothing of interest to report by this patrol	[initials]
"	29		Battalion in the front line trenches.	
			A patrol which went out this evening was fired at and challenged near ARGUS	[initials]

A7092 Wt. W128 9/M1293. 750,000. 1/17. D. D & L. Ltd. Forms/C2118/14.

Instructions regarding War Diaries and Intelligence Summaries are contained in F. S. Regs., Part II. and the Staff Manual respectively. Title pages will be prepared in manuscript.

WAR DIARY
or
INTELLIGENCE SUMMARY.
(Erase heading not required.)

Army Form C. 2118.

17th (S) Batt. The Welsh Regt.
December 1917

Place	Date	Hour	Summary of Events and Information	Remarks and references to Appendices
			Ref map HANDECOURT Ed. 5 Special Sheet	
CROISILLES	30.		Battalion in the front line This evening a patrol went out, accompanied by a R.E. demolition party who destroyed a hostile pill box.	[illegible]
"	31		Battalion in the front line A patrol went out in evening and reported that FAG ALLEY was unoccupied, and that no enemy patrols appeared to be about.	[illegible]

F. E. Bradshaw
Major
17th Welsh Regt.

Instructions regarding War Diaries and Intelligence Summaries are contained in F. S. Regs., Part II. and the Staff Manual respectively. Title pages will be prepared in manuscript.

WAR DIARY
or
INTELLIGENCE SUMMARY.
(Erase heading not required.)

119/40

Army Form C. 2118.

Vol 20

Place	Date	Hour	Summary of Events and Information	Remarks and references to Appendices
			War Diary 17th Bn Welsh Regt January 1918	

20 D
15 sheets

A7092). Wt. W12839/M1295 750,000. 1/17. D. D & L., Ltd. Forms/C2118/14.

Army Form C. 2118.

WAR DIARY
or
INTELLIGENCE SUMMARY.
(*Erase heading not required.*)

*Instructions regarding War Diaries and Intelligence Summaries are contained in F. S. Regs., Part II. and the Staff Manual respectively. Title pages will be prepared in manuscript.

Place	Date	Hour	Summary of Events and Information	Remarks and references to Appendices
CROISILLES (SECTOR)	1918 JAN 1st		The Bn holding the Front Line Trenches. Our Own Artillery were fairly active, Hostile quiet. This Bn was relieved by the 18th Bn The WELSH Regt during the evening, and went into Brigade Support at RAILWAY RESERVE. The following list of honours were granted to Officers. Warrant Officers N.C.O's and Men of this Bn for devotion to duty and gallant conduct in and around BOURLON WOOD on the 23rd 24th & 25th of NOVEMBER 1917 Major H.P.B. GOUGH M.C. - Bar to M.C. CAPT C.R. EVANS - MILITARY CROSS " A.P. LLOYD - do do LIEUT D.A.H. MOSES (Bn M.O) - do do 2/Lt T.T. DAVIES - do do " D.M. DAVIES - do do " P. HAY - do do " K.L. JONES - do do 26056 C.S.M. T. ABBOTT. - DISTINGUISHED CONDUCT MEDAL 26010 Cpl. T. BAILEY. - do 25788 LCpl F. MORRIS. - do 26728 " J.T. DUNN. - do The following were MENTIONED in NEW YEARS HONOURS. Lieut D.A.H. MOSES (Bn M.O.) 25688 Pte G. MOCK. 2/Lt G.R. JACKMAN (dec'd)	C Stanley Thomas 2/Lt
do	JAN 2nd		The Bn in Brigade Support at RAILWAY RESERVE and during the day were marched off under Company arrangements to St LEGER to have baths, the remainder of the day devoted to cleaning up.	

(A7092). Wt. W12839/M1293. 750,000. 1/17. D. D. & L., Ltd. Forms/C.2118/14.

Instructions regarding War Diaries and Intelligence Summaries are contained in F. S. Regs., Part II. and the Staff Manual respectively. Title pages will be prepared in manuscript.

WAR DIARY
or
INTELLIGENCE SUMMARY.
(Erase heading not required.)

Army Form C. 2118.

Place	Date	Hour	Summary of Events and Information	Remarks and references to Appendices
	1918.			
CROISILLES SECTOR.	JAN 2nd		2/Lt H.T. DALE complimented by the G.O.C. 40th DIVISION upon his PATROL ~~up~~ made on the night 16-17/12/1917.	C.O.T.
do	JAN 3rd		Bn in Brigade Support at RAILWAY RESERVE. Men employed during the day in improving TUNNEL TRENCH and the C.T.'s going up to THE FRONT LINE. also in cleaning up their equipment and having their boots ~~and~~ clothing mended if required.	C.O.T.
do	JAN 4th		Bn in Brigade Support at RAILWAY RESERVE. Men employed during the day in improving the condition of TUNNEL TRENCH (FRONT LINE) and the C.T.'s going up to ~~same~~ when not so employed they had their boots + clothing attended to.	C.O.T.
do	5th		Bn in Brigade Support at RAILWAY RESERVE. Working Parties were furnished and employed on Front Line Trenches. In the afternoon the men generally cleaned up their Quarters + Equipment. During the late afternoon the Bn moved up	

(A7092). Wt. W12839/M1293. 750,000. 1/17. D. D. & L., Ltd. Forms/C.2118/14.

Instructions regarding War Diaries and Intelligence Summaries are contained in F. S. Regs., Part II. and the Staff Manual respectively. Title pages will be prepared in manuscript.

WAR DIARY
or
INTELLIGENCE SUMMARY.
(Erase heading not required.)

Army Form C. 2118.

Place	Date	Hour	Summary of Events and Information	Remarks and references to Appendices
CROISILLES (SECTOR)	1918		into the Front Line relieving the 18th Bn THE WELSH Regt. Our B & D Coys manned the front line Posts. Patrol work was carried out during the hours of darkness.	C.J.T.
do.	JAN 6th		Bn in the FRONT LINE TRENCHES. Artillery on both sides active. During the night Patrol work was carried out along the Bn front well in front of our wire but no hostile movement was observed	C.J.T.
do	7th		Bn holding the Front Line Trenches. As the Brigade on our right was carrying out a semi daylight raid Our Artillery opened out to give the Infantry support. This naturally drew the Enemy fire so that for a period both Our Own & Hostile artillery were active. Inter-Company relief A and C Companies relieving B & D Coys respectively. Lieut G. J. Greer appointed O.C. of "C" Company during the absence of Capt. Grant ~~who~~ on leave.	C.J.T.

(A7092). Wt. W12839/M1293. 750,000. 1/17. D. D. & L., Ltd. Forms/C.2118/14.

Instructions regarding War Diaries and Intelligence Summaries are contained in F. S. Regs., Part II. and the Staff Manual respectively. Title pages will be prepared in manuscript.

WAR DIARY
or
INTELLIGENCE SUMMARY.
(Erase heading not required.)

Army Form C. 2118.

Place	Date	Hour	Summary of Events and Information	Remarks and references to Appendices
	1918			
CROISILLES	JAN 8th		Bn in the Front line Trenches. Our Own Artillery was fairly active all day whereas the Enemy's was quiet. Patrol work was carried out all night through. 2/Lts FRANKLIN, ROBERTS, and GRAY (?) together with an Officer from the R.E.'s went out into NO MAN'S LAND and blew up a DUG OUT with M.G. Emplacement at top which in an advance on the Enemy's line would be a dangerous obstacle if left untouched. This Emplacement was discovered by 2/Lts FRANKLIN and ROBERTS whilst on patrol on the night of 5-6/12/17. 2/Lt J.O. HILL appointed A/Captain whilst in charge of a Company.	C.O.T.
do	9th		Bn in the Front Line Trenches. Hostile Artillery fairly active also our own. 2/Lt FRANKLIN took out a day light Patrol to find and bring back a GERMAN who had been seen in NO MAN'S LAND but he was not to be found. Patrol work was carried out during the hours of darkness but no Enemy were encountered. 2/Lt R.S. McCartney was killed whilst on duty in the Front line Trenches. Sugar tickets first issued to Officers and Men going on leave to England.	C.O.T.

(A7092). Wt. W12839/M1293. 750,000. 1/17. D. D. & L., Ltd. Forms/C.2118/14.

Instructions regarding War Diaries and Intelligence Summaries are contained in F. S. Regs., Part II. and the Staff Manual respectively. Title pages will be prepared in manuscript.

WAR DIARY
or
INTELLIGENCE SUMMARY.
(Erase heading not required.)

Army Form C. 2118.

Place	Date	Hour	Summary of Events and Information	Remarks and references to Appendices
CROISILLES	1918 Jany 9th		(cont from previous page) Major F. E. Bradshaw appointed a/Lieut Colonel. During the evening the Bn were relieved by the 18th Bn The WELSH Regt and went into Brigade Reserve at MORY (NORTH CAMP)	C.O.T.
MORY	10th		Bn at MORY (NORTH CAMP.) as Bn in Brigade Reserve. The Companies were at the disposal of the Coy Commanders who paraded their men, and gave them Platoon, Section, and Arms drill. Working Parties were employed inside and outside the Camp making improvements and carrying out new work. In the morning the men were employed in cleaning up generally.	C.O.T.
do	11th		Bn at MORY (NORTH CAMP) as Bn in Brigade Reserve. The various Companies were at the disposal of the Company Commanders who carried out Platoon, Section, & Arms drill. Working Parties were furnished & employed in carrying out improvements and new work inside and outside the camp.	C.O.T.

(A7092). Wt. W12839/M1293. 750,000. 1/17. D. D. & L., Ltd. Forms/C.2118/14.

Instructions regarding War Diaries and Intelligence Summaries are contained in F. S. Regs., Part II. and the Staff Manual respectively. Title pages will be prepared in manuscript.

WAR DIARY
or
INTELLIGENCE SUMMARY.
(Erase heading not required.)

Army Form C. 2118.

Place	Date	Hour	Summary of Events and Information	Remarks and references to Appendices
MORY.	1918 JAN 12th		Bn in Brigade Reserve at MORY (NORTH CAMP) The Companies were marched off under Company Officers and to times given out in B.R.O to Baths at St LEGER. The rest of the day was spent with Companies at the disposal of the Coy Commanders who gave the men Platoon. Section and Arms drill.	C.A.T.
do	13th		Bn at MORY (NORTH CAMP) as Bn in Brigade Reserve. The day was devoted to Church Parades in the morning in the afternoon the time was devoted to generally cleaning up of Equipment and Quarters. At 4 pm. the Bn moved forward to relieve the 18th Bn The WELSH REGt who were holding the LINE. The relief was completed without any mishap. The Trenches were found to be in a fairly good state only owing to the thaw having set in the sides of the trenches had started to cave in in places. Patrol work was carried out during the hours of darkness. B & D Coys were holding the FRONT LINE TRENCH.	C.A.T.
CROISILLES.	14th		Bn in the Front Line Trenches. Our Own Artillery was quiet Hostile Artillery was fairly active shelling our C.T's. No further thaw having set in Patrol work was possible Trenches in a fairly good condition.	

(A7092). Wt. W12839/M1293. 750,000. 1/17. D. D. & L., Ltd. Forms/C.2118/14.

Army Form C. 2118.

Instructions regarding War Diaries and Intelligence Summaries are contained in F. S. Regs., Part II. and the Staff Manual respectively. Title pages will be prepared in manuscript.

WAR DIARY
or
INTELLIGENCE SUMMARY.
(Erase heading not required.)

Place	Date	Hour	Summary of Events and Information	Remarks and references to Appendices
CROISILLES SECTOR	1918 JAN 10th (CONT)		2/Lt K.L. Jones appointed a/Captain whilst in charge of a Company	C.S.T.
do	15th		Bn in the Front Line Trenches Hostile Artillery fairly quiet Trenches in a fairly good condition but owing to rain & thaw there was a fair amount of water about. C.T.'s were in fairly good order but showed signs of caving in in places which grew worse as the day progressed and during the night. Patrols were able to go out at dusk and remained out watching and searching the Bn front until dawn.	
			2/Lt W.E. NORRIS killed whilst on duty in the front line Trench through the collapse of a Trench Shelter which had been erected in one of the Posts (No 28)	
			Lt H.E. CHRISTY posted as Transport Officer to the 119th M.G. Coy.	
			2/Lt R.A. GRAY takes over command of "A" Coy during the absence of 2/Lt K.L. JONES M.C. (on leave)	
			Inter Company relief "A" & "C" Coys relieving "D" & "B" respectively.	C.S.T.

(A7092). Wt. W12839/M1293. 750,000. 1/17. D. D. & L., Ltd. Forms/C.2118/14.

Army Form C. 2118.

Instructions regarding War Diaries and Intelligence Summaries are contained in F. S. Regs., Part II. and the Staff Manual respectively. Title pages will be prepared in manuscript.

WAR DIARY
or
INTELLIGENCE SUMMARY.
(Erase heading not required.)

Place	Date	Hour	Summary of Events and Information	Remarks and references to Appendices
CROISILLES (SECTOR)	1918 JAN 16th		Bn in the Front Line Trenches. Hostile Artillery fairly quiet. Enemy Snipers were busy and fired at any target given them. White ~~flares~~ lights which when in the air burst into two white stars appeared to be a Signal fired from his Front Line to his Artillery when any great movement in our lines was seen. Movement was caused on top because the C.T.'s were full of mud. Condition of ground too bad for Patrol work. A Working Party at work in BOW LANE were shelled and suffered 6 casualties 3 killed + 3 wounded (men were not of the Bn) ~~Inter Company relief~~	C.D.T.
do	17th		Bn in the Front Line Trenches. Hostile Artillery + M.G's fairly active and Sniping whenever possible at movement over the top. The C.T.'s being impassable owing to mud from recent thaw after severe frosts + rain, over the top was the only means of getting water and food from the rear Trenches to Front Line System. In the evening this Bn was relieved by the 18th Bn The Welsh Regt and went into Brigade Support at RAILWAY RESERVE	C.D.T.

(A7092). Wt. W12839/M1293. 750,000. 1/17. D. D. & L., Ltd. Forms/C.2118/14.

Instructions regarding War Diaries and Intelligence Summaries are contained in F. S. Regs., Part II. and the Staff Manual respectively. Title pages will be prepared in manuscript.

WAR DIARY
or
INTELLIGENCE SUMMARY.
(Erase heading not required.)

Army Form C. 2118.

Place	Date	Hour	Summary of Events and Information	Remarks and references to Appendices
	1918		(Continued from previous page)	
CROISILLES (SECTOR)	JAN 17th		The following Officers were posted to this Bn. 2/Lt E. TATTON. 2/Lt T.E. WILSON 2/Lt E.H. WILSON 2/Lt G.H. HOBBY.	C.S.T.
do	18th		Bn in Brigade Support at RAILWAY RESERVE and the Companies distributed as usual. B.H.Q. & 2 COYS in RAILWAY RESERVE. 1 at MAN SUPPORT, 1 in RAILWAY EMBANKMENT (MAIDA VALE) The Bn were marched off under Company arrangements to St LEGER to have baths. The remainder of the day was spent in generally cleaning up.	C.S.T.
do	19th		Bn in Brigade Support at RAILWAY RESERVE. The men were employed in working parties clearing the C.T.'s going up to the Front Line System of all mud that had fallen in owing to the recent thaw & rain.	C.S.T.
do	20th		Bn in Brigade Support at RAILWAY RESERVE. The men being employed as on the previous day in clearing the C.T's up to Front Line System. Hostile Artillery active & shelled "C" Coy who were in the	

(A7092) Wt. W12839/M1293. 750,000. 1/17. D. D. & L., Ltd. Forms/C.2118/14.

Instructions regarding War Diaries and Intelligence Summaries are contained in F. S. Regs., Part II. and the Staff Manual respectively. Title pages will be prepared in manuscript.

WAR DIARY
or
INTELLIGENCE SUMMARY.

(*Erase heading not required.*)

Army Form C. 2118.

Place	Date	Hour	Summary of Events and Information	Remarks and references to Appendices
CROISILLES (SECTOR)	1918 JAN 20th		(continued from previous page) RAILWAY EMBANKMENT 1 man being killed and 6 wounded.	C.D.T.
do.	21st		Bn in Brigade Support at RAILWAY RESERVE. Day spent in finding Working parties for the front line and C.T's leading there to in the morning. In the afternoon men employed in cleaning up themselves and their Quarters. During the evening the Bn moved forward and relieved the 18th Bn THE WELSH Regt who were in the front line. The relief was carried out without any casualties "B" & "D" Coys occupying the front line "C" Coy in Support & "A" Coy in Reserve. Some of the C.T's were found to be nearly clear of mud.	C.D.T.
do.	22nd		Bn holding the front line System of Posts Ref Map CHERISY (Special map) U. 14. a. 70. 10. to U. 20. b. 70. 80. Hostile and Our Own Artillery fairly active. Fair amount of Sniping on both sides, owing to the fact that the Trenches were not clear in many places so the overland track had to be used. Patrol work was impossible so protection was carried out by a system of Listening Posts outside our wire.	C.D.T.

(A7092). Wt. W12859/M1293. 750,000. 1/17. D. D. & L., Ltd. Forms/C.2118/14.

Instructions regarding War Diaries and Intelligence Summaries are contained in F. S. Regs., Part II. and the Staff Manual respectively. Title pages will be prepared in manuscript.

WAR DIARY
or
INTELLIGENCE SUMMARY.
(Erase heading not required.)

Army Form C. 2118.

Place	Date	Hour	Summary of Events and Information	Remarks and references to Appendices
CROISILLES (SECTOR)	1918 JAN 23rd		Bn holding the Front Line System of Posts in front of TUNNEL TRENCH The Artillery fire was active on both sides. We were shelling new work in COPSE TRENCH & Working Parties. The Bosche endeavoured to find our Battery positions but failed, his shots falling short of them. Sniping was again indulged in like the previous day. The Enemy also appeared to be nervous as he fired off a large number of Very lights during the hours of darkness. Patrolling was again of no use as the ground was too heavy for good & silent work. The Bn front was therefore guarded by a system of Listening Posts pushed well in front of our wire Inter Company relief "A" "C" Coys relieving "D" "B" respectively.	C.O.T.
do	24th		Bn holding the Front Line System of Posts in front of TUNNEL TRENCH Our Artillery were very active especially in the early morning about 7 a.m. They then fired Salvoes at intervals. At 11 a.m. Our artillery had a practise shoot against a prospective aircraft (low flying) attack. Hostile Artillery was fairly quiet only he fired periodically on our C.T's. Our Snipers & Observers were fairly active both in rifle shooting & getting the Artillery on to targets. Listening posts were pushed well outside our wire to guard the Bn Front against Hostile attacks	C.O.T.

(A7092). Wt. W12839/M1293. 750,000. 1/17. D. D. & L., Ltd. Forms/C.2118/14.

Instructions regarding War Diaries and Intelligence Summaries are contained in F. S. Regs., Part II. and the Staff Manual respectively. Title pages will be prepared in manuscript.

WAR DIARY
or
INTELLIGENCE SUMMARY.
(Erase heading not required.)

Army Form C. 2118.

Place	Date	Hour	Summary of Events and Information	Remarks and references to Appendices
CROISILLES (SECTOR)	1918 JAN 25th		Bn in the ~~Front~~ Line our Artillery were fairly active firing on COPSE ROAD & working Parties along COPSE TRENCH. HENDECOURT also received their attention. Hostile Artillery was active & shelled our C.T's and Left Front Line Coy's H.Q.s where men were at work clearing the Trench of mud. We suffered casualties to the extent of 1 killed and 2 wounded. A fair amount of movement was observed in enemy lines & which was fired upon either by rifle or Artillery fire. This Bn was ~~...~~ relieved during the evening by the 18th Bn The WELSH REGt and proceeded to MORY (NORTH CAMP) as Bn in Brigade reserve.	C.J.T.
MORY	26th		Bn as Bn in Brigade reserve at MORY (NORTH CAMP). During the morning men were allowed time to clean themselves and their equipment. Under Coy arrangements men were marched off to the Baths at MORY. LIEUT. COLONEL F.E. BRADSHAW left the Bn and was succeeded by Major SWEET.	C.J.T.
do	27th		Bn at ~~MORY~~ (NORTH CAMP) as Bn in Brigade Reserve during the morning the men paraded for Divine Service & 2 Coys for C.O's inspection. A Coy also went to the Musketry Range. In the afternoon the remaining 2 Coys were paraded for C.O's inspection. In the evening a large Working Party of 5 Officers & 200 O.R. were sent up to C.7.a.8.8. to dig trenches.	C.J.T.

(A7092). Wt. W12839/M1293. 750,000. 1/17. D. D. & L., Ltd. Forms/C.2118/14.

Instructions regarding War Diaries and Intelligence Summaries are contained in F. S. Regs., Part II. and the Staff Manual respectively. Title pages will be prepared in manuscript.

WAR DIARY
or
INTELLIGENCE SUMMARY.
(Erase heading not required.)

Army Form C. 2118.

Place	Date	Hour	Summary of Events and Information	Remarks and references to Appendices
CROISILLES	1918 JAN 31st (cont.)		Own shelled the Enemy Front Line at intervals. Bn Front was watched during the night by a system of Listening Posts with 2 Patrols searching NO MANS LAND in front. Inter Coy relief "A" & "C" Coys relieving "D" & "B" respectively.	C.O.T.

Fred Swett
Major.
Commanding 17th (S) Bn Welsh Regt

(A7092). Wt. W12839/M1293. 750,000. 1/17. D. D. & L., Ltd. Forms/C.2118/14.

Instructions regarding War Diaries and Intelligence Summaries are contained in F. S. Regs., Part II. and the Staff Manual respectively. Title pages will be prepared in manuscript.

WAR DIARY
or
INTELLIGENCE SUMMARY.

(Erase heading not required.)

Army Form C. 2118.

Place	Date	Hour	Summary of Events and Information	Remarks and references to Appendices
MORY ~~CROISELLES~~	1918 Jan 28th		Bn at MORY (NORTH CAMP) as Bn in Brigade Reserve. During the day the men under Coy arrangements were marched off to the Baths to undergo the foot treatment as laid down by Brigade Order. Men employed during the afternoon doing work in and around the Camp. In the evening the Bn Band gave an Entertainment which was quite a success.	C.J.T.
do	29th		Bn at MORY (North Camp). Battalion inspected by Colonel R. Benzie of the 12th S.W.B.s a/c Brigadier General of the 119th Infantry Brigade in close Order & at drill. The afternoon was devoted to cleaning up of Quarters & themselves. The Bn moving forward at 4.30 pm. to relieve the 18th Bn The WELSH Regt who were holding the line. The Relief was carried out without mishap. "B & D" Coys in the front Trench.	C.J.T.
CROISELLES	30th		Bn holding the front line System of Trenches. Hostile Artillery was active in the early morning. Our Artillery was quiet. The Bn front was patrolled during the night, and also Listening Posts were pushed out well in front of wire. no hostile movement was noted	C.J.T.
do	31st		Bn holding the front line system of Posts & Trenches. Hostile Artillery was active during the morning shelling our C.T's. Our	

(A7092). Wt. W12839/M1293. 750,000. 1/17. D. D. & L., Ltd. Forms/C.2118/14.

Army Form C. 2118.

Instructions regarding War Diaries and Intelligence Summaries are contained in F. S. Regs., Part II. and the Staff Manual respectively. Title pages will be prepared in manuscript.

WAR DIARY
or
INTELLIGENCE SUMMARY.

(Erase heading not required.)

Vol 21

Place	Date	Hour	Summary of Events and Information	Remarks and references to Appendices
			War Diary. February 1918. 17th Welsh Regt.	

21.D
8 sheets

A7092). Wt. W12839/M1293. 750,000. 1/17. D. D & L., Ltd. Forms/C2118/14.

Instructions regarding War Diaries and Intelligence Summaries are contained in F. S. Regs., Part II. and the Staff Manual respectively. Title pages will be prepared in manuscript.

WAR DIARY
or
INTELLIGENCE SUMMARY.
(Erase heading not required.)

Army Form C. 2118.

Place	Date	Hour	Summary of Events and Information	Remarks and references to Appendices
			List of O.R. presented with MILITARY MEDAL for gallantry in BOURLON WOOD NOVEMBER 23rd 24th + 25th 1917	
			25978 Pte J. BARRETT — BAR TO HIS MILITARY MEDAL: 8806 Pte J. DAVIES	
			44343 " E. MORGAN	
			26181 Cpl J. GRIFFITHS	
			25835 Cpl H. THOMAS	
			37803 Pte W. GALPIN	
			25523 " I. MORRIS	
			15427 " J.B. O'NEILL	
			51685 " H. DAVIES	
			36001 " E. IRELAND	
			15302 " W. FLOOD	
			25691 SERGt E. THOMAS	
			26126 " P. REES	
			14887 L/Cpl D. LLOYD	
			19141 Pte W. WRIGHT	C.O.T.

A7092 Wt. W128.9/M1293. 750,000. 1/17. D. D & I. Ltd. Forms/C2118/14.

Instructions regarding War Diaries and Intelligence Summaries are contained in F. S. Regs., Part II. and the Staff Manual respectively. Title pages will be prepared in manuscript.

WAR DIARY
or
INTELLIGENCE SUMMARY.
(Erase heading not required.)

Army Form C. 2118.

Place	Date	Hour	Summary of Events and Information	Remarks and references to Appendices
CROISILLES.	1918 Feb 1st		Bn in the Front Line System of Trenches. Hostile Artillery was active during morning but quieted during the day. Our Artillery was also active shelling known Targets. During the day our Snipers were out in NO MANS LAND, and during the night a System of Listening posts were put out in front of the wire along the Bn front, with Patrols reconnoitering & Searching NO MANS LAND well over towards the Enemy lines.	C O Thomas
do	Feb 2nd		Bn in the Front Line System of Trenches. Hostile & Our Own Artillery fairly active. During the evening the Bn were relieved by the 18th Bn THE WELSH REGT. and moved into Brigade Support at RAILWAY RESERVE. Owing to a new system of Organization this was the last day the Bn as a Bn would be in the Front Line System of Trenches.	C.O.T
do	Feb 3rd		Bn were in Billets in RAILWAY RESERVE as Bn in Bde Support. The men were employed in furnishing working parties to clean & repair the Front Line System of Trenches, when they returned to their Dug Outs they cleaned themselves after their tour of duty in the Trenches.	C.O.T

A7092 Wt. W128 9/M1293. 750,000. 1/17. D. D & L. Ltd. Forms/C2118/14.

Instructions regarding War Diaries and Intelligence Summaries are contained in F. S. Regs., Part II. and the Staff Manual respectively. Title pages will be prepared in manuscript.

WAR DIARY
or
INTELLIGENCE SUMMARY.

(Erase heading not required.)

Army Form C. 2118.

Place	Date	Hour	Summary of Events and Information	Remarks and references to Appendices
CROISILLES	1918 Feb 4th		Bn at RAILWAY RESERVE as BN in Brigade Support. The men were employed all day in finding working parties to repair & clear the front line system of Trenches.	C.J.T.
do.	Feb 5th		Bn at RAILWAY RESERVE as Bn in Bde Support and moved in the evening to L'ABBAYE CAMP, MORY as Bn in Divisional Reserve. No working parties were furnished as owing to the Bn being disbanded to suit the new system of Organization a draft of 10 Officers and 200 O.R. were posted to the 18th BN THE WELSH REGt. The names of the Officers posted were. Capt. W.P. STRATTON. 2/Lt. D.M. DAVIES M.C. Lieut. G.J. EVANS. 2/Lt. P. HAY M.C. 2/Lt a/Capt. J.O. HILL 2/Lt. A. EVANS. 2/Lt C.S. THOMAS 2/Lt. J. STRONGMAN 2/Lt A.T. FRANKLIN 2/Lt. T.E. MITFORD	C.J.T.
MORY	6th		Bn at L'ABBAYE Camp MORY as Bn in Divisional Reserve. The day was spent in the men cleaning up and were paraded and inspected under Company Arrangements.	C.J.T.

A7092 Wt. W128:9/M1293 750,000. 1/17. D. D & L. Ltd. Forms/C2118/14.

Army Form C. 2118.

Instructions regarding War Diaries and Intelligence Summaries are contained in F. S. Regs., Part II. and the Staff Manual respectively. Title pages will be prepared in manuscript.

WAR DIARY
or
INTELLIGENCE SUMMARY.
(Erase heading not required.)

Place	Date	Hour	Summary of Events and Information	Remarks and references to Appendices
MORY	1918 Feb 7th		Bn were at L'ABBAYE CAMP, MORY as BN in Divisional Reserve men were paraded under Company arrangements and lists of deficiencies were compiled.	C.A.T.
do	8th		Bn at L'ABBAYE CAMP, MORY as BN in Divisional Reserve men were paraded & inspected under Company arrangements. A draft of 2 Officers and 50 O.R left the BN to join the 9th BN THE WELSH REGT The names of the Officers were Lieut W. G. JONES 2/Lieut R. A. GRAY	C.A.T.
MORY and BAILLEULMONT (9 miles S.W. of ARRAS)	9th		Bn at L'ABBAYE CAMP, MORY until 10 am when they embussed in Motor Lorries & G.S. Waggons for BAILLEULMONT which place was reached at 1 p.m. the route taken was via ERVILLERS, BOYELLES, BOISLEUX-AU-MONT, FICHEUX, BEAUMETZ, BASSEUX, to BAILLEULMONT and were lodged in BILLETS in the Village.	C.A.T.
BAILLEULMONT	10th		Bn at BAILLEULMONT as SURPLUS PERSONNEL to VI CORPS The men were paraded & inspected under Company arrangements they also underwent Physical Training, Close & Open order drill a draft of 2 Officers & 50 O.R left to join the 2nd Bn THE WELSH REGT The	

Instructions regarding War Diaries and Intelligence Summaries are contained in F. S. Regs., Part II. and the Staff Manual respectively. Title pages will be prepared in manuscript.

WAR DIARY
or
INTELLIGENCE SUMMARY.
(Erase heading not required.)

Army Form C. 2118.

Place	Date	Hour	Summary of Events and Information	Remarks and references to Appendices
	1918 10th (cont.)		names of the Officers were 2/LIEUT A J. LEWIS 2/LIEUT E TATTON.	C.S.T.
BAILLEULMONT	11th		Bn at BAILLEULMONT as SURPLUS PERSONNEL to VI CORPS. The men paraded and inspected after which they went for a route march	C.S.T.
do	12th		Bn at BAILLEULMONT as VI CORPS SURPLUS PERSONNEL. The whole Bn paraded en mass and were inspected by the Commanding Officer after the inspection Coys carried out close order & Arms drill.	C.S.T.
do	13th		Bn at BAILLEULMONT as VI CORPS SURPLUS PERSONNEL. Men paraded in the morning and given P.T. & B.F until it started to rain when Lectures were delivered by Company Officers to them. In the afternoon men excused parades. Officers paraded in Recreation Hut and were given a lecture by Commanding Officer.	C.S.T.
do	14th		Bn at BAILLEULMONT as VI CORPS SURPLUS PERSONNEL. Men paraded and marched to BAILLEULVAL for Baths under Coy arrangements. The Officers were lectured by C.O upon Topography.	C.S.T.

A7092 Wt. W128 9/M1293 750,000. 1/17. D. D & L. Ltd. Forms/C2118/14.

Instructions regarding War Diaries and Intelligence Summaries are contained in F. S. Regs., Part II. and the Staff Manual respectively. Title pages will be prepared in manuscript.

WAR DIARY

or

INTELLIGENCE SUMMARY.

(*Erase heading not required.*)

Army Form C. 2118.

Place	Date	Hour	Summary of Events and Information	Remarks and references to Appendices
BAILLEULMONT	1918 Feb 15th		Bn at BAILLEULMONT The men were paraded under Company arrangements & were given Open & Close order drill also Arm drill. During the morning the Commanding Officer & Adjutant attended a meeting when a Scheme was put before them in which the majority of the Officers & O.R. remaining were merged into an Entrenching Battalion. The list of Officers posted to this new (No 9) Entrenching Bn is as follows Major H.P.B. GOUGH M.C. Lieut H.O. CHRISTY " H.E. COOKE 2/Lt A/Capt K.L. JONES 2/Lt L. PHILLIPS 2/Lt Y.T. JONES 2/Lt A.T. GOODSON 2/Lt S. GRAHAM 2/Lt T. WILLIAMS 2/Lt J.D. GREEN 2/Lt J.I. HOPE-EVANS 2/Lt C.G. ROBERTS 2/Lt G.H. HOBBY M.M. Lieut G.J. Greer left the Bn for ENGLAND for 6 MONTHS ~~[illegible]~~ Tour of Duty.	C.O.T.
do	16th		Bn at BAILLEULMONT The men were allotted to their new Coys in the new Bn The following Officers left for the BASE to be reposted to Regiments as required.	

Instructions regarding War Diaries and Intelligence Summaries are contained in F. S. Regs., Part II. and the Staff Manual respectively. Title pages will be prepared in manuscript.

WAR DIARY
or
INTELLIGENCE SUMMARY.
(Erase heading not required.)

Army Form C. 2118.

Place	Date	Hour	Summary of Events and Information	Remarks and references to Appendices
	1918 16th Feb	Cont	~~2/Lt H.W.M. WILLIAMS~~ · 2/Lt L.A. TUGBY 2/Lt D.R. MORGAN · 2/Lt S.J. GRAY 2/Lt H. DALE · 2/Lt A.W. HORDIDGE 2/Lt H.W. GAMMON · 2/Lt D.J. EDWARDS ~~2/Lt A.R. SMEATHERS~~ · 2/Lt L.O. GRIFFITHS 2/Lt F.C. TAYLOR · 2/Lt E.A. WILSON 2/Lt H.W.M. WILLIAMS & 2/Lt A.R. SMEATHERS posted to the 5th & 12th Bns South Wales Borderers, respectively. The Bn (17th WELSH) ceased today to be an Unit. [signature] Major Commanding 17th Bn Welsh Regt	C.O.T.

A7092 Wt. W128 9/M1293 750,000. 1/17. D. D & L. Ltd. Forms/C2118/14.

The Attack on BOURLON WOOD

Ref MOEUVRES. Special Sheet 1/20,000.

On November 23rd 1917, the 119th Infantry Brigade with the assistance of "Tanks" and Artillery attacked the enemy positions in BOURLON WOOD. At the same time BOURLON VILLAGE was attacked by the 120th Infantry Brigade on our left and FONTAINE-NOTRE-DAME by the 51st Division on our Right.

The 119th Infantry Brigade attacked on a two Battalion Front the 19th R.W. Fusiliers on the right and the 12th S.W. Borders on the left. The dividing line between the 2 Battalions was roughly the road running N & S through the wood the road itself being given to the 19th R.W.F.

The 17th Welsh was in Support
The 18th Welsh was held in Reserve in and about GRAINCOURT.

— " —

On the evening of Nov 22nd the 17th Welsh Regiment moved forward from DOIGNIES and spent the night 22/23rd Nov in the Sunken Road in E.30.c.

Shortly before ZERO hour (10.0am 23/11/1917) the Battalion moved forward to its assembly position A & D Companies through ANNEUX to the E edge of the CAMBRAI Road in F.19 central, B & C Companies to the sunken road in E.24 B.

Orders were issued to Company Commanders as follows:-

(1) A & D Companies to support the 19th R.W.F.
(2) C & B Companies to support the 12th S.W.B.
(3) "D" Company to secure the Sunken road through F.14 and establish a Strong point there.
(4) "B" Company to establish a Strong point at about E.18.A.1.9.
(5) All 4 Companies to be prepared to throw out defensive flanks and to keep touch with troops on right & left.
(6) The advance to be checked on the road running E & W through F.13. a & b and posts left to secure a position on the high ground on that General line.

When the 2 leading Battalions entered the Wood A & C Coys moved forward in Artillery Formation followed at 200 yards distance by D & B Companies.

Early in its advance "A" Company became aware of a large party of the enemy on its right flank directing fire against the Division operating on our right. This party was successfully attacked, and fifty prisoners taken, without materially interfering with the forward movement of our troops.

After "A" Company had passed North of the Old Quarry /in

in F 14 c two small parties of the enemy appeared behind them and opened fire. These were successfully dealt with by 'D' Company several being killed and sixteen captured. Except for occasional Snipers and a few small enemy parties no further resistance was encountered on the right until the first objective (Road E & W through F 13. a & b) was reached by A Company at 11.45 am 23/11/1917.

On the left little opposition was met by C & B Companies. A few Snipers were accounted for and 'B' Company cleared up a dugout the bag being 30 prisoners including an Officer and a Machine Gun. "C" Company reached the first Objective at 11.55 am 23/11/1917 and "B" Company established a Strong point at about E. 18 a 1.9 by am.

At an early hour on the 23rd it became evident that the attack on BOURLON VILLAGE was not progressing satisfactorily and the O/C "B" Company (Lieut A. R. JONES. M.C) was ordered to send another platoon to reinforce the garrison of the Strong point on the left and form a defensive flank on the S.W edge of the Village.

By 11.30 am the 12th S.W.B were hard pressed by the enemy in the N.W portion of the wood and Captain DUNN (O/C. "C" Company) sent up 2 platoons under Lieut ENSOR to reinforce them. Enemy pressure increasing still further. Captain DUNN took the two remaining platoons of his Company forward into the firing line with the result that the Enemy advance was for the time being "checked". Meanwhile the enemy was counter attacking vigorously from BOURLON VILLAGE and the O/C. "B" Company was ordered to move his remaining two platoons to the left flank. The whole of 'B' Company was then hotly engaged and did splendid work under the leadership of Lieut A. R. JONES. M.C.. 2nd Lieutenant T. T. DAVIES of this company fought hard in an endeavour to save the path of the Middlesex Regiment on his left but without avail, and in a little while "B" Coy were fighting hard to maintain its own ground against the ever increasing pressure of Enemy troops debouching from the village.

The condition of affairs on the left flank had now become very serious and at 1.30 pm a message was sent back asking for reinforcements. The 12th S.W.B and the 2 Companies of the 17th Welsh though disputing every inch of ground were, being forced slowly back when at pm the 18th Welsh arrived. Enemy progress was immediately stayed and our troops in their turn began to gain ground. For sometime the line swayed backwards and forward but when night fell and the fighting ceased our troops held all the High Ground and were within sight of the houses of BOURLON VILLAGE.

On the right rapid progress was made at first but at 12.45 pm. a message was received from the 19th R.W.F. asking for reinforcements to be sent to the Eastern edge of the wood. This request had been anticipated One Company having been ordered to make good the N.E portion of the wood as soon as it became known that the R.W.F had passed beyond the N edge. Owing to the left of the line being driven back from the N. Eastern portion of BOURLON VILLAGE the R.W.F were forced to drop back to the N. edge of the wood and being subjected to considerable enemy pressure were reinforced by 2 platoons of A Company 17th Welsh.

An attempt was made to dig in along the N & NE edges of the wood but heavy shell fire and M. Gun fire forced the line to drop back to a position about 100 to 150 yards inside. This line was worked on during the night of 23/24th November.

Towards evening however the right centre had been driven back and a message was sent to O/C A Company instructing him to throw his left back towards the track running diagonally through F.13.b and link up with the right of C Company. At midnight 23/24th November this junction was effected and the line was ~~effected~~ continuous from F.7.b.2.6 to F.8.c.5.4 and thence by means of posts to the Sunken road at F.14.a.3.3

This operation was rendered the more difficult because by this time the 17th Welsh and 19th R.W.F were very much mixed up and reorganisation was hampered by darkness.

At about 9.0pm 23rd November the left of "C" Company was at F.7.b.2.6 and touch had been lost with "B" Company 17th Welsh and 18th Welsh and the 12th S.W.B.. Before midnight the right of the 18th Welsh had been located at F.7.c.5.5 and instructions issued for O/C 'C' Coy 17th Welsh to establish posts along the road running from N.E to S.W. through F.7.c & for the 18th Welsh to throw back and extend their right in order to gain touch. This was satisfactorily effected and the whole line was then continuous.

At dawn on the 24th November the enemy delivered a very heavy counterattack along the greater part of the front but mainly against the centre. In the heavy fighting that followed "B" & "C" Company 17th Welsh lost all their remaining Officers and the Companies suffered very heavy losses. On the right centre the line was driven back a considerable distance and the remnants of A & D Companies in the N.E & E portions of the wood were completely cut off. These two companies were almost surrounded and though putting up a determined resistance suffered very heavy losses.

The arrival of reinforcements stiffened the defence and despite all efforts of the enemy the whole of the High Ground in the wood remained firmly in our hands. During the day two efforts were made, by Dismounted Cavalry and A & S.H, to recover the Eastern portion of the wood where some parties of A & D Companies 17th Welsh were still holding out. These efforts failed but at dusk a considerable number of our men continued to get back and join up with the troops holding the main line of resistance on the High Ground.

At about midnight 24/25th November a Battalion of Scots Guards and some Kings Own Royal Lancs were brought up in an endeavour to re-establish our line round the edge of the woods. The Kings Own proceeded along the main road running N & S through the wood with the object of securing the N edge.

The Scots Guards proceeded to the Sunken road at F.14.c.3.3 with the intention of securing the Eastern edge of the wood. On arrival at the Sunken road it was at once evident that the enemy held that portion of the wood East of the road running from N.W to SE through F.7.d very strongly, and it was deemed advisable to wait till the morning before endeavouring to clear it. The attempt was made on the morning 25th November but was only partially successful and the Guards withdrew once again to the High Ground.

At 3pm 25th a general advance of the line was ordered. Progress was made by the Scots Guards on the right of their attack & by the units of the 119th Infantry Brigade on their left. The Guards' left & the 119th Infantry Brigades right however were able to make little or no progress and the attack came to a standstill.

During the 24/25th November an immense amount of work was done in reorganising groups of leaderless men of different units and sending them back to the firing line as fighting units under a recognised leader. The promptness with which this was done, and the alacrity with which orders were obeyed alone rendered it possible to stiffen the line of resistance at the critical periods, and enabled our troops to hold on to the all important High Ground in the wood. The astonishing valour and tenacity displayed by all units of the 119th Infantry Brigade in face of extremely heavy shelling, and continuous counter attacks, ~~made it possible~~ and the valuable aid rendered by ~~help of~~ the Scots Guards and Dismounted Cavalry, enabled the 119th Inf Bgde to hold the important tactical position BOURLON WOOD, until handed over to the 62nd Division on the night 25/26 November 1917

H P B Gough Major

Commanding 19th (Service) Battalion The Welsh Regt

O.C. 119th Inf. Bde. No.[illegible]

12th S.W.B.
17th Welsh. 119th M.G.Coy.
18th Welsh. 119th T.M.B.

DISPOSITIONS FOR WHITE FORCE.

TACTICAL EXERCISE 12th NOVR. 1917.

12th S.W.B. will find the Outpost Line, and will be in position by 10-30 a. m.

1 Section M.G.Coy is placed at the disposal of O.C. 12th S.W.B.

18th Welsh Regt. are billeted in [illegible] (imaginary)

17th Welsh Regt. Bde H.Q., 119th M.G.Coy., 119th T.M.B. are billeted in LE SOUICH (imaginary)

A Battery R.F.A. is at LE SOUICH (imaginary) at disposal of G.O.C.

18th Welsh Regt. at 10-30 a. m. will pass through the Outpost Line and will drive the enemy out of FORET DE LUCHEUX on front covered by Outpost Line. Simultaneously an advance (imaginary) is being carried out on Right & Left flanks by "X" Division and 121st Brigade.

17th Welsh Regt. 119th M.G.Coy; 119th T.M.B will be in Brigade Reserve at N. 33. c. central (approximately) and will be in position by 10-30a. m.

Outposts will close by companies when FORET DE LUCHEUX is reported clear of enemy on our Front, and will become Brigade Reserve.

O.C.12th S.W.B. will report position of his H.Q. (Outpost) at 10-30 a. m.

Fullest communications to be established.

Bde. HQ. N.33. c. central, in first ins tance.

(signed)

Captain
Brigade Major.
119th Infantry Brigade.

10th Nov 1917.

S P E C I A L O R D E R O F T H E D A Y.

B Y

BRIGADIER-GENERAL F.P.CROZIER.,D.S.O.

COMMANDING 119th INFANTRY BRIGADE.

Nov.27th.1917.

The G.O.C. 119th Infantry Brigade wishes to congratulate all ranks of the Brigade on the results of their efforts in action on 23rd,24th & 25th November, 1917.

The valour and endurance displayed was beyond all praise.

A most important tactical position in BOURLON WOOD was assaulted and taken on 23rd and held against countless counter attacks and ceaseless pressure till handed over, consolidated and intact, to 186th Infantry Brigade on the night of 25/26th November.

The flanks were kept secure despite abnormal difficulties.

The enemy attacked up to the last moment of relief.

The difficult duties of maintenance of communications and supply of S.A.A. and rations were carried out by all concerned in a very efficient manner despite very heavy shelling; and reflect great credit on 119th Infantry Brigade Signal Section, Battalion Signallers and runners, and Brigade & Battalion Transport Officers and personnel.

The evacuation and tending of wounded was carried out under most trying circumstances, by all concerned, in the most self sacrificing manner.

Over 500 prisoners were taken by the Brigade from 214th and 3rd Guard Divisions, which, in itself, is proof of the strength of the enemy facing the Brigade, and the importance he attached to his lost positions.

These results could not have been achieved had not all done their utmost for the common cause - beating the Bosche.

17th (S) Battalion The Welsh Regiment

Officers Casualties

RANK	NAME	DATE OF CASUALTY	NATURE OF CASUALTY	REMARKS
Lt a/Capt	ELMITT A.J.	24-11-17	KILLED	
2/LIEUT	MATHIAS J.H.T.	25-11-17	"	
"	BAILEY H.P.A.	24-11-17	"	
LIEUT	JONES A.R. MC	23-11-17	WOUNDED	
2/LIEUT	DAVIES T.T.	" " "	"	
LT COL.	ANDREWS R.J. DSO MC	24-11-17	"	
LT a/CAPT	LLOYD A.P.	" " "	"	
LIEUT	DUKE S.C.L.	" " "	"	
2/LIEUT	DAVIES T.	" " "	"	
"	HANSON R.D.	" " "	"	
"	GRIFFITHS J. MC	25-11-17	WOUNDED AND MISSING	
LIEUT	ENSOR J.G.	23-11-17	WOUNDED	DIED OF WOUNDS 26-11-17
CAPT	DUNN G.M.	25-11-17	MISSING	BELEIVED KILLED
LIEUT	O'MALLEY E.	25-11-17	"	
2/LIEUT	MORGAN D.R.	" " "	WOUNDED	
	LEWIS F.S.J.M.	" " "	MISSING	
LIEUT	MOULD W.J.		"	

COPY.

SPECIAL. DIVISIONAL ORDER

The Commander-in-Chief personally informed the Divisional Commander that he wished all ranks of the 40th Division to be congratulated on his behalf, on their recent success.

Great credit is due, not only to Infantry Brigades who gave proof of fine fighting qualities and endurance, but also to the loyal co-operation and untiring energy shown by Royal Artillery (including the Divisional Ammunition Column), the Royal Engineers, 12(S) Battalion Yorkshire Regiment (Pioneers) the 40th Divisional Train, the Field Ambulances, and the Army Ordnance Corps.

(Signed) W. G. Charles
Lieut Colonel.
General Staff 40th Division

28th November 1917.

17TH. (SERVICE) BATTALION THE WELSH REGIMENT.

TRAINING PROGRAMME FOR THURSDAY. NOVEMBER 1ST. 1917. –

17th (GLAM) Bn. – THE WELSH REGT.
01 NOV 1917
No. 359

BATTALION AND LOCATION OF HEADQUARTERS	DESCRIPTION OF TRAINING	TIME	REMARKS.
COULLEMONT.	PHYSICAL TRAINING.	7.15 – 7.45 AM	
NOV. 1ST. 1917.	BATTALION DRILL. (U.3. a. 5. 8)	9.30 – 10.0 AM	BATTALION TO PARADE AS STRONG AS POSSIBLE DRESS – DRILL ORDER.
	SECTION IN THE ATTACK } PLATOON IN THE ATTACK }	10.15 – 11 A.M.	"A", "C" & "D" COMPANIES
	BOMBING.	10.15 – 11 A.M.	"B" COMPANY
	MUSKETRY	11.10 – 11.50 AM	"A", "B" & "D" COMPANIES
	BOMBING	11.10. – 11.50 AM	"C" COMPANY
	GAS DRILL	12.0 – 12.30 PM	"A" & "B" COMPANIES
	JUDGING DISTANCE	12.0 – 12.30 PM	"C" & "D" COMPANIES
	POINT TO POINT RUN BY PLATOONS	2.0 – 4.0 PM	"C" & "D" COMPANIES — DRESS – FIGHTING ORDER. STARTING POINT Bn. O
			ROUTE "C" COMPANY SOMBRIEN – WARLU… BACK TO STARTING…
			"D" COMPANY WARLUZEL – SOM… BACK TO START…
	BOMBING	2.0 – 3.0 PM	"A" COY
	MUSKETRY	2.0 – 3.0 PM	"B" COY
	BAYONET FIGHTING	3.0 – 4.0 PM	"A" & "B" COMPANIES

CAPT + ADJT

17TH (S) BN. THE W.

17TH.-(SERVICE) BATTALION THE WELSH REGT.

TRAINING PROGRAMME FOR FRIDAY NOVEMBER 2ND. 1917.

BATTALION AND LOCATION OF UNIT.	DESCRIPTION OF TRAINING.	TIME.	REMARKS.
COULLEMONT. NOVEMBER 1ST 1917	PHYSICAL TRAINING.	7.15 - 7.45 A.M.	
	BATTALION DRILL.	9.30 - 10.30 A.M.	BATTALION TO PARADE AS STRONG AS POSSIBLE DRESS – DRILL ORDER.
	COMPANY IN THE ATTACK.	10.45 - 11.45 A.M.	"A", "B" "C" & "D" Coys.
	MUSKETRY.	12.0 - 12.30 P.M.	"A", "B" "C" & "D" Coys.
	BOMBING	2.0 - 3.0 P.M.	"A" & "D" Coys.
	BAYONET FIGHTING.	2.0 - 3.0 P.M.	"B" & "C" Coys.
	INSPECTION AND BOX RESPIRATOR DRILL.	3.0 - 3.30 P.M.	"A", "B", "C" & "D" Coys.
	VISUAL TRAINING AND JUDGING DISTANCE	3.30 - 4.0 P.M.	"A" "B" "C" & "D" Coys.

[signature]
CAPTAIN
& ADJUTANT
17TH (S) BN. THE WELSH REGT.

17th (Service) Battalion The Welsh Regt.

Training Programme for Saturday November 3rd 1917.

Place and location of Unit.	Description of Training.		Time	Remarks.
Coullemont. Nov. 2nd. 1917.	Physical Training		7.15. - 7.45 a.m.	
	Batallion Drill	U.3. d. 5.8.	9.30. - 10.30 a.m	Bn. to Parade as strong as possible. Dress Drill Order
	Company in the attack.	U.3. d. 5.8.	10.45. - 11.45 a.m	"B", "C" & "D" Coys.
	Bombing.	O.33. c. 9.1.	12.0 - 12.30 P.M.	"B" Coy.
	Bayonet Fighting	U. 4. A. 2.3.	12.0 - 12.30 P.M.	"C" & "D" Coys.
	Point to Point Run by Platoons.		2.0 - 4.0 P.M.	"C" & "D" Coys. Dress Fighting Order. Starting point. B^n O. Room. Route "C" Coy. Sombrin - Warluzel - Back to Starting point. "D" Coy. Warluzel - Sombrin - —do—
	Musketry	U.3. d. 5.8	2 - 3 p.m.	"B" Coy
	Bayonet Fighting	-do-	3 - 3.30 p.m	"B" Coy.
	Company Drill.	-do-	3 - 30 - 4 p.m	"B" Coy.
	Musketry Course.	T. 6. A. 2.1.	All Day.	"A" Coy. The Coy. Cooker will be taken. O.C. "A" Coy. will arrange that those not actually shooting carry out. (a) Instruction in Musketry. (b) Bayonet Fighting. (c) visual training & judging Distance. (d) Gas Drill etc.

N.B. The above programme is to be strictly complied with & no alterations to be made without previous reference to these ~~of~~ Headquarters.

Captain
& Adjutant
17th (S) Bn. The Welsh Regt.

14th (S) Bn The Welsh Regt.

Training Programme for Monday Nov 5th 1917.

Place & location of unit	Description of Training	Time.	Remarks
	P. T.	7.15 – 7.45	C. D Coys.
COULLEMONT	Coy in the attack, followed by outposts. (neighbourhood of U 3 d 5.8)	2 – 4	A Coy. O.C. A Coy for this purpose will submit to the H.Q. before 8.0 pm tonight Nov 4. a short scheme giving a general & special idea. (N.B. It is most important that when carrying out any tactical exercise, if even only on quite a small scale, that a situation be made up, so that all ranks carrying out the exercise can have an idea of what is intended.)
	Bombing 0 33 C. 7.1.	3 – 4	B Coy.
	Coy drill. U 3 d 5.8	9 am – 10 am	C. D Coys.
	Musketry. U 3 d 5.8.	10 am – 11 am	D Coy.
			N.B. The Battn is halting tomorrow Nov 5 at LUCHEUX. 3 Coys are being inspected by Bde Gas N.C.O on Bn drill ground U 3 d 5.8. (Auth: Ltr of Bde 38/1775/G.L. d 4/11/17) Times of parade vide B.R.O para [illegible] dated 4/11/17.

17th (S) Battalion The Welsh Regiment

Training Programme for Tuesday November 6th 1917

Date & Location of HQ	Description of Training		Time	Remarks
GUILLEMONT	Physical Training		7.15 AM to 8.45	All Coys
	Battalion Drill	U 3. d. 5. 8.	9.30 – 10.30	DRESS Drill Order
	Bombing	U 3 3 c 9 1	10.45 – 12.30	D Coy
	Outpost Scheme	U 3. 6.	10.45 – 12.30	B. Coy
	Musketry (including Rapid Loading)	U 3. d. 5. 8.	10.45 – 11.15	A Coy
	Bayonet Fighting		10.45 – 11.15	C Coy
	Musketry (including Rapid Loading)		11.15 – 11.45	C ″
	Bayonet Fighting		11.15 – 11.45	A Coy
	Coy. Drill & Platoon Drill		12 noon – 12.30	A & C Coys
			PM	
	Outpost Scheme	″ 3. 6.	2 — 4	C Coy.
	Bombing	″ 3 3 c. 9 1.	2 — 4	A Coy
	Bayonet Fighting	U 3 d 5 8	2 – 2.30	B ″
	Musketry (including Rapid Loading)		2 – 2.30	D ″
	Bayonet Fighting		2.30 — 3	D ″
	Musketry (including Rapid Loading)		2.30 – 3	B
	Coy Drill and Platoon Drill		3.15 – 4	B & D. Coys.

The Bde. Staff Sergt instructors will be at the disposal of this Battalion for Bayonet Fighting etc.

NB

[illegible]
Captain
& Adjutant
17th (S) Battalion Welsh Regt.

SECRET.

Copy No 11

17th. Welsh Order No. X

War Diary

6th. November 1917.

Ref. Map France 51c.
1/40,000.

1. **INFORMATION.**

(a) Reliable information has been received that the enemy has retired to the line, GRAND- ROLLECOURT-SOMBRIEN-SAULTY.

(b) Our main Body is at LUCHEUX, where it will remain for the night 6/7 November.

The 119th. Infantry Brigade (advanced guard to the 40th. Division) has reached the line SUS-St. LEGER-WARLUZEL - COULLEMONT.

The G.O.C. 119th. Infantry Brigade has received orders to establish outposts in front of this line, and has allotted to the O.C. 17th. Welsh Regt. a frontage from about U.10 central to O 33. d. 3. 5. The No. Battn. Berks will continue the line to the South. The 12th. S.W.B. to the North.

2. **INTENTION.**

I intend to hold this line with 3 companies and 1 Company in Reserve.

3. **INSTRUCTIONS.**

(a) Right Company. "A" Company from U.10 Central to about U.4.D. 1.7.

Central Company. "C" Company thence to U.4.A.1.9.

Left Company. "D" Company thence to N.E. edge of wood at about O.33.D.3.5.

Actual boundaries between Companies will be pointed out on the Ground.

"B" Company will be held in Reserve in the village of COULLEMONT at about U.3.B.1.2.

(b) The piquet line will be the line of resistance and will be held at all cost.

(c) No Cooking will be done and no fires will be lit in the Outpost Line.

(d) The Reserve Company will provide ration and carrying parties.

(e) The Battalion will be relieved at 5.0.a.m. on the morning of Nov. 7th.

(f) A Regtl. Aid Post will be established at U.3.B.1.1.

(g) The Regtl. Transport will be parked at U. 3.C.0.5.

(h) Bn. H.Q. and report centre will be established at U.3.B.1.2. at 10.30 a.m. 6th. November 1917.

4. ACKNOWLEDGE.

Captain
& Adjutant.
17th. (S) Bn. The Welsh Regt.

Dictated at 10.15 a.m.
6th. November 1917.

Copy No. 1. to 4. "A", "B", "C", "D" Companies.
" 5,6 & 7. M.O., Q.M., and T.O.
" 8. Brigade Hqrs. by runner.
" 9. 12th. S.W.B. by runner.
" 10. No. Berks. by runner.
" 11. War Diary.
" 12. File.

17th (Service) Battalion The Welsh Regiment.

Training Programme for Wednesday 7/11/17.

Battalion & Location of H.Q	Description of Training	Time.	Remarks.
COULLEMONT. 6.11.17.	Physical Training.	a.m. 7.15 – 7.45	All Companies.
	Battalion Route March	9.30. a.m.	Route. COURTRELLE – SAULTY – SOMBRIN – WARLUZEL. Starting Point – B.H.Q. Dress. Full marching Order.
	Recreational Training in the afternoon.		N.B. "B" Company and Battalion Snipers will fire on range at 1.6.a.2.1. all day. The Company Cookers will be taken

Captain
~~Lt~~ ~~Adjutant~~
17th (S) Bn. The Welsh Regt.

11.17.

17th (S) Battalion The Welsh Regiment

TRAINING PROGRAMME FOR THURSDAY NOVEMBER 8th. 1917

LOCATION OF UNIT	DESCRIPTION OF TRAINING	TIME	REMARKS
COULLEMONT	A.M. PHYSICAL TRAINING BATTALION DRILL U3.d 5.8. OUTPOST SCHEME N.E. OF COULLEMONT	A.M. 7.15. — 7.45. 9.30. — 10.30. 10.45.	ALL COYS. DRESS DRILL ORDER. REPEAT AS FOR 6/11/17. CHANGE — DISPOSITIONS AS FOLLOWS:— RIGHT D COY CENTRE A COY LEFT B COY RESERVE C COY. ALL DETAILS TO BE IN POSITIONS BY 11.30 A.M. O.C. RESERVE COY. WILL DETAIL PARTIES TO TAKE RATIONS TO A.B. and D COMPANIES

CAPTAIN
& ADJUTANT
17th (S) BATT THE WELSH REGT.

17th (Service) Bn [illegible] the Irish Regt.

Training Programme for Friday Nov 9th 1917

Battalion and location of H.Q.	Description of Training	Time	Remarks
COULLEMONT	Brigade in Attack	7.30 am	As per programme attached S.L. 56/ [illegible] Brew [illegible] Before [illegible] Sections or [illegible] Parade on [illegible] L. G. [illegible] will be taken.
		10.30 am	[illegible]

W.P. [illegible] Captain
for Adjutant
[illegible] The Irish Regt

Copy No. 9

19th Welsh Order No X2

Reference. France 51c. 1/40,000.

I Information

(a) Enemy force (strength unknown) is reported to have passed South of ST POL – TINQUES road and to have established his outposts on the general line of the REBREUVIETTE-AVESNES-LE-COMTE road. Enemy patrols are reported to have been seen in the neighbourhood of GRAND-ROULLECOURT SOMBRIN and SUS-ST-LEGER.

(b) The 40th Division is moving Northwards along the route COUTERELLE-COULLEMONT, GRAND RULLECOURT. The 119th Infantry Brigade will form the Advance Guard and will establish an outpost line N of GRAND RULLECOURT.

The G.O.C 119th Infantry Brigade has detailed the 19th Welsh Regt to act as Vanguard and to take up an Outpost line from O2. central to O4. central

2 Intention

I intend to march to GRAND ROULLECOURT tomorrow the 13/11/1917 via road junction U.3 b.9.5. WARLUZEL and take up the outpost line referred to above with 3 Companies holding 1 Company in reserve in the N end of GRAND RULLECOURT.

3 Instructions

(a) For the march

ADV GUARD – A Coy (Lieut A.P.Lloyd)

(a) (Contd).

Main Body. – B.C + D Coys less 1 Platoon
Starting Point – U 36.q.5.
Hour 9.30 am.

{ Rt. Fl Guard "B" Coy will form an officer patrol
{ Lt Fl Guard "C" Coy will form an officer patrol
(names of officers in charge to be furnished to B.H.Q by 9 am. 13/11/17)

Rear Guard 1 Platoon "D" Coy (2/Lt W.R Morgan)

Transport L.G. limbers accompany respective companies
Remainder will follow 300 yds behind main body.

3. Outpost

1 Right Section – O.4 central to O.3.b.8.2 B. Coy.
Central Section O.3.b.8.2 to O.3.a.2.2 A. Coy.
Left Section O.3.a.2.2 to O.2 Central C. Coy.

Actual boundaries will be pointed out
Reserve "D" Company. on the ground.

2 Picquet post will be line of resistance and will be held at all costs.

(3) Transport will be parked in the first instance at O.9.c.9.1.

(4) Report centre at church GRAND RULLECOURT

(5) Positions of dressing stations will be notified later

(6) ACKNOWLEDGE

Issued at pm
12 · 11 · 1917

[signature]

Captain
& Adjutant.
17th Welsh Regt.

Copies 1·4. O^s C^s A.B.C + D. Coys
5·7. Q.M. M.O T.O.
8. H.Q.rs 119th Inf Bde
9. War.
10 File

17th (Service) Battn The Welsh Regt

Training Programme for Week Ending 17th November 1917

Place and location of UNIT	Description of Training	Time	Remarks
COULLEMONT Mon. 12th Nov.	Brigade Scheme		
Tues. 13th Nov.	Battalion Advance Guard Scheme.	9.0 am – 4.0 pm	Cookers will accompany the Battn
Wed. 14th Nov. 252	Musketry Wood fighting Organised mopping up of a village. Recreational Training	All day. 9.0 am – 12.30 pm 9.0 am – 12.30 pm Afternoon.	T.G.A. [illegible] Coy (Coy cooker will be taken) (A Coy (Area U 3 A + C) (B Coy (Area U 9 B + U 10 A) D Coy Area: Village of COULLEMONT)
Thurs. 15th Nov.	Brigade Scheme.		
Friday 16th Nov.	Battalion as a rearguard.	9.0 am – 4.0 pm	Cookers will accompany Battn.
Saturday 17th Nov.	Musketry Battalion Close Order Drill	All Day. 9.0 am – 10.0 am 10.15 – 11.30	(T.G.A) D Coy. Coy Cookers will be taken to meet. U 3 D. A B & C Coys. Various Practice in rapid deployment U. 3. D A B C Coys
11th Nov 1917.			[illegible] Captain & Adjutant 17th (S) Bn The Welsh Regiment

17th Welsh Order No X. 2.

Ref. France 51 C. 1/40,000

Copy No.

(1) INFORMATION

(a) Enemy Force (strength unknown) is reported to have passed south of [illegible] Road and to have established his outposts on the general line of the [illegible] Road. Enemy patrols are reported to have been seen in the neighbourhood of GRAND [illegible]COURT, [illegible] ST. [illegible].

(b) The 40th Division is moving northwards along the route [illegible], [illegible], GRAND [illegible]COURT. The 119th Infantry Brigade will form the Advance Guard and will establish an Outpost Line N. of GRAND [illegible]COURT.

The G.O.C. 119th Inf Bde. has detailed the 17th Welsh to act as Vanguard and to take up an Outpost Line from [illegible] central to O.4. central.

(2) INTENTION.

I intend to march to GRAND [illegible]COURT 13/11/17 via Rd. junction O.3.B.9.5. [illegible] to-morrow and take up the Outpost Line referred to above with 3 Coys. holding 1 Coy. in Reserve in the N. end of GRAND [illegible]COURT.

(3) INSTRUCTIONS.

(a) For the march

Advance Guard	A. Coy (Lt. [illegible] Lloyd)
Main body	B.C.D. Coys less 1 Platoon. Starting point O.3.B.9.5. Hour 9-30 a. m.
Rt. Fl.Gd.	B Coy will find an Officers patrol
Lt. Fl.Gd.	C " " " " " " (Names of Officers i/c to be furnished to B.H.Q. by 9.0 a.m. to-morrow 13/11/17)
Rearguard.	1 Platoon D. Coy (2/Lt D.R. [illegible])
Transport.	L.G. Limbers will accompany respective Coys. Remainder will follow 800 yards behind Mainbody

(b) OUTPOST.

(1) Right Section O.4. central to O.3.[illegible] B Company

Centre Section O.3.B.8.[illegible] to O.[illegible] A Company.

Left Section O.3.[illegible] to O.2. central C Company.

[illegible] boundaries will be pointed out on the ground.

Reserve D Company.

(2) Picquet Line will be the Line of Resistance and will be held at all costs.

(3) Transport will be parked in the first instance at O.3.C.9.1.

(4) Report Centre at Church GRAND [illegible]COURT.

(5) Position of Dressing Station will be notified later.

(6) ACKNOWLEDGE.

Issued at 7 p. m.
12/11/17.

Copies

1-4 O.C.'s A.B.C.D. COYS.
5-7 [illegible] T.O.
8 119th Inf Bde.
9 War Diary
10 File

Captain & Adjutant
17th(S) Bn Welsh Regt.

www.ingramcontent.com/pod-product-compliance
Lightning Source LLC
Chambersburg PA
CBHW082011220426
43670CB00014B/2600